IMAGES
of America

HARDIN AND LARUE COUNTIES 1880–1930

IMAGES
of America

HARDIN AND LARUE COUNTIES 1880–1930

Carl Howell and Don Waters

ARCADIA
PUBLISHING

ISBN 978-0-7385-4282-9

Published by Arcadia Publishing
Charleston, South Carolina

Printed in the United States of America

Library of Congress Catalog Card Number: 98-86767

For all general information contact Arcadia Publishing at:
Telephone 843-853-2070
Fax 843-853-0044
E-mail sales@arcadiapublishing.com
For customer service and orders:
Toll-Free 1-888-313-2665

Visit us on the Internet at www.arcadiapublishing.com

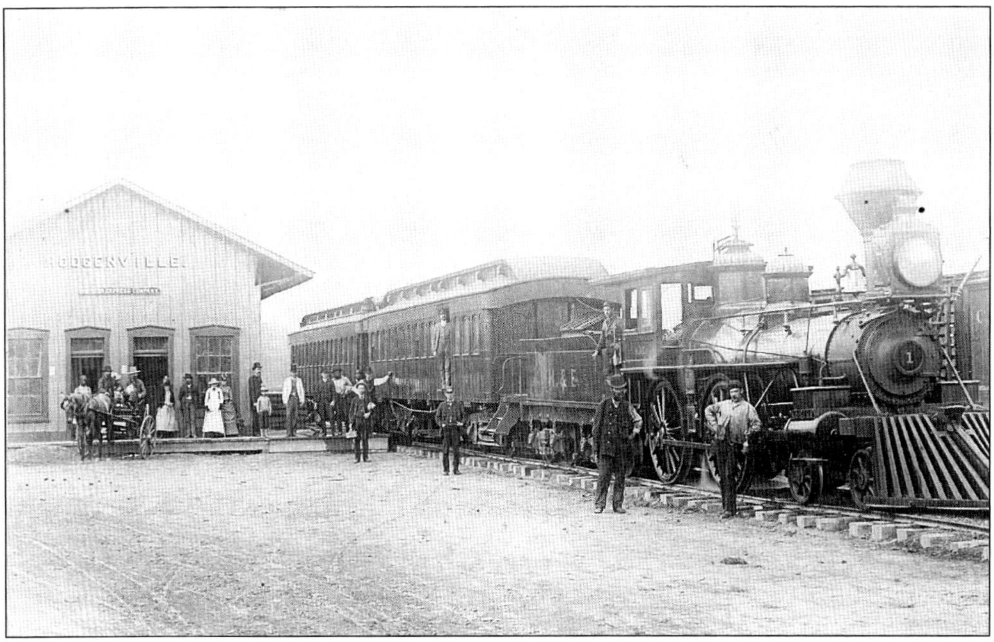

THE HODGENVILLE DEPOT AND AN H&E LOCOMOTIVE AND TRAIN, C. 1888. On March 14, 1888, an H&E locomotive (Engine Number One) and train made the first run from the new Hodgenville depot through Tonieville and on to Elizabethtown. H.D. LaRue was the first station master, and the first train crew was composed of James Conners (conductor), John Eagleby (engineer), Bill Bethel (fireman), John Clarke (brakeman), and C.T. Riney (express messenger). United States Presidents Theodore Roosevelt, William Howard Taft, and Woodrow Wilson all came by special trains to this depot when they traveled to Hodgenville to visit the birthplace of Abraham Lincoln in 1909, 1911, and 1916, respectively.

Contents

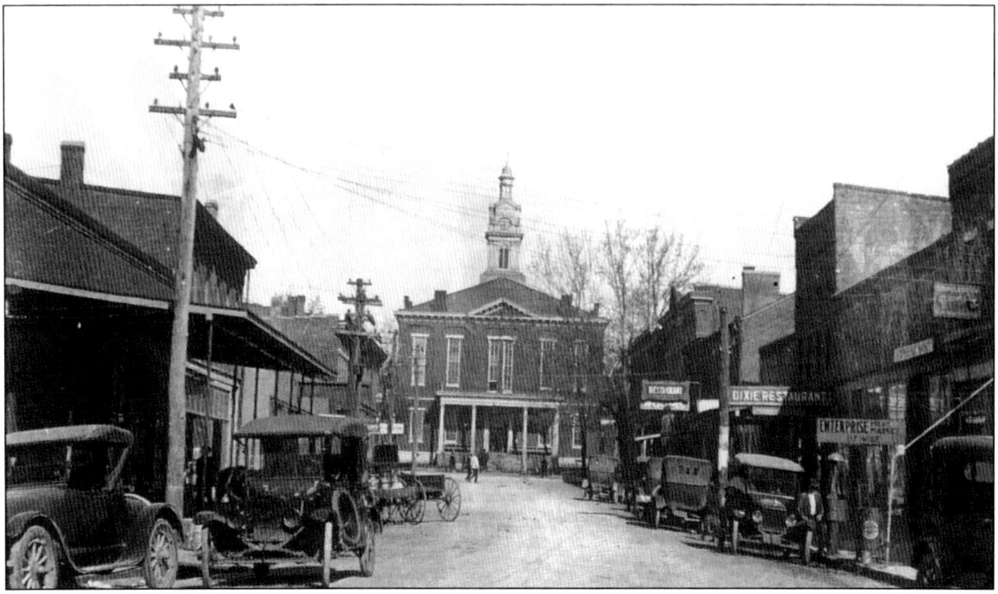

THE HARDIN COUNTY COURTHOUSE, VARIOUS BUSINESS ESTABLISHMENTS, AND SEVERAL AUTOMOBILES DURING A BUSY DAY IN ELIZABETHTOWN IN 1925.

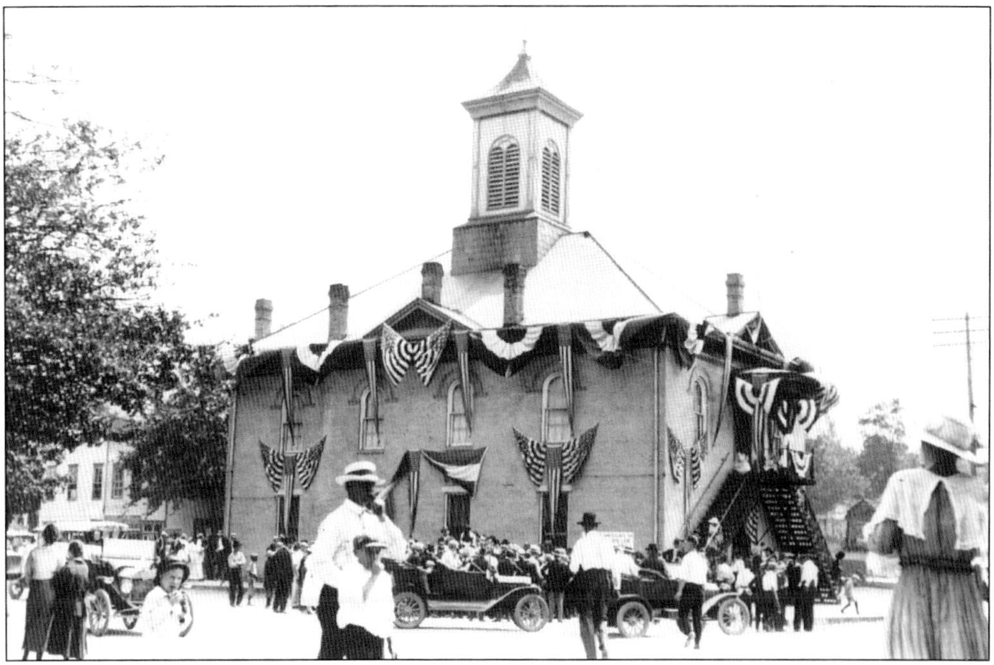

THE LARUE COUNTY COURTHOUSE DURING PRESIDENT WOODROW WILSON'S VISIT TO HODGENVILLE AND ABRAHAM LINCOLN'S BIRTHPLACE ON SEPTEMBER 4, 1916.

INTRODUCTION

Hardin County was formed from Nelson County in 1792, the year Kentucky was granted statehood from Virginia. It was named for Colonel John Hardin, an early Kentucky explorer who was a veteran of the Revolutionary War. Elizabethtown, named after the wife of one Mr. Hynes, who laid out the town, was established as the county seat.

LaRue County was formed from Hardin County in 1843. It was named for John LaRue, who had settled at Phillips Fort, the county's first settlement. Hodgenville, named for Robert Hodgen (LaRue's brother-in-law and another resident of Phillips Fort, who later built and operated Hodgens Mill), was established as the county seat.

Abraham Lincoln, Kentucky's most famous and revered native son, was born near Hodgenville in Hardin County, now LaRue County, on February 12, 1809. These two counties have numerous other Lincoln connections which are little known but are of singular historical significance.

It is our primary desire that this book serve as an educational illustrated history of Hardin and LaRue Counties from 1880 to 1930, as well as to highlight and explain the times and events of this period and its people.

Celebrations that occurred at places which have become historic sites are revealed in vivid detail to enable the viewer to feel the excitement and atmosphere of the particular event in a way that words alone could never portray. Public gathering places such as courthouses, train depots, and mills, which have long been destroyed but have been discovered on postcard images and in family photographs, have been included. Many of the photographs and postcard scenes have been selected due to their intrinsic historical interest and content. Others simply provide, for the first time, an accurate and informative thread of everyday life and scenery as it really was, in a more relaxed and "laid-back" time. Many of the images have only recently been discovered and reveal scenes and individuals heretofore known only to a few people. Some were simply put away in drawers and forgotten, while others were placed in family albums many years ago, with little thought given to their content or historical relevance. Many of these photos meant little or nothing to their owners, while to others they were valued as prized heirlooms handed down by prior generations. Although historically significant, one of these photographs depicts an event we wish had never happened.

Lifestyles and occupations now nonexistent and long forgotten are presented in a nostalgic combination of early photography and text. There are people who were leaders of the small-town communities in which they lived as well as hard-working farmers, merchants, and other ordinary people trying to simply eke out a living. From blacksmith to tinsmith, from simple country stores to detailed images of specialty shops, the array of subjects and scenes places a premium on variety and visual content.

The evolution of transportation in Kentucky, from horses, wagons, buggies, and carriages to the advent of the automobile, is chronicled in a way that reflects the rapid changes in methods of travel as they took place in central Kentucky during the early 20th century. Together with documentation of buildings, institutions, local landmarks, and architecture now gone, this book is intended to create and bring to life a new dimension in the already rich heritage of Hardin and LaRue Counties.

Rather than having separate Hardin and LaRue County sections, we have elected to portray the towns, areas, and scenes alphabetically in the first chapter to create for the reader a broader overall perspective of the two counties.

Our primary wish, however, is that the legacy left to us by our forebears will be rekindled and that the fascinating history of this period, together with much of the area's rural beauty and tranquillity, will be promoted by this book and preserved for future generations.

Lengthy chapters and even entire books could be written about many of the images depicted in this volume. Despite the constraints of space, we are extremely pleased with the result and hope that you, the reader, will find the contents interesting and informative.

Perhaps even an occasional chuckle will occur, as it did with us when we were doing research for one of the images and read about this letter President Lincoln received from a Hardin County job applicant: "I feel purfickly qualerfied to be Minister to England or any foron post, but if you dont have one vacant, I will take the Post Office at Buck Snort, Hardin County, Kentucky."

One

Towns, Communities, and Neighborhoods

Panoramic scenes and close-up views of buildings, activities, celebrations, and other events in Hardin and LaRue County towns, communities, and even rural neighborhoods with well-established names are depicted here with descriptive text. Many of the communities and neighborhoods are no longer known by the names which were in common usage during part or all of the period from 1880 to 1930. Included in alphabetical order on the following pages are Athertonville, the Barren Run community, Buffalo, Cecilia, Colesburg, the Corinth neighborhood, Dever's Hollow, Eagle Mills, East View, Easy Gap, Elizabethtown, Franklin Crossroads, Gleanings, Glendale, Harcourt, Hardin Springs, Hodgenville, near Howardstown (LaRue/Nelson), Howevalley, Leafdale, Magnolia, Malt, Mt. Sherman, Nolin, Red Mills, Rineyville, Roanoke, Solway, Sonora, St. John, Star Mills, Stephensburg, Stithton, Summit, the Talley neighborhood, Tonieville, Tunnel Hill, Upton, Vertrees, Vine Grove, West Point, and White Mills.

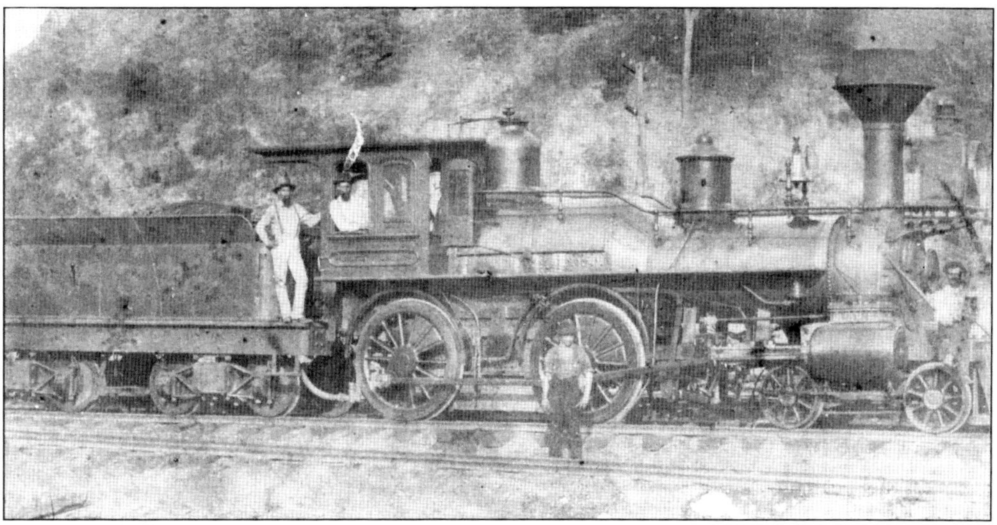

Hill Engine Number 34. Shown here in 1882 at Colesburg, in northeastern Hardin County, is hill engine number 34. Standing on the tender, near the cab, is fireman Lev Purcell. Engineer Frank Ryan leans out the cab window. Agent A.H. Roy stands at the side of the engine, and "Pat" Feathers sits on the cow-catcher. This is one of the earliest known examples of the early steam engines that helped build Hardin and LaRue Counties.

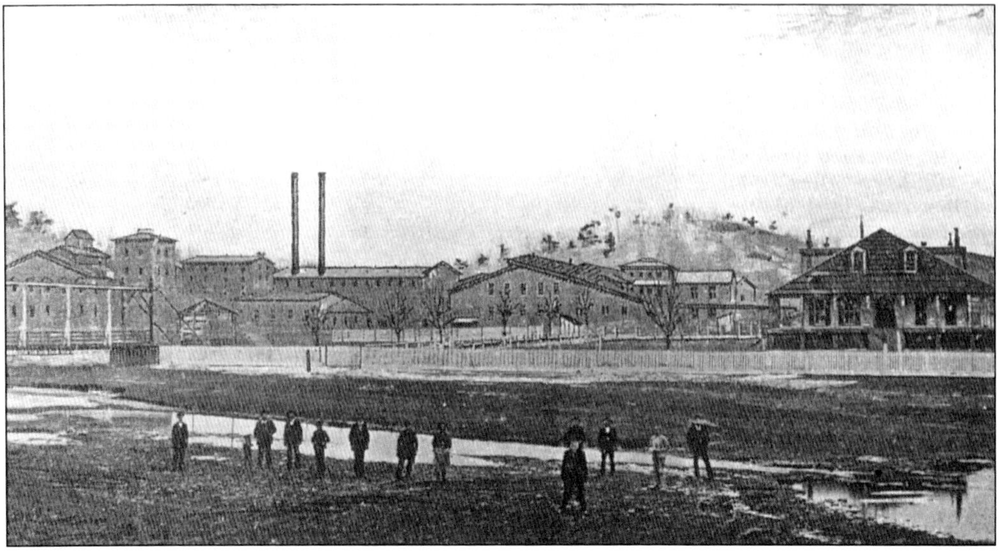

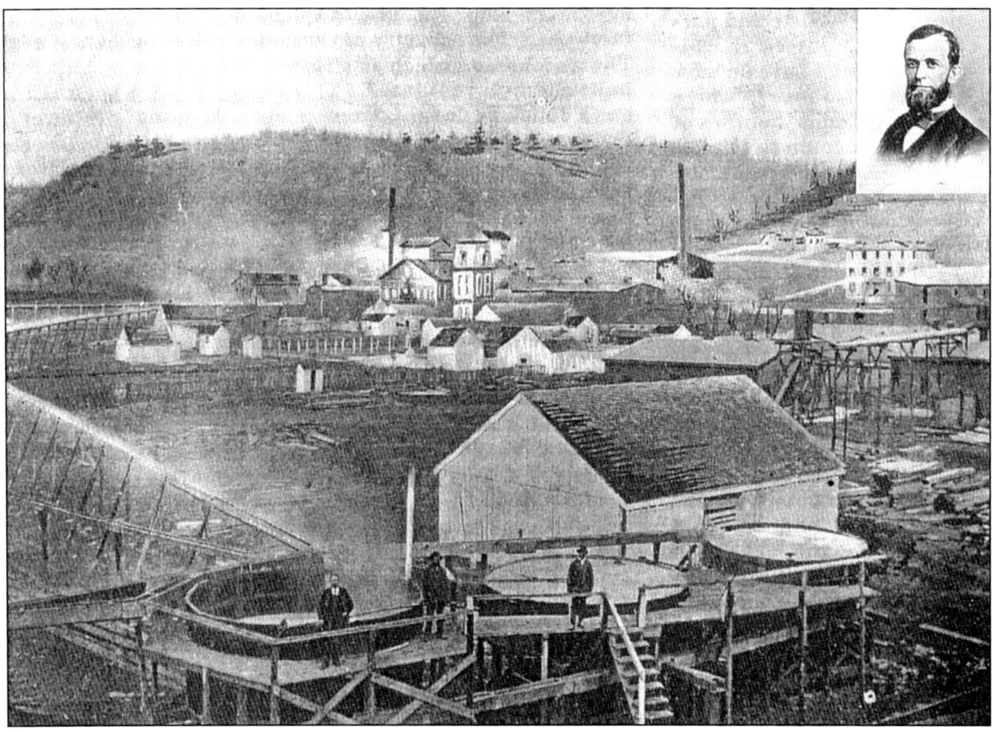

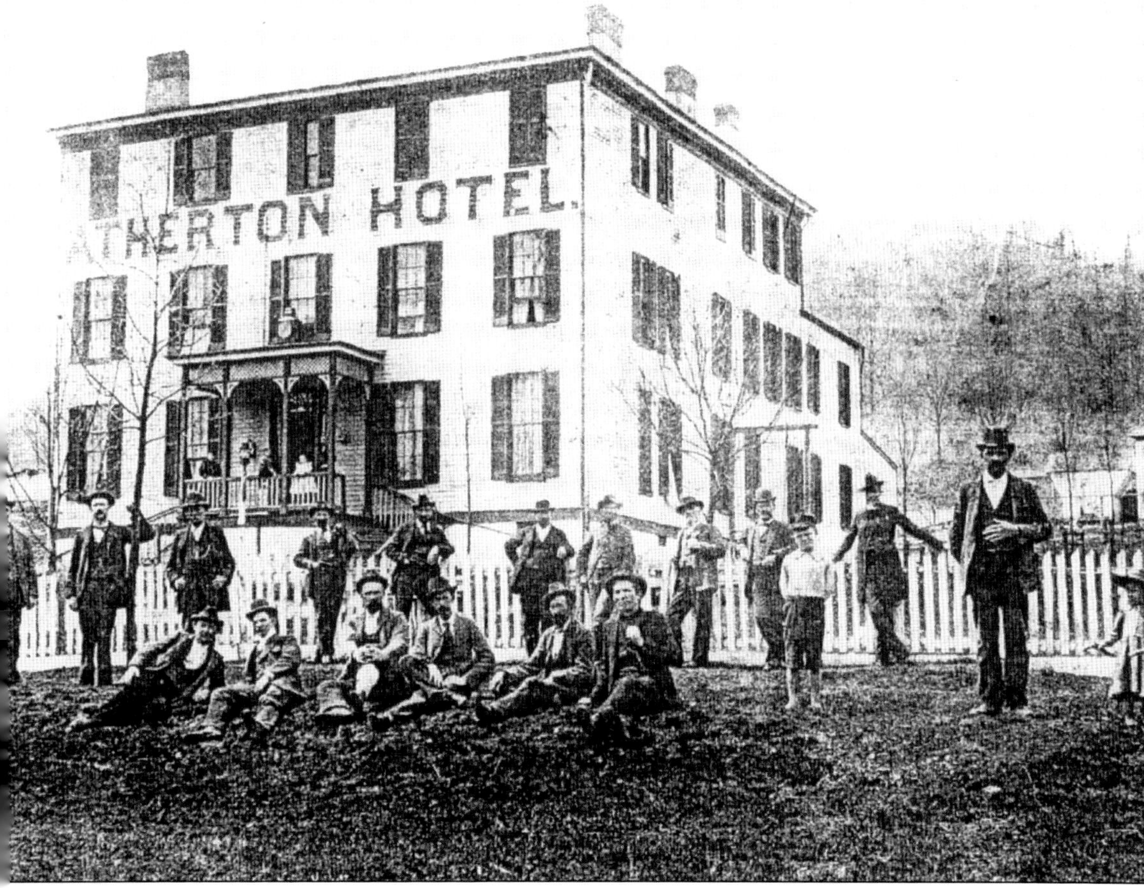

ATHERTON DISTILLERIES AND THE ATHERTON HOTEL, C. 1890. John M. Atherton (opposite page, bottom image, inset) operated two large distilleries in Athertonville, one on each side of Knob Creek. The Mayfield Distillery (opposite page, top image) and the larger J.M. Atherton Distillery (opposite page, bottom image) are pictured as they appeared about 1890. Popular brands of whiskey produced by the two LaRue County distilleries were Atherton, Mayfield, Clifton, Windsor, Howard, Carter, Kenwood, Brownfield, and Baker. On a daily basis, at the height of its capacity, the J.M. Atherton Distillery used 2,200 bushels of grain and produced about 6,600 gallons of whiskey. At one time, it was recognized as the biggest sour mash distillery in the world. The Atherton plant had bonded storage capacity of over 150,000 barrels. The largest employer in LaRue County, Atherton employed over two hundred men at the plant. He also built his own depot in Athertonville, a spur railroad line to the L&N Railroad at New Haven, and a large store known as "The Fair." In 1899, Atherton sold the buildings, equipment, brand names, and warehoused whiskey to the Kentucky Distilleries and Warehouse Company, which continued the business until 1919, when the Volstead, or Prohibition Act, was enacted. The magnificent Atherton Hotel, which John M. Atherton built in Athertonville in the 1880s (above), further reflects the magnitude of his accomplishments during this period. Except for Hodgenville, Athertonville was the most heavily populated town in LaRue County during the 1890s.

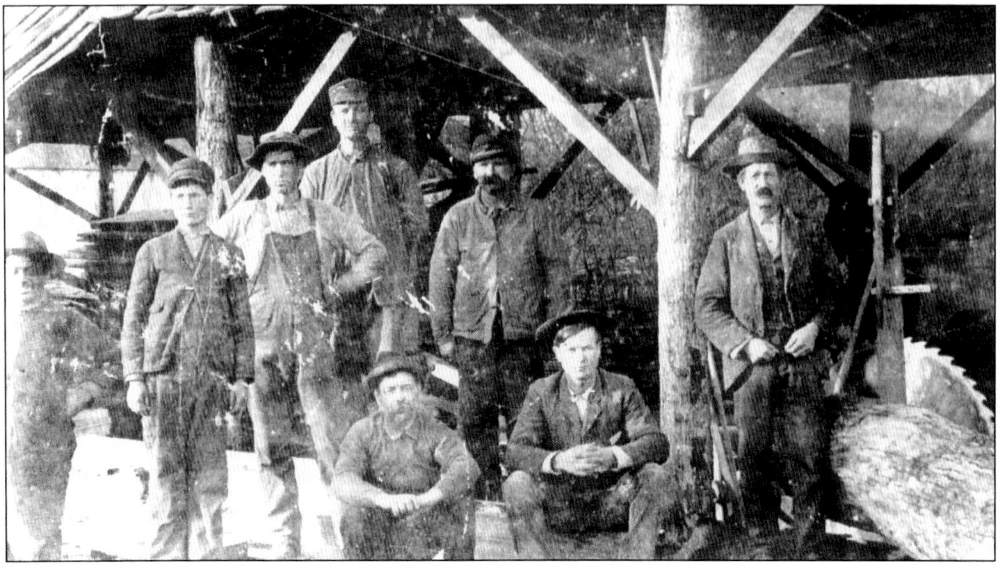

THE MARCUM SAWMILL, C. 1915. From left to right, George, Jesse P., Hardin A., John David, and Sylvester are the five Marcums posing in this picture taken at Marcum's Sawmill in Athertonville. The Marcum family (father and four sons) began doing business at this location in 1905. Sawing logs into marketable lumber provided a good source of income for these LaRue County men and their families for many years.

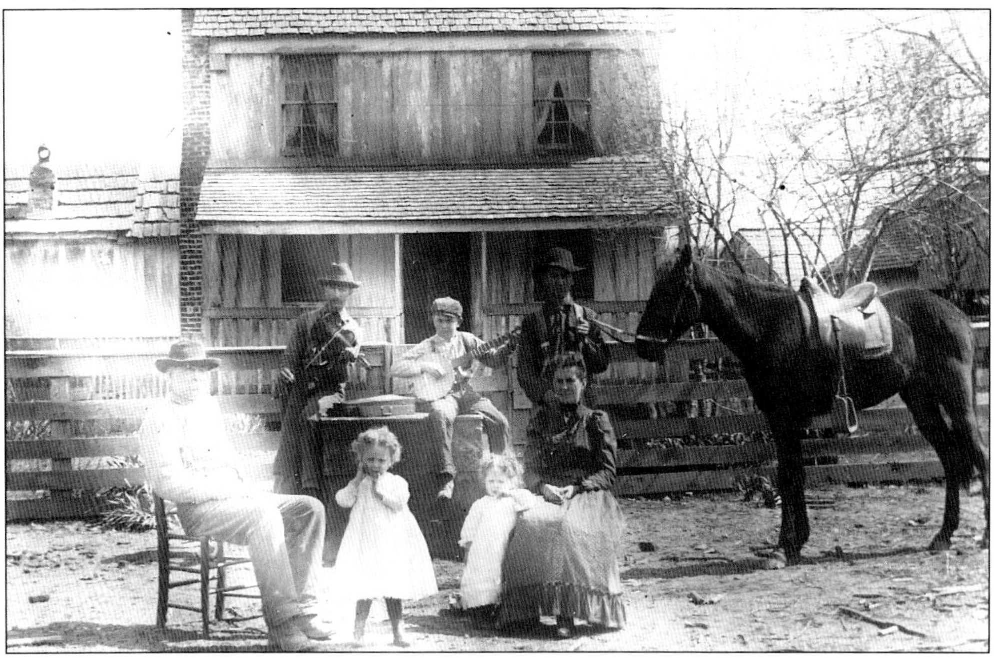

THE ROUTT FAMILY IN BARREN RUN, 1899. The Routt family poses in front of their two-story frame residence in the Barren Run community of LaRue County. Seated at left is William Purd Routt, who was a Union Soldier in the Civil War. His second wife, Sarah Della (Reynolds) Routt, is seated at right. From left to right are John Routt (with fiddle), Henry Kaufus "Cap" Routt (with banjo), and Stiles Routt (with horse). The two small girls are Bertha Lee Routt (left) and Edna Routt.

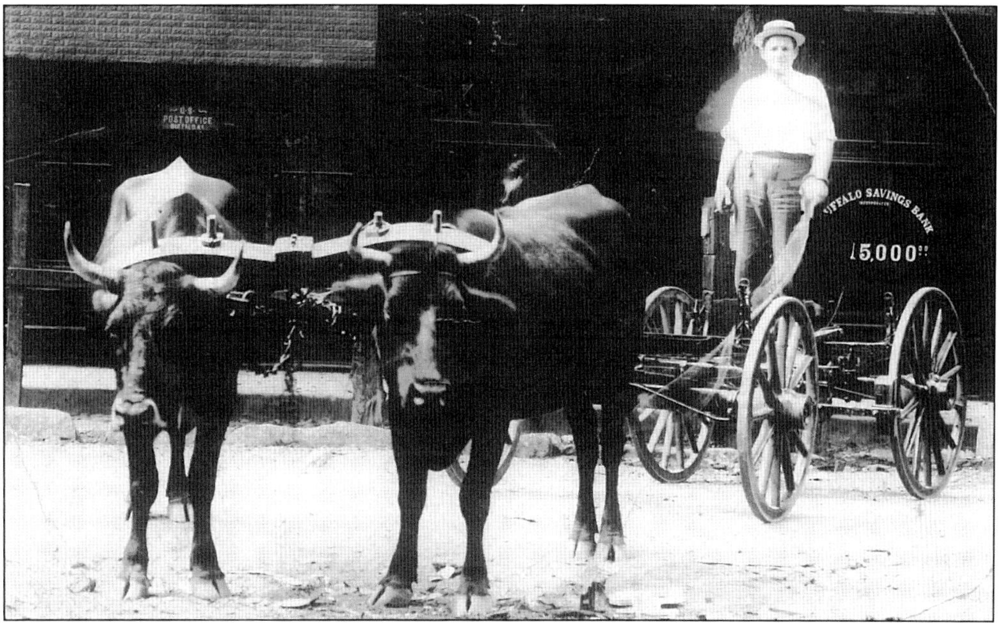

RAPID TRANSIT IN BUFFALO, APRIL 1909. Donohue Ferrill stands in his wagon, pulled by a team of oxen, in this real-photo postcard scene. The Buffalo Post Office is at left, and the Buffalo Savings Bank (now Bank of Buffalo), founded in 1901 by his father, E.S. Ferrill, is at right. Donohue Ferrill later became the owner and operator of the Donohue Ferrill Motor Company, located in the square in Hodgenville.

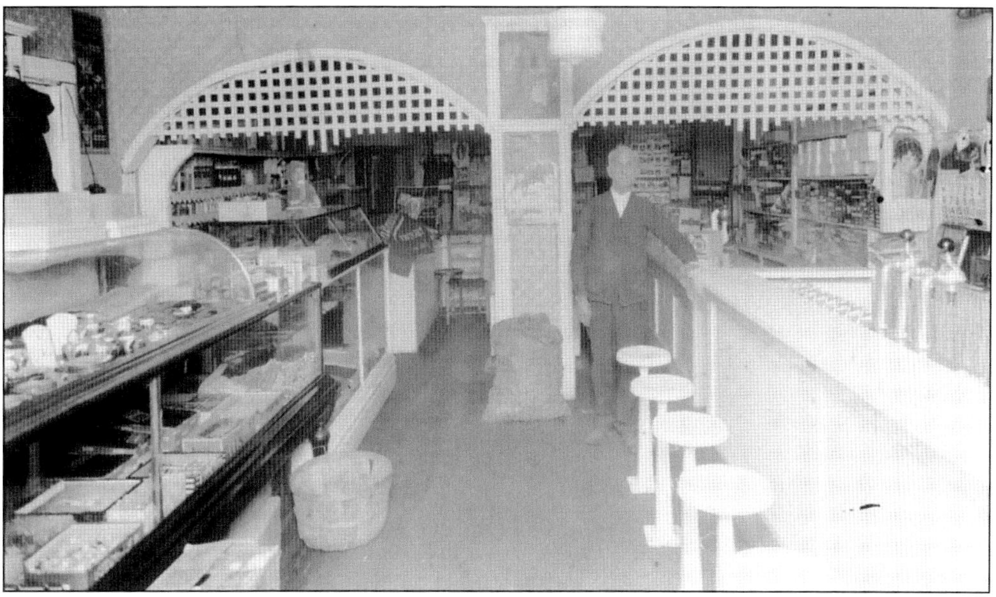

JACOB STROUS AND STORE, C. 1929. German immigrant Jacob Strous stands next to the ice cream parlor and soda fountain in his store in Buffalo. Judelle Vance Puckett, a lifetime Buffalo resident, fondly recalls being one of many children who frequently stopped by to purchase soft drinks, candy, and delicious maple walnut ice cream. Originally a grocery store when he purchased it in 1922, Strous also sold a few grocery items and had an icehouse at the rear of the building.

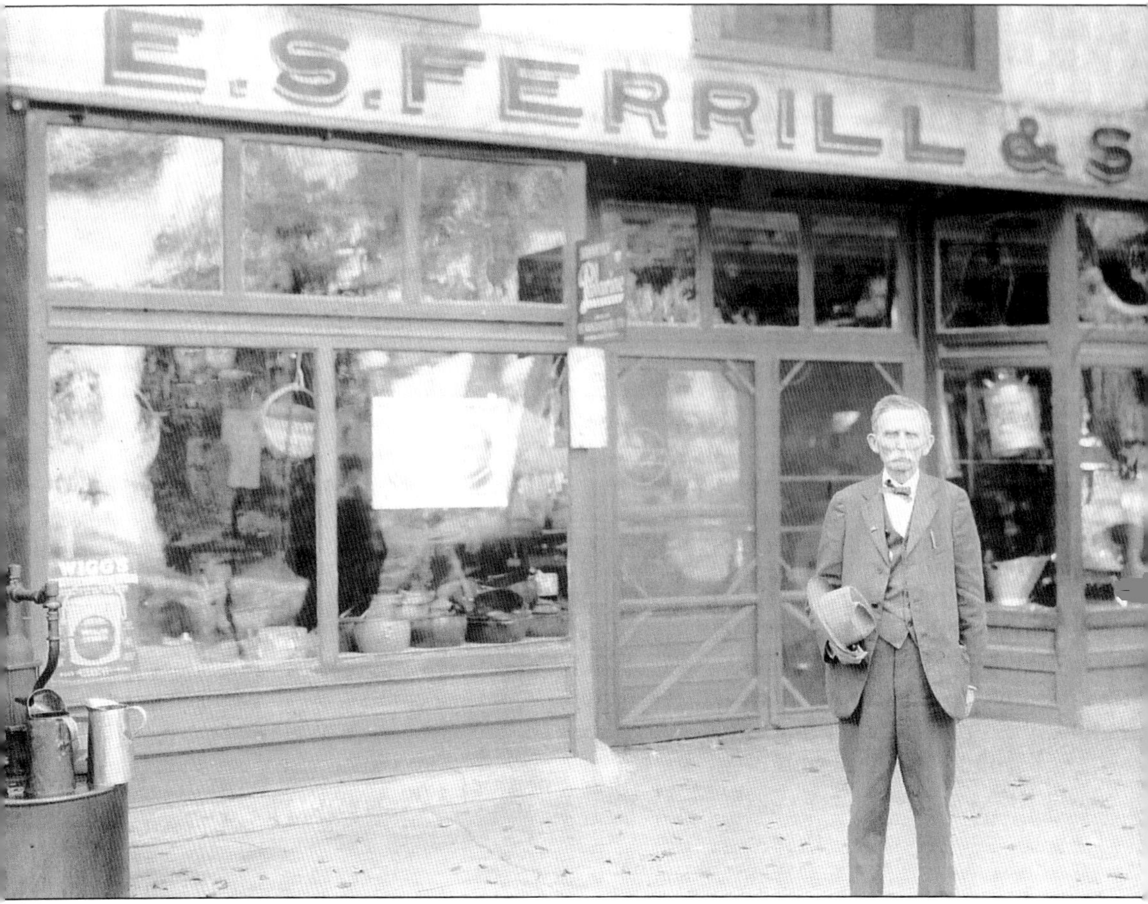

E.S. Ferrill and Store, c. 1928. Edward Stanton "E.S." Ferrill was LaRue County's leading merchant and businessman during the first 45 years of the 20th century. His entire business operation was located in Buffalo, with his first commercial enterprise being a drug store which he established in 1883. He sent for some books that he studied, and was soon able to pass a state examination which enabled him to obtain a pharmacist's diploma. Ferrill started his wholesale operations by buying barrels of salt in Louisville and selling them to farmers and other store owners in and around LaRue County. For many years during his remarkable career, he ran the drug store, a hardware store, and the Buffalo Savings Bank in adjoining buildings. His wholesale grocery business was located on the other side of the street. He dealt in surreys, buggies, farm implements, fertilizer, and numerous other commodities. He also had a lumberyard and a stove factory. Sam Underwood Jr., a lifetime Buffalo resident and former Ferrill employee, recalls that, for many years, Ferrill routinely made deliveries to farmers and stores in 30 surrounding counties. Doing business as E.S. Ferrill and Son, he kept an enormous stock of goods which was contained in his seven spacious warehouses in Buffalo, from which he shipped merchandise using 12 large trucks which were painted a bright red with "E.S. Ferrill and Son, Buffalo, Kentucky" on the sides. Longtime Buffalo resident John T. Meers Jr. advises that, due to the number of warehouses and his consistently large stock of merchandise, Ferrill established his own fire department and employed a roving policeman to provide security at night. The Great Depression was not a setback for him but, instead, proved to be an opportunity, because he was never in debt. In one year during the Depression, his annual gross revenue soared from $250,000 to $1,250,000, while other businesses in the area were failing. Ferrill died in 1945 at his home, "Ferrilland," in Buffalo, at the age of 83.

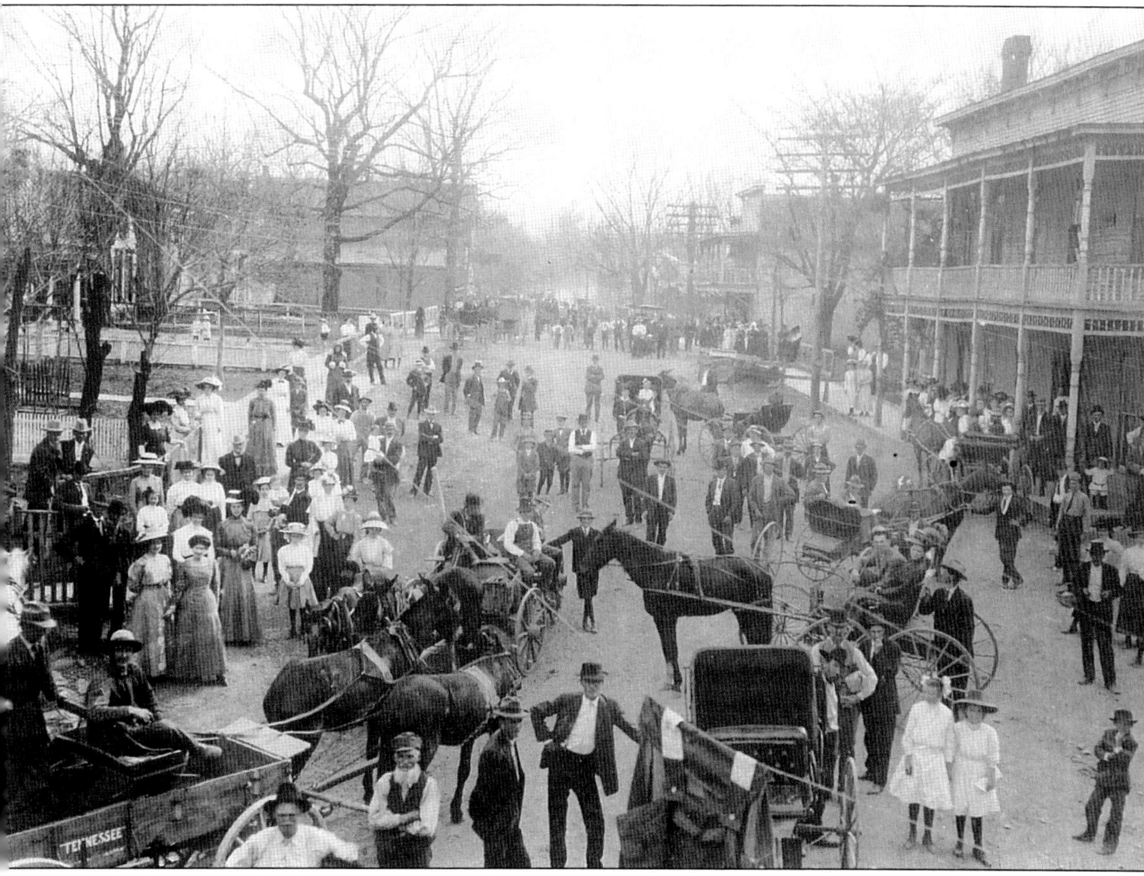

A Saturday Afternoon in Buffalo, c. 1912. The people congregated in downtown Buffalo were there for a special occasion. Local businessman E.S. Ferrill was conducting a promotional raffle to give away one of the new surreys that he sold at his store. The name drawn as the lucky winner was that of a ten-year-old girl who was in attendance. Her father, however, traded the girl's new surrey for a disk that he needed for his farming operation. This picture was taken from the top of the old Upton Building. In the right foreground is the Beauchamp Hotel, later known as the Bales Hotel. The Buffalo Baptist Church can be seen at left.

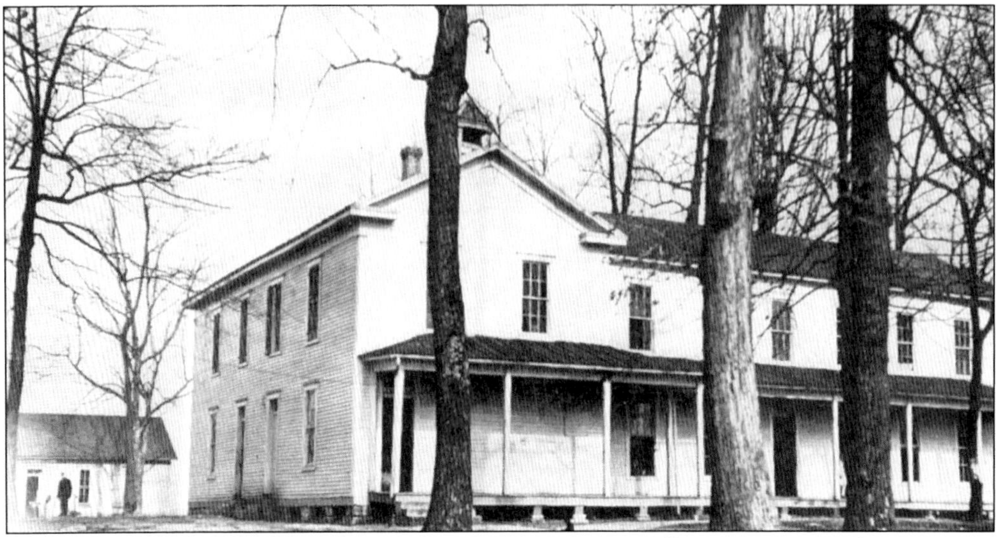

The East Lynn College Building, c. 1925. East Lynn College, incorporated January 16, 1880, was the educational and social center of the community. Built in 1879 and named for Benjamin Lynn, a Baptist minister and early explorer of LaRue County, the college was a two-year, private boarding school located adjacent to the site where Buffalo Grade School is now located. The college conferred degrees in philosophy, science, arts, business, and pedagogy (teaching). East Lynn's annual announcement for 1897–98 advertised that Buffalo is "a prohibition town," "one of the most quiet, moral, and religious towns in Kentucky," and "is celebrated for its excellent mineral water." The Buffalo High School building is pictured above, c. mid-1920s, and was the same building formerly occupied by East Lynn College. Pictured below is a close-up of the right section of the school building and the Buffalo schoolchildren in 1924.

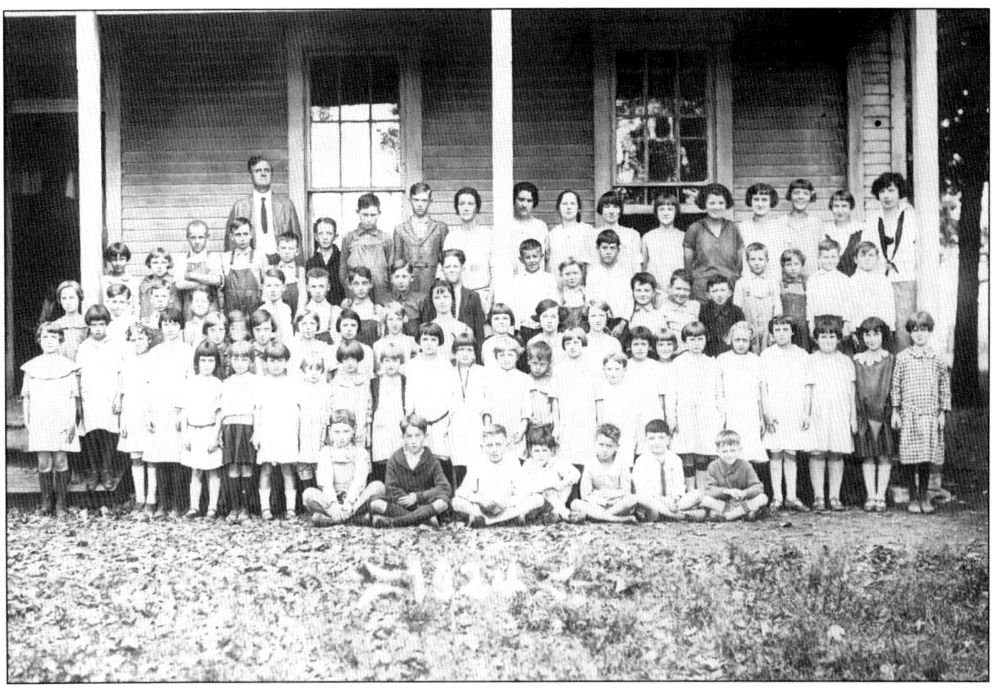

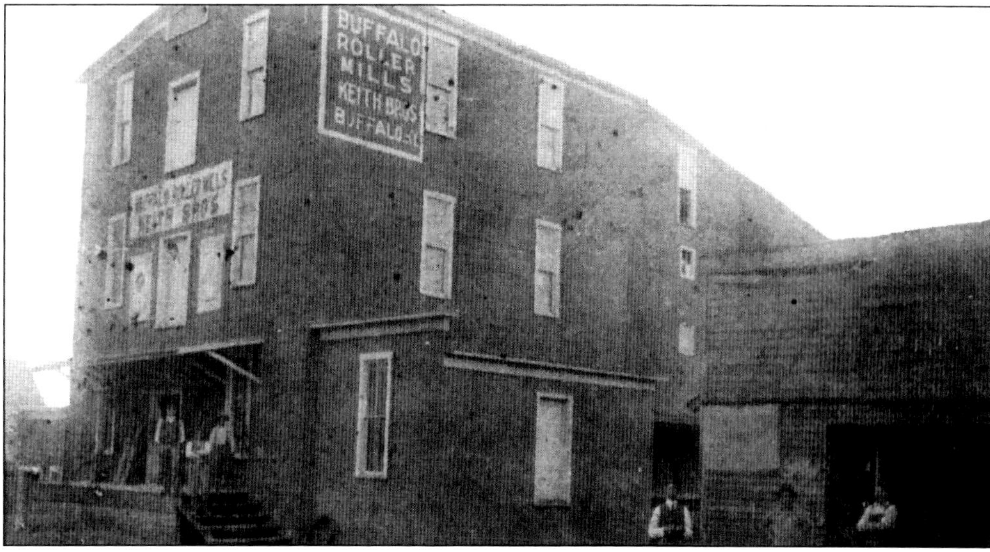

The Buffalo Roller Mill, 1916. This mill served Buffalo and nearby areas in LaRue County for many years. Standing on the porch, from left to right, are Edgar Keith, O.W. Keith, and Ollie Noe. During this time, the popular "Sea Foam" was the mill's best-selling brand of flour. Standing at right, in front of the adjoining blacksmith shop, are Claude "Pink" Miller and Charlie McClain, with arms folded.

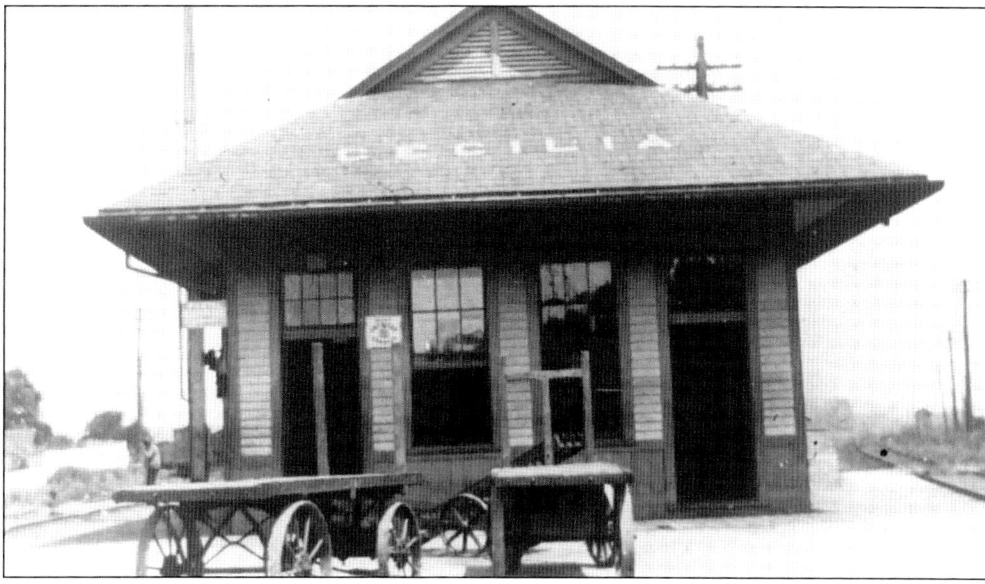

The Cecilia Depot, 1908. The Elizabethtown and Paducah Railroad was chartered on March 5, 1867, under the direction of Elizabethtown millionaire Samuel Beale Thomas. Construction began in Elizabethtown in 1869, and by the spring of 1870 the first 39 miles of track were completed. By September 6, 1872, the entire line was completed to the western Kentucky city of Paducah. The "Cecilian Branch," extending from Cecilia to Louisville, was opened on September 1, 1874. The line was later operated as the Chesapeake, Ohio, and Southwestern Railroad. On August 1, 1896, it became the property of the Illinois Central Railroad. The line from Cecilia to Elizabethtown became a branch line, which later extended to Hodgenville. Cecilia became Hardin County's largest "railroad town."

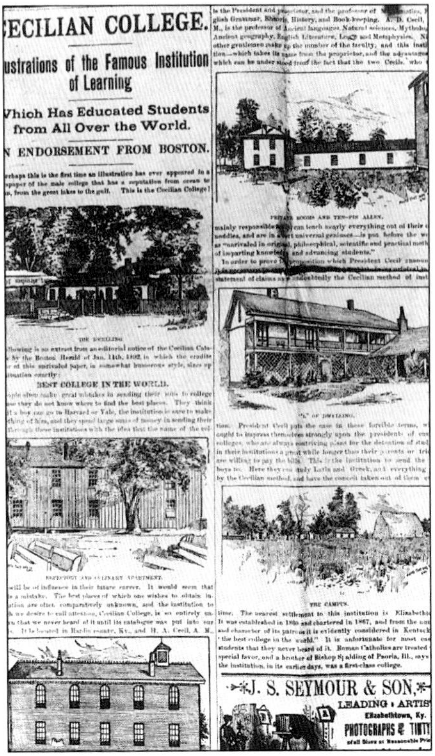
ECILIAN COLLEGE.
ustrations of the Famous Institution of Learning
Which Has Educated Students from All Over the World.
N ENDORSEMENT FROM BOSTON.
BEST COLLEGE IN THE WORLD.
J. S. SEYMOUR & SON,
LEADING ARTIS
Elizabethtown, Ky.
PHOTOGRAPHS & TINTY

THE CECILIAN COLLEGE, 1892. Long before the Elizabethtown and Paducah Railroad was constructed through the Cecilia area, the once-famous Cecilian College was gaining high recognition and respect. First known as "St. Nathan," the school was founded in 1860 and chartered in 1867. It was operated by three highly educated brothers: Henry Cecil (president), and Charles and Ambrose Cecil (assistant professors). The college was an all-male boarding school, attended by students from across the country. Henry Cecil, or "Old Pres," as he was fondly known, was the backbone of the institution. A mathematical genius, his advice was often sought by bankers and businessmen. The school closed shortly after his death in 1893. The town of Cecilia derived its name from the Cecil family. These newspaper illustrations are the only known images of the college buildings.

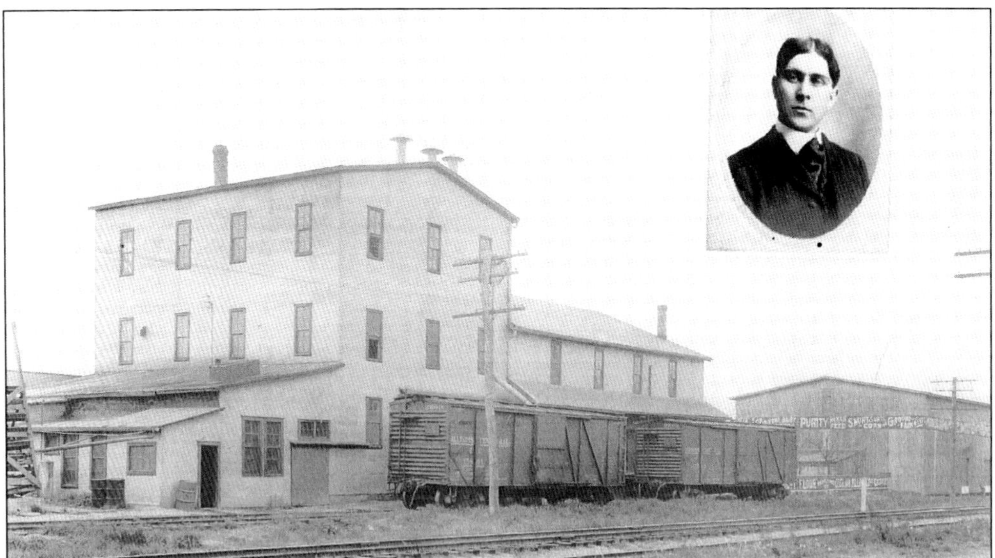

THE CECILIAN MILLING COMPANY, 1920. Established in 1904, this famous mill was located on the south side of the Illinois Central Railroad tracks in Cecilia. On May 20, 1909, Merten A. Cooper (inset) purchased the mill and successfully transformed the small-town milling business into one of the largest and most respected roller mills in Kentucky. Here was made the famous "White Dove" flour, which became a household name for more than 40 years. It was the town's largest industry to date, and was operated by the Cooper family until it was destroyed by fire in 1936.

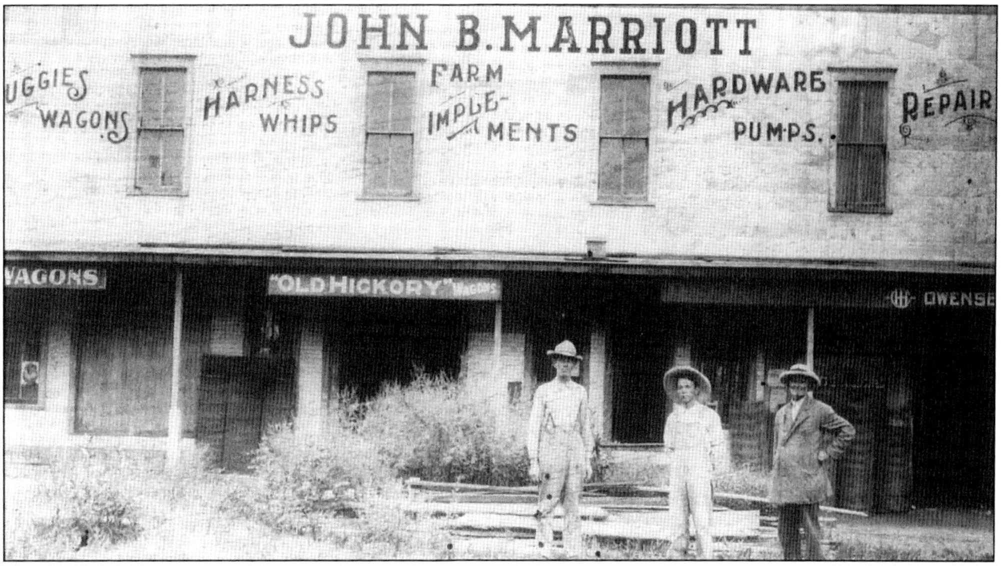

The John B. Mariott Hardware Store, 1912. John B. Mariott built this large hardware and implement store in the heart of Cecilia in 1911, and operated it for many years. In more recent years, it was operated under the title of "Cecilia Center." The building continues to be a familiar landmark. Shown here in this 1912 photo, from left to right, are John B. Mariott II (owner), Ralph Mariott, and an unknown man.

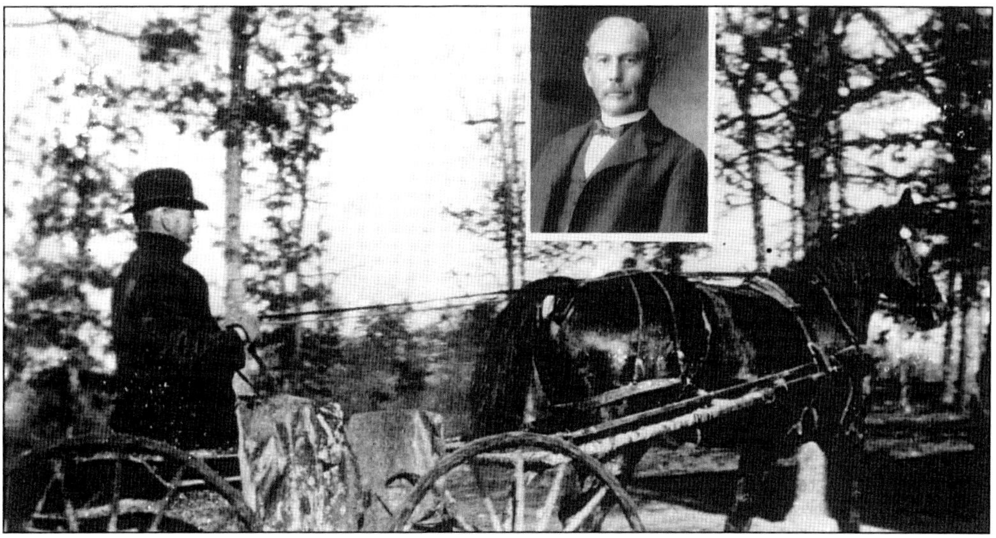

The Country Doctor, 1910. With his faithful horse and buggy that he used for making house calls, Dr. Charles Zachary Aud (inset) was one of Cecilia's leading residents. He came to Cecilia as local surgeon and general physician for the E&P Railroad, as it was nearing completion in 1871. Aud also served as physician for the students of Cecilian College and Bethlehem Academy. He served as health officer in Hardin County for 28 years, was a member of the state board of health under three governors, and was president of the Kentucky State Medical Association in 1906. He is credited for introducing the hypodermic syringe, clinical thermometer, and x-ray into medical service in Hardin County. He was highly instrumental in the early development of Cecilia, and was one of the founders of the Cecilian Bank in 1903, serving as its president for several years.

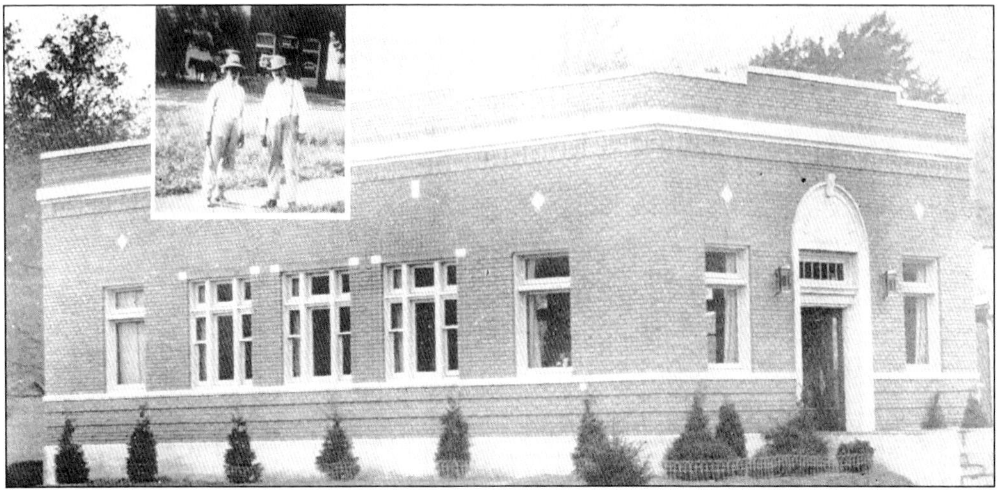

The Cecilian Bank, 1929. The Cecilian Bank first opened for business on May 23, 1903, with Allen Ament as president, Wood English as vice-president, and J.C. Cardwell as cashier. The first bank (inset) was a small brick structure located on the corner of Methodist Street. In 1929, the bank moved to its present main office location across the street from the original bank. The building has undergone many changes through the years to better serve the needs of its depositors. It is one of only two early Hardin County banks that have remained locally owned and operated.

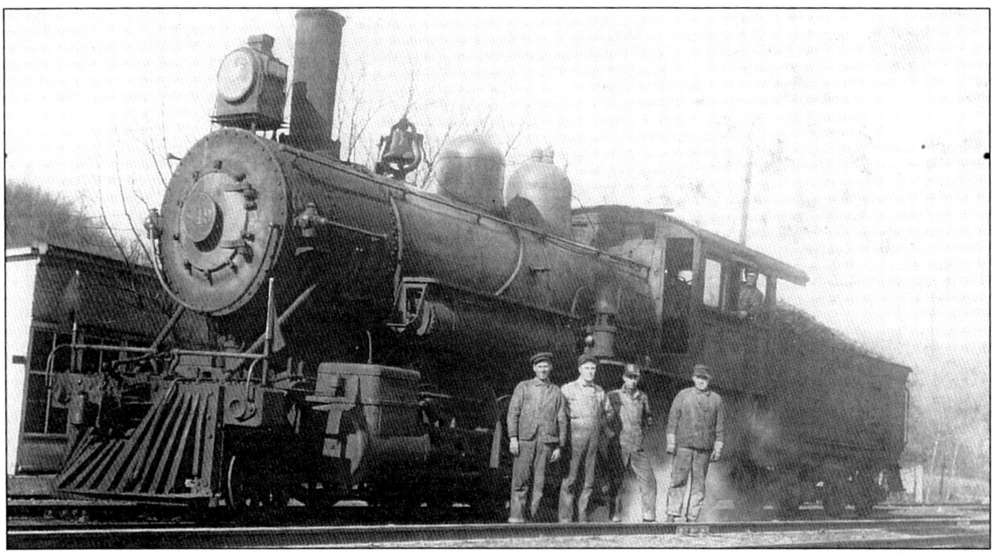

Old Hill Engine Number 849, 1906. When the L&N Railroad made its way through the Clear Creek Valley in 1854, two powerful steam locomotives used in pulling the long trains up the steep 5-mile incline to Elizabethtown were stationed in a building near the base of Muldraugh Hill. The need for these "helper engines" and their crews gave birth to the small railroad community of Colesburg. First known as Robertsonville, a post office was established here on August 19, 1856. The town's name was changed to Colesburg in 1877, to honor one of the town's founders, William Cole. With the decline of steam power and the advent of the diesel engine, the hill engines were removed. In this photo, taken in front of J.W.G Stark's Store, engineer James T. Larkin leans out of the cab of Engine # 849, while other crew members stand below.

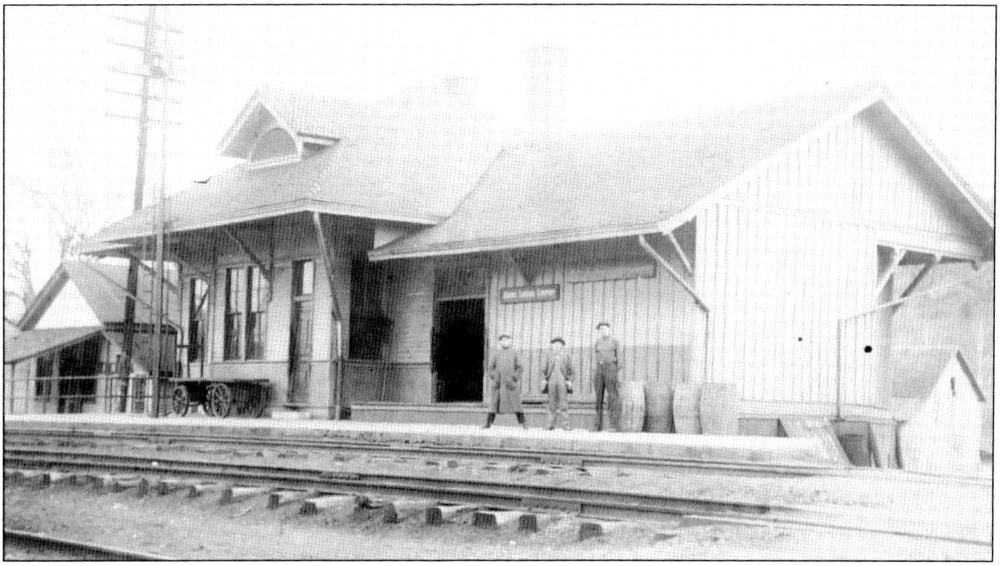

THE COLESBURG DEPOT, 1910. The L&N Depot at Colesburg was built in 1858 by Samuel L. Purcell. In 1882, the L&N Railroad Company purchased the building from the Purcell family. It was remodeled and enlarged around 1908, making it one of the most attractive depots in the county. Due to the decline of passenger service, and heavy damage from the 1937 flood, the depot was torn down in 1939.

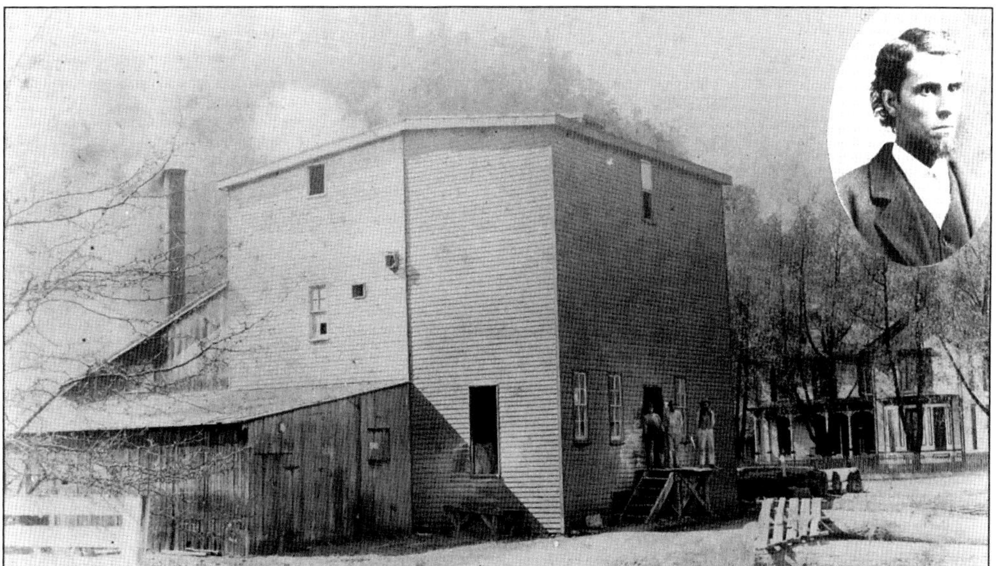

THE PARDEE MILL AND LUMBER YARD, 1904. Casius M. Pardee (inset) and his wife, Susan, moved to Colesburg in 1876. He immediately began construction of a large steam-powered gristmill and a sawmill to accommodate the farmers in the vicinity. Pardee also owned a small farm on top of the hill beside his home. He constructed a wooden log flume on the hill that he used to carry logs to the mill at the bottom, where they were processed and sold. Pardee and his sons, Clarence, George, and Robert, operated the mill until 1919, when the property was sold out of the family. The mill was torn down in 1928. The Pardee home is seen here to the right of the mill.

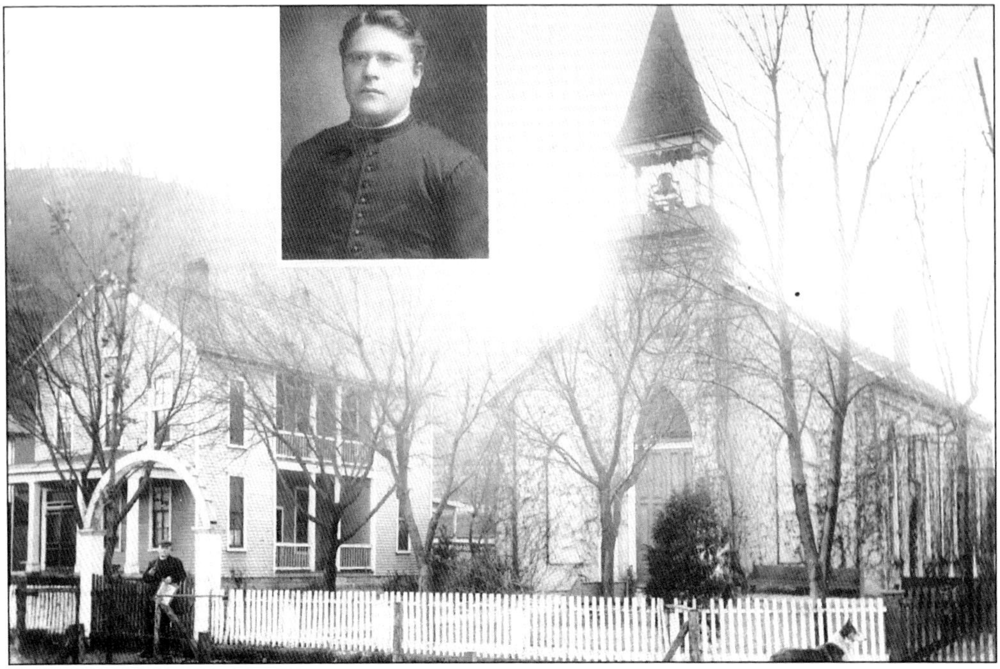

The St. Clare Catholic Church, 1914. Established in 1808, St. Clare is the oldest Catholic church in Hardin County. Rev. Charles Nerinckx, a pioneer priest of Kentucky, built the first log church for the Clear Creek congregation with his own hands, on a small knoll about a mile from the present town of Colesburg. The church's cemetery is still located there today. By 1842, a small brick structure had replaced the original church. With the arrival of the railroad through the valley in 1854, a small village began to take form. In 1873, work was begun on the present church of St. Clare, which was located in the growing town of Colesburg. The old church was dismantled, and the bricks were used in the new one. In 1878, Rev. J.J. Abell had a rectory built next to the church, and he became the town's first resident pastor. Rev. John Gastaldi (inset), pastor from 1901 to 1928, stands at the front gate of the church in 1914.

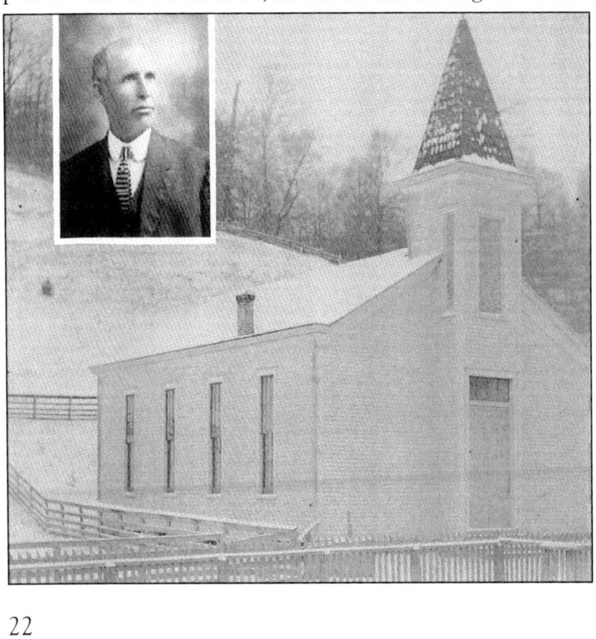

The Colesburg Baptist Church, 1906. The Baptists in the Colesburg community began holding services in the town's one-room schoolhouse around 1880. By 1891, their numbers had grown to the point that they organized their own church on May 2, 1891, with 31 charter members. Rev. B.P. Robinson was the first pastor, and local merchant Leven Purcell (inset) was selected as church clerk, a position he held until his death in 1918. The church was built on a lot directly across from the school. In its early years, the church was served by students of the Southern Baptist Seminary in Louisville.

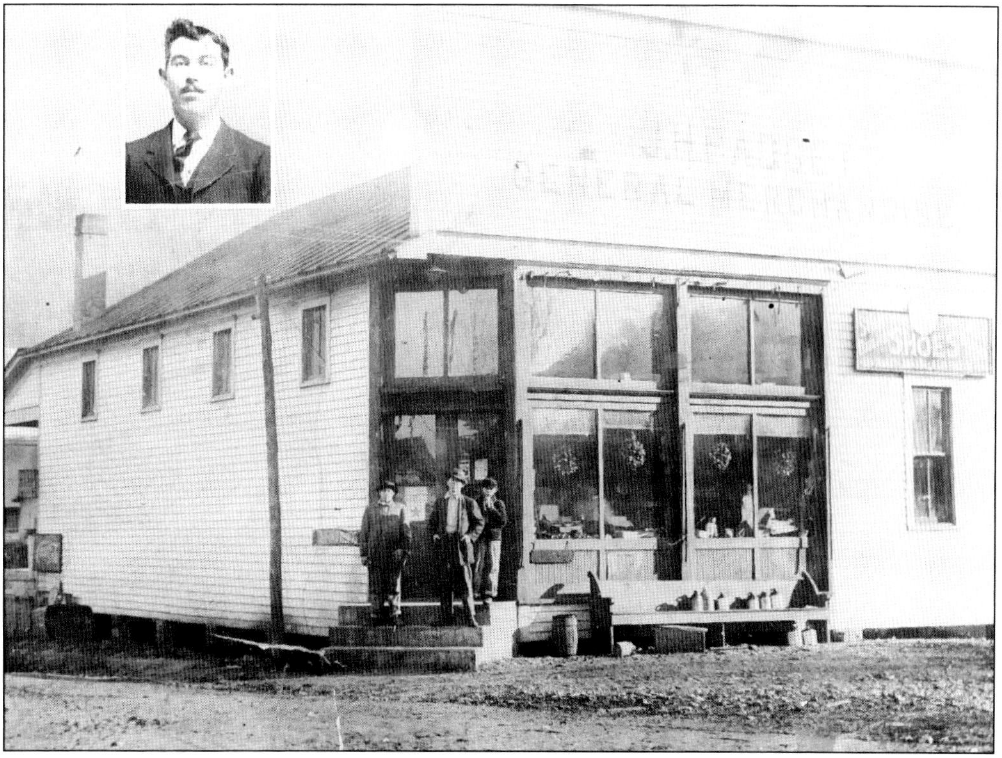

J.H. Padgett's General Store, 1914. James H. Padgett (inset) built this store beside his home in Colesburg in 1911. Later, after purchasing another store owned by his father-in-law (B.F. Brian), Padgett moved his store building and combined the two stores into one building, operating it with his brother-in-law, Jerome Brian, as the Brian and Padgett General Store. Padgett later became sole owner, operating the store and post office until 1943. His daughter, Veronica "Sis" Padgett, ran it for a few years before selling it to Jerome Brian. Brian's wife, Mayme, was the last to own the store before it was removed by the Hardin County Road Department in 1956, to straighten the county road. Mr. Padgett's endless generosity helped many Colesburg residents through the Depression. Standing on the steps of the store are J.H. Padgett (center) and his sons, Gerald (left) and Marvin (right).

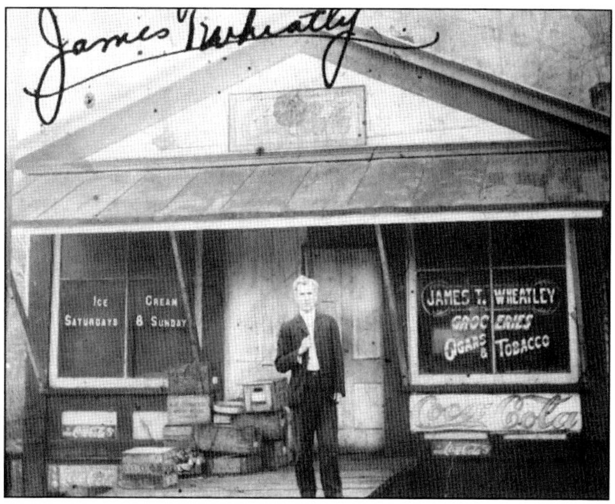

James T. Wheatley's Store, 1910. This photo was taken in front of James T. Wheatley's General Store in Colesburg. It stood on the east side of the L&N Railroad tracks, about two doors north of the depot. Mr. Wheatley is pictured standing in front. The rear portion of this building once housed the drug store of James Alfred Stovall. Note the advertisement on the window for ice cream on Saturday and Sunday. The building was torn down in the early 1940s.

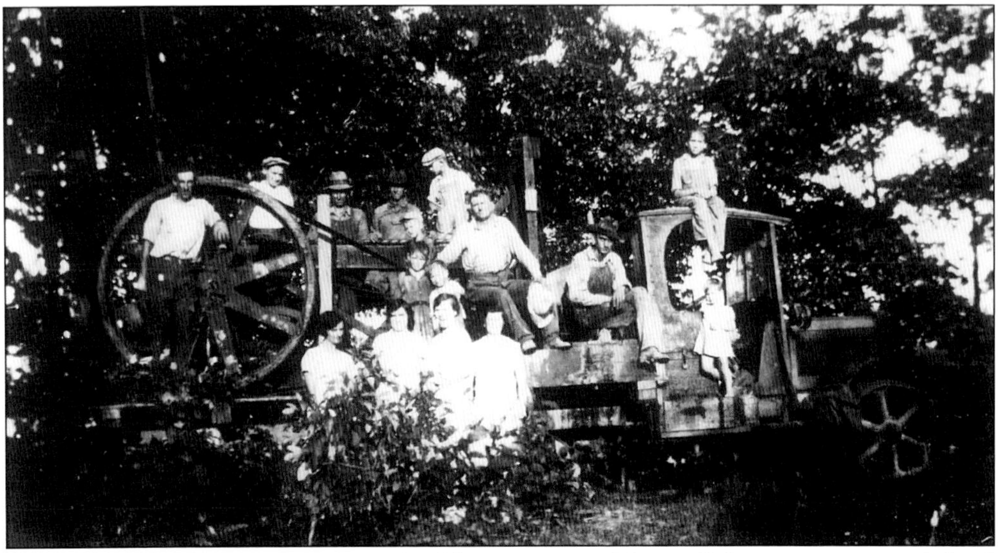

WELL-DIGGING NEAR CORINTH, C. 1930. The operators of this well-digging rig pose with local children and residents of the Corinth neighborhood in the Hibernia community of LaRue County. Two Taylor County men were digging a well that day at the Corinth Schoolhouse. Among the observers are Ike Skaggs, Willard Skaggs, Jess Howell, Mack Skaggs, Woodrow Thompson, and John Henry Skaggs.

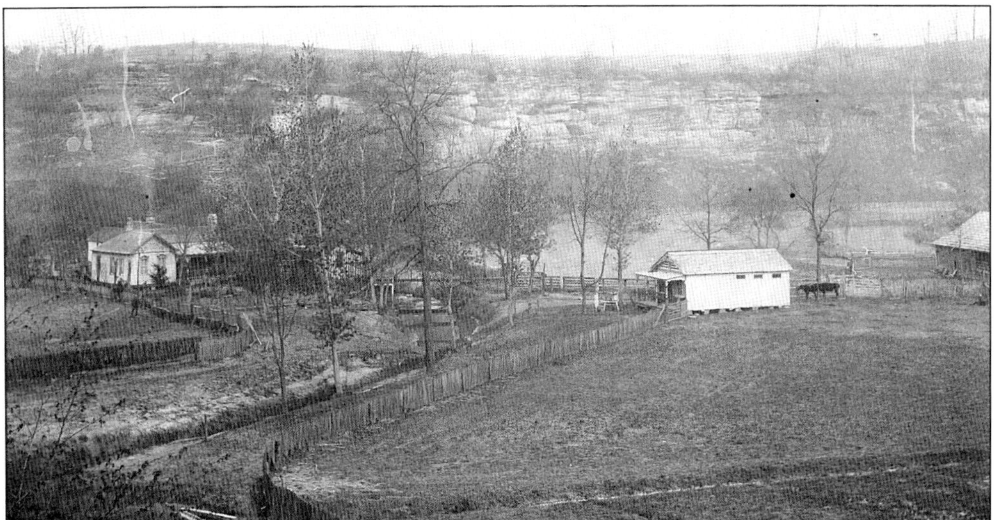

DEVER'S HOLLOW, 1900. William A. Dever came to this hollow, near the town of Summit, shortly after the Civil War, and built a home for his family. He farmed the approximately 40-acre valley, which was surrounded on all sides by natural rock walls. Dever spent countless hours exploring every nook and crevasse of the area, unearthing many Native-American artifacts, which he displayed in his own museum. This photo is a panoramic view of the hollow, with Dever's home at left and his "Black Hoof Museum" located across the creek. Today, nothing remains that would suggest anything but nature ever existed here.

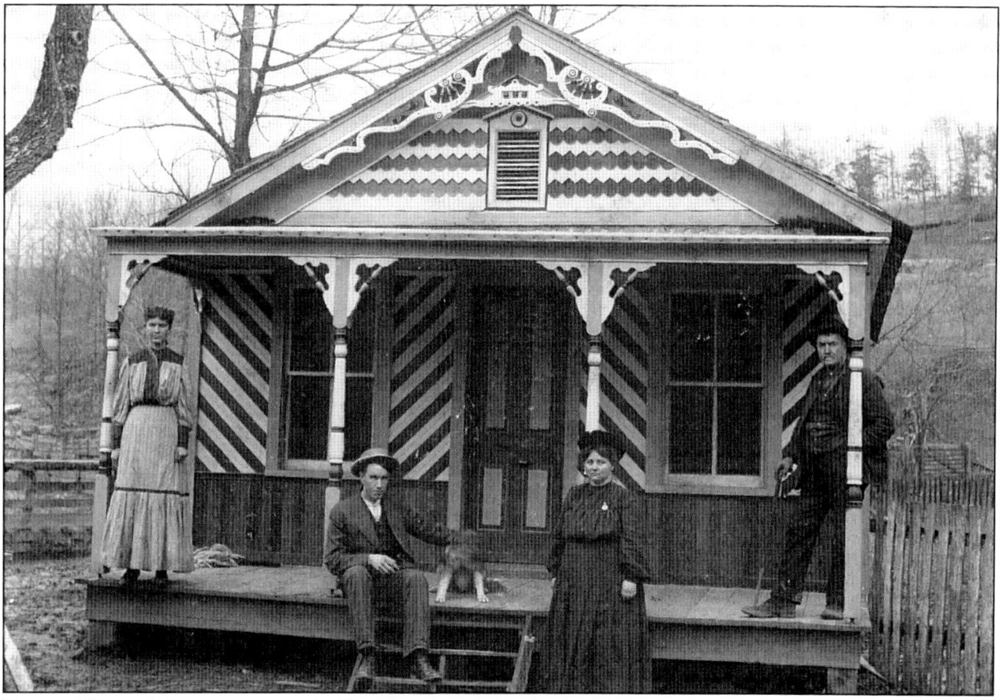

Black Hoof Museum, 1905. Shown posing in front of the museum, from left to right, are Minnie Dever, John Dever (son of W.A. Dever), Melvina Young Dever (wife of W.A. Dever), and William A. Dever. The front of the building was an example of Dever's imagination and craftsmanship. Known as the "jack-knife genius," he decorated the building with many of his intricate carvings, and named it Black Hoof Museum, after an old Native-American chief. Dever's collection was so unique that he was asked to display it at the St. Louis World's Fair in 1904. After his death, the collection was sold to various individuals and museums across the country.

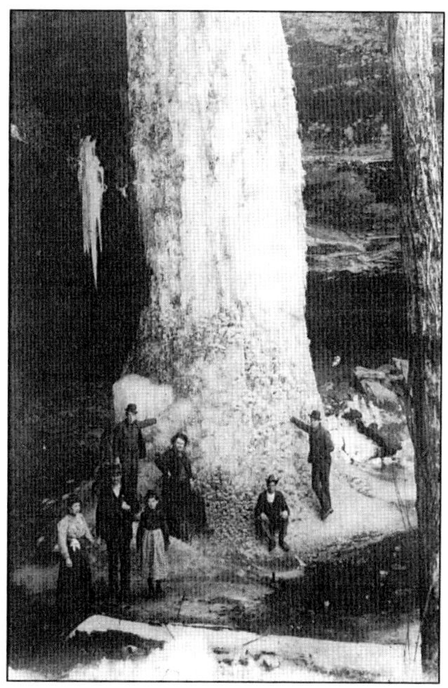

A Frozen Waterfall at Dever's Hollow, 1903. W.A. Dever (standing third from the right) and several family members pose in front of a 72-foot frozen waterfall on his Dever Hollow farm in 1903. A cave, located behind the waterfall, is where Dever found many of the Native-American artifacts that he displayed in his museum. The family stored ice from the waterfall to use during the warmer months.

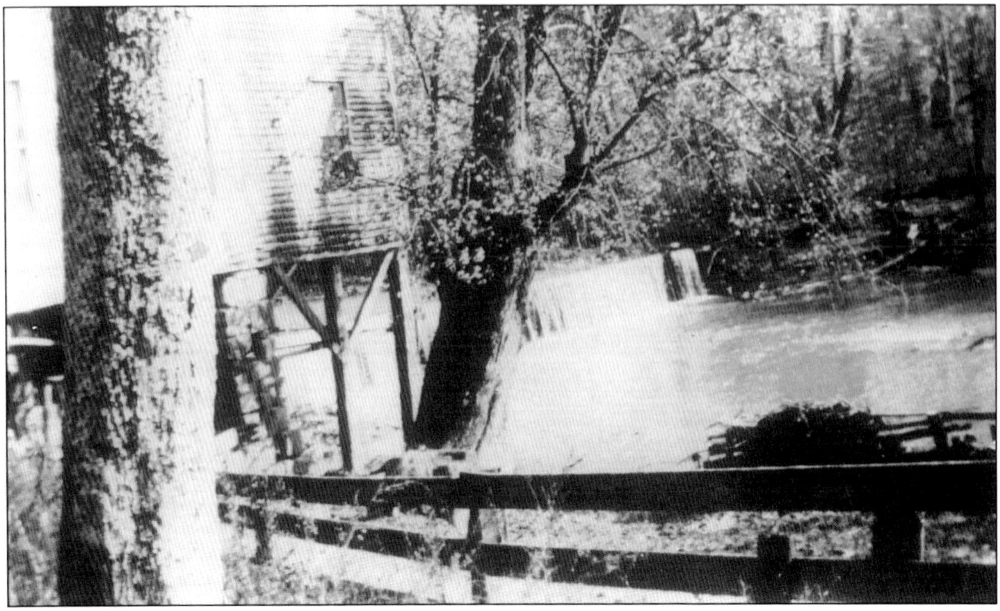

Eagle Mills, c. 1920. Located on Nolin Creek in LaRue County, this was one of the earliest mills in the area. During the Civil War, and at the time of Confederate General Braxton Bragg's invasion of Kentucky, part of his army camped at Eagle Mills. One of the Confederate officers, Captain Pittman, took charge of the mill and used it for grinding corn for the army. The corn was hauled in from the farms of the neighborhood and the mills were run day and night during the time the army was staying there and at nearby Red Mills. Eagle Mills was operated at that time by the grandfather of Mr. James Atwood. The mill and farm were sold during the early 1900s by Albert Watkins and W.J. Boyd to J.B. Bunch, who moved to the farm and took over operation of the mill. It was very successful until 1918, when J.B. Bunch sold the mill, a small acreage of land, and a five-room house to J.C. O'Banion and a Mr. Ennis, who moved to the property and operated the mill during their ownership of the property. The dam and a portion of the mill are pictured above, and the bridge leading to the mill is pictured below.

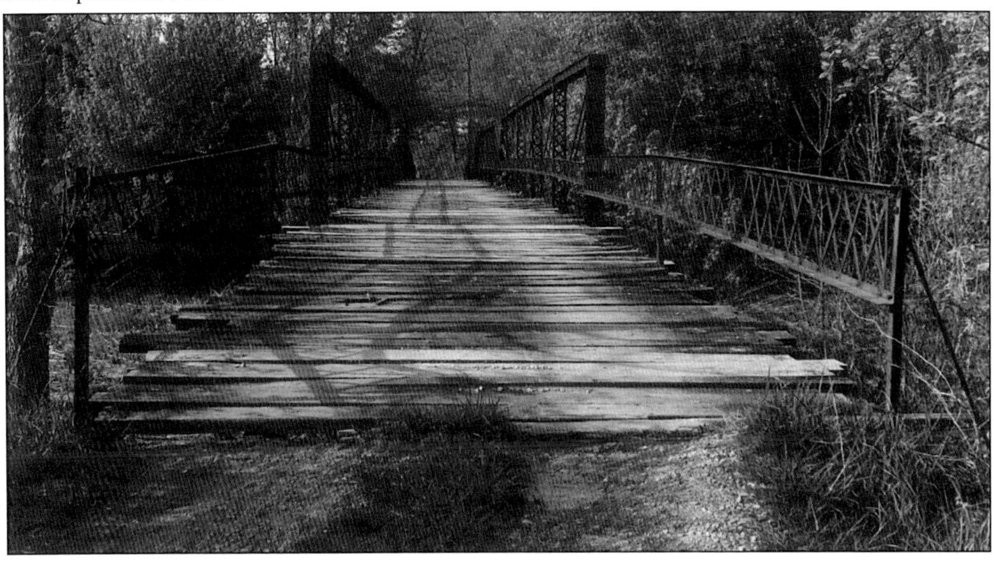

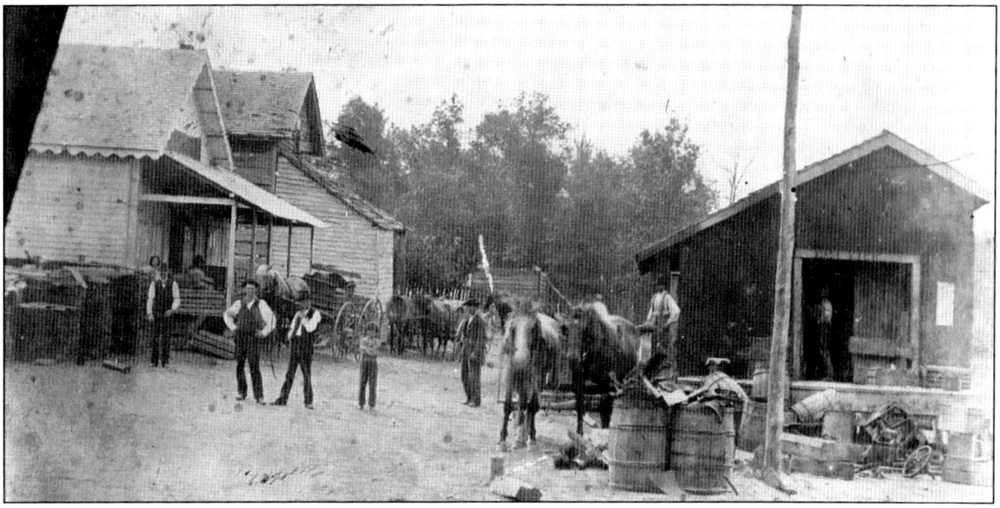

AN EAST VIEW STREET SCENE, 1889. The town of East View took form shortly after the E&P Railroad was built through the area in 1870. Around the turn of this century, East View boasted a school, Baptist church, three general stores (operated by Jeff Beeler, John Hoover, and M.S. Ragland), a furniture and hardware store (operated by C.G. Bluit), a doctor's office (Dr. J.W. Brandon, physician), a gristmill (operated by John Daugherty), a train depot, stock yards, and a sumac factory. On September 1, 1920, Leslie Ragland, Alex Montgomery, and Claud Givan opened the East View Bank. It was purchased by the First Hardin National Bank, and closed in 1932. Visitors to both the Hardin Springs and White Mills summer resorts arrived and departed at the East View Depot. The post office has been in continuous operation here since April 6, 1871.

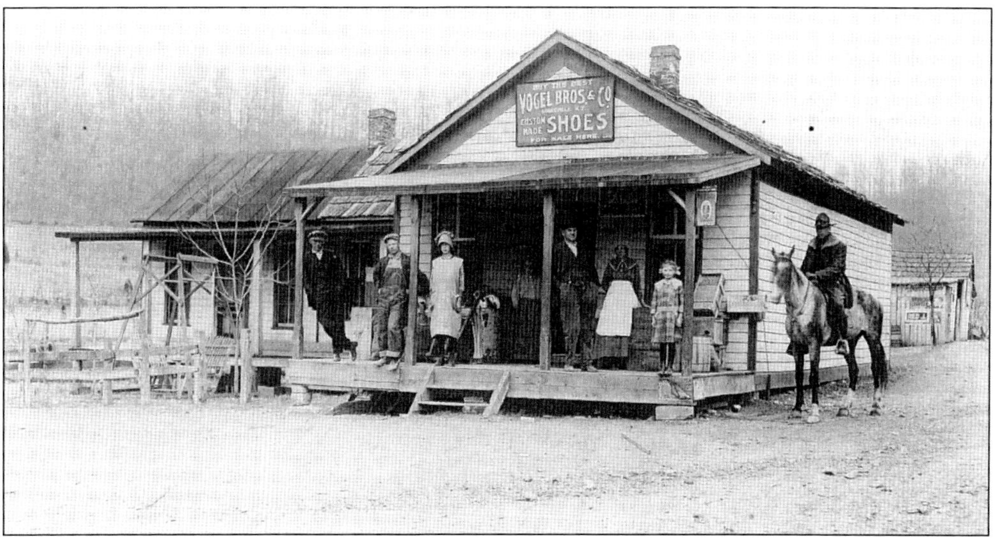

THE J.L. HARRIS GENERAL STORE, 1914. James Lewis Harris purchased this store at Easy Gap, near the Salt River in northern Hardin County, in 1912, and operated it with his wife, Sally. In 1918, they moved to the town of Nolin and operated a large general store. Easy Gap had a post office from 1890 to 1907. The entire town was later consumed as part of the Fort Knox Military Reservation. Shown standing below the Vogel Brothers shoe sign are J.L. Harris, Sally (his wife), and their daughters, Georgia (left) and Ethel (right). Others in the photo are unidentified. The family lived in the house connected to the left side of the store.

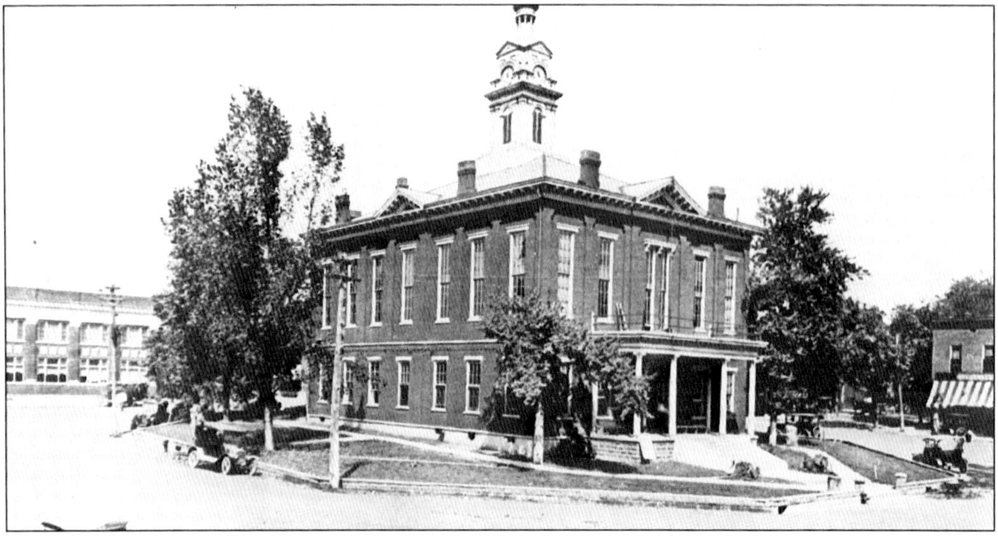

THE HARDIN COUNTY COURTHOUSE, 1905. The first Hardin County Courthouse, a log structure, was built in 1795. The next was a small brick building, which stood on the southwest corner of public square, facing north. The beautiful building shown here was constructed in 1872, and was the first courthouse located in the center of the town's square. A majestic cupola graced the top of the building, which later housed a large clock, consisting of four faces, that could be seen from any point on the square. The building was heavily damaged by fire on December 5, 1932, after which the present courthouse was built on the site.

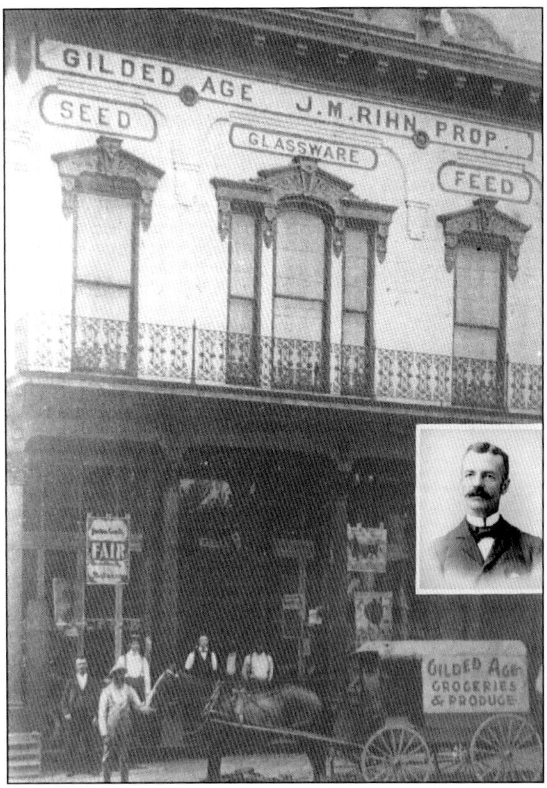

THE GILDED-AGE GROCERY, 1900. This elaborate building was constructed in 1877 for the notorious Philip Arnold, who was known throughout the country for his famous diamond swindle of the mid-1800s. The first business in the city to have plate-glass windows, the building's ornate facade and iron railings were unique to the area. It was occupied by James M. Rihn's "Gilded Age Grocery and Produce Store" from 1886 to 1920. Rihn (inset) was a charter member of the Knights of Columbus Council Number 1455, which formed in the city in 1909. An upper room in the building served as the Knights of Columbus Meeting Hall from 1910 to 1916. The building remains standing today, although greatly altered.

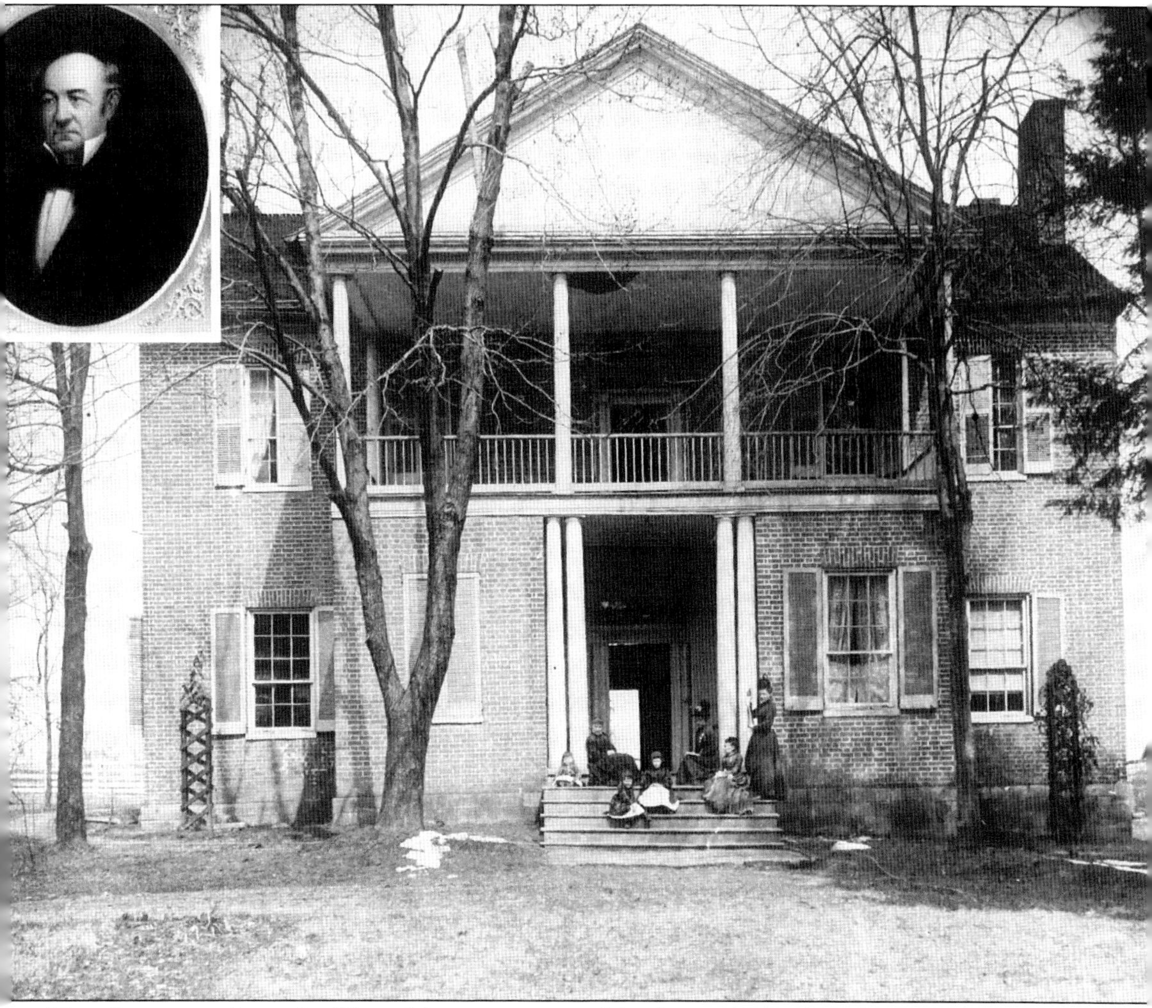

THE GOVERNOR JOHN L. HELM MANSION, 1890. John Larue Helm (inset), a wealthy and prominent lawyer and statesman, purchased his paternal grandfather's home place from an uncle and began construction of this stately mansion in 1831, using slave labor. It was built on or near the site of Captain Thomas Helm's fort, which was one of the three original forts that comprised the Severn's Valley Settlement, long before Elizabethtown was established. In this house, John and Lucinda Helm raised a large family. He became involved in state and local politics, being elected lieutenant governor of Kentucky in 1848. When Governor John J. Crittenden resigned office on July 31, 1850, Helm assumed the title until September 5, 1851. He then turned his efforts to the establishment of the Louisville and Nashville Railroad Company, which he was elected president of from 1854 to 1860. Helm proudly rode the first train through Hardin County and Elizabethtown in 1859. On August 7, 1867, at age 65, Helm was elected governor of his beloved state. However, his laborious campaign had weakened him to the point that the installation ceremonies were conducted at his mansion in Elizabethtown, on September 3, 1867, where he died a few days later. The house and property then passed on to his son, John L. Helm II. The property was sold out of the Helm family in 1919. Today, the Helm farm has been consumed by business and housing projects, and the altered mansion is used as a doctor's office.

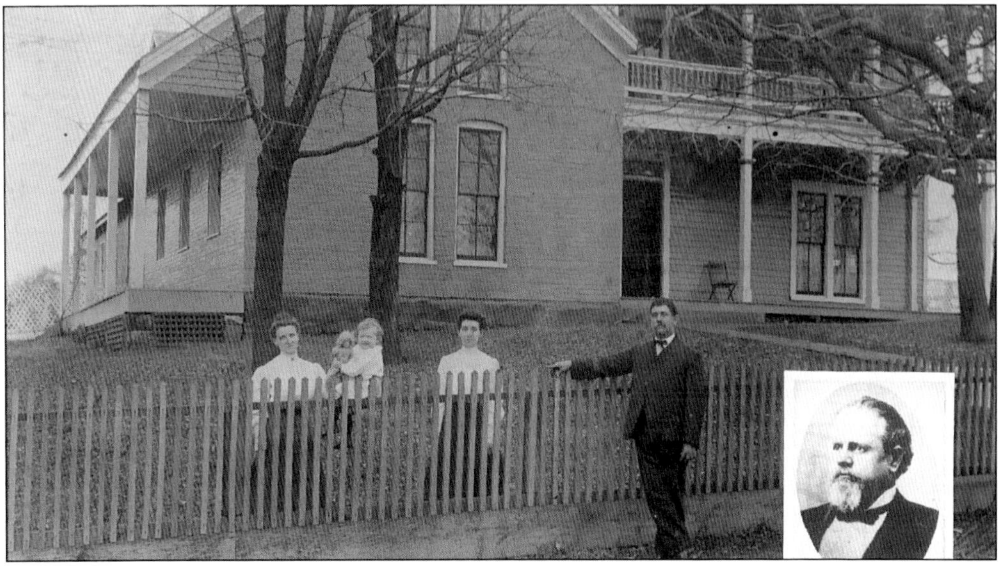

THE BIRTHPLACE OF GOVERNOR JOHN YOUNG BROWN, 1908. This home, located in the now-defunct Claysville community, was the birthplace of Kentucky Governor John Young Brown (inset) on June 28, 1835. Brown enjoyed a successful law practice in Elizabethtown, before entering politics. He was elected to Congress four times, and served as governor from 1891 to 1895. The Adams family lived in the home from 1898 to 1940. It was torn down in 1941. Shown here, from left to right, are Mrs. Clarence Adams, Lila Adams Dykes, Bertha Bishop (sister to Mrs. Adams), and Clarence Adams.

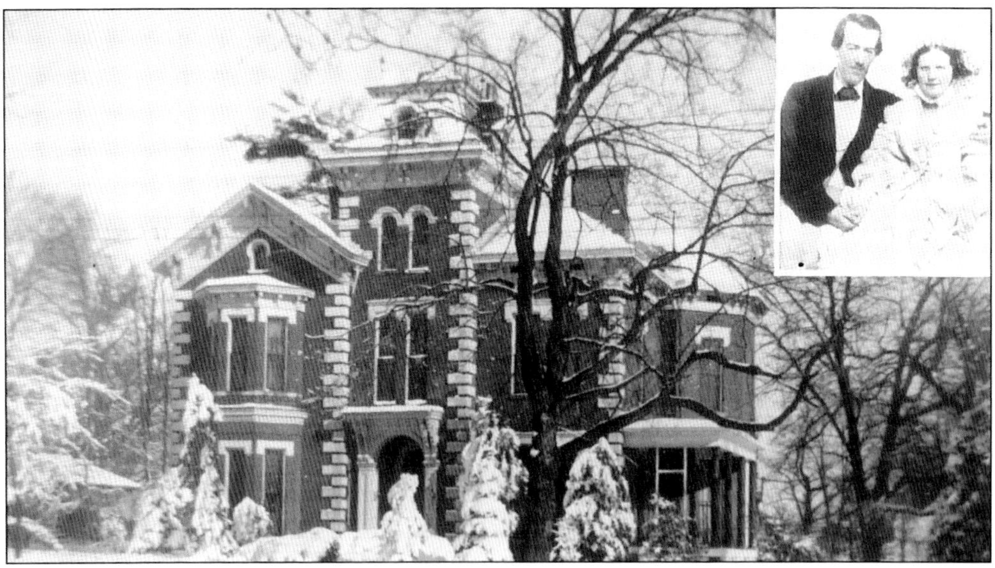

THE COLONEL JAMES B. PAYNE HOME, 1920S. Construction of this exquisite home began late in 1872, and lasted two years. It was built in the front right corner of Samuel B. Thomas's (Elizabethtown's first millionaire) front yard, and presented to his daughter Elizabeth and her husband, James B. Payne (inset), as a gift. Colonel Payne died in 1919, and the home was sold out of the family. In 1953, Logan Haycraft rented the home and operated a restaurant there known as "The Stagecoach Inn." In 1954, the house was sold to the Pan American Oil Company, which tore it down and built a gas station on the property.

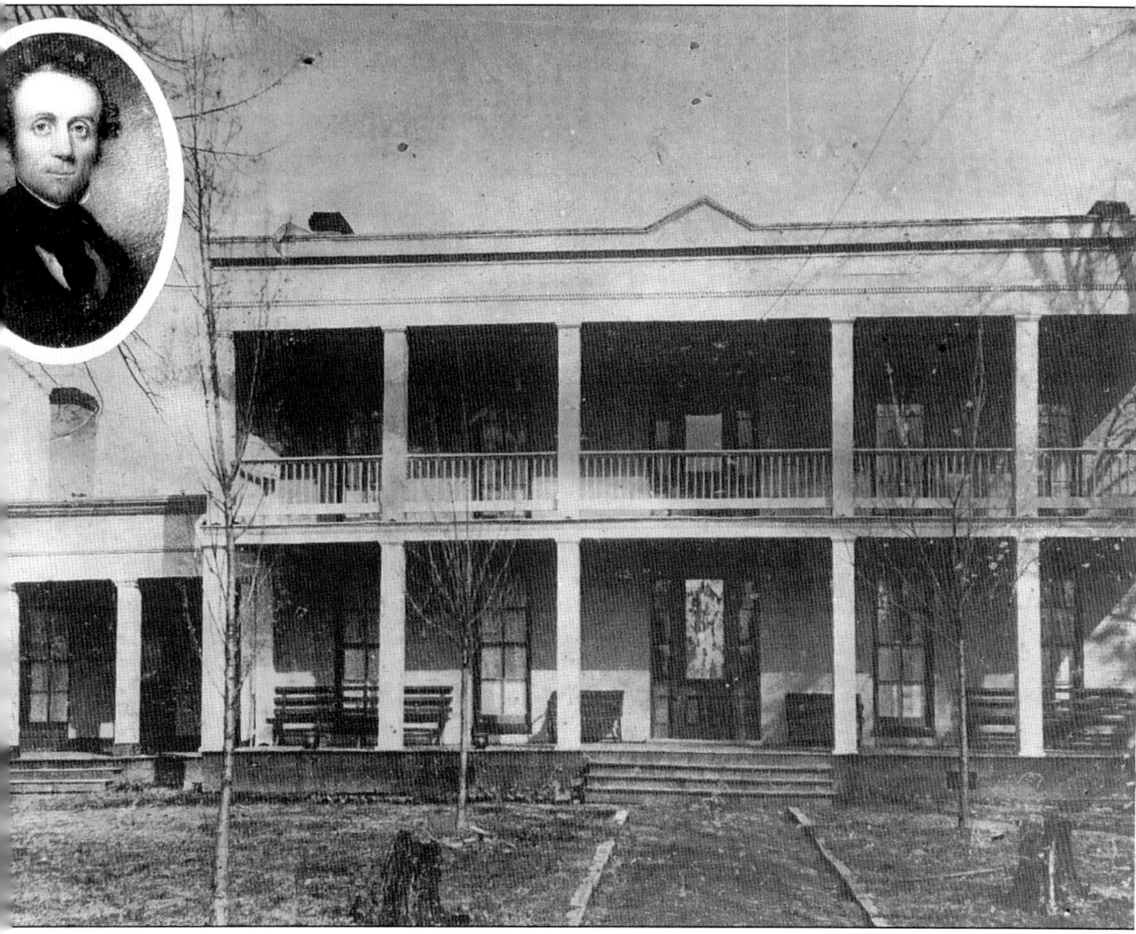

THE SAMUEL BEALE THOMAS HOME, 1890S. Built by Archibald Chaffin in 1842, this home was purchased by Elizabethtown's first millionaire, Samuel Beale Thomas (inset), in 1844. Thomas, who had been residing in the town of West Point, was operating a large and profitable stagecoach route on the old L&N Pike, which happened to pass directly in front of his new home. When noted personalities, such as famous opera singer Jenny Lind, traveled through the area, Thomas would drive the stagecoach. Headquartered in the Galt House in Louisville, the company had over 1,600 horses in use daily. After moving to Elizabethtown, Thomas joined forces with other prominent local figures, such as John L. Helm, to establish the Louisville and Nashville Railroad Company, which was built through the county from 1854 to 1859. A man of great influence and foresight, Thomas also headed the effort to build a railroad extending westward from Elizabethtown to the town of Paducah. Chartered on March 5, 1867, as the Elizabethtown and Paducah Railroad, with Thomas as its first president, the new company had its main offices and repair shops located in Elizabethtown. By 1870, the entire line was operational, and by 1873, another line connecting at Cecilia extended on to Louisville. When Thomas died in 1874, a special funeral train carried his body from Louisville to Elizabethtown for burial. Along the route, great crowds of mourners stood along the tracks to pay tribute to the man who, in realizing his dream, had improved the lives of so many people. Thomas's home remained in the family for a number of years before being sold. The large, two-story porches were removed in 1946. The house remains today on Poplar Street as a reminder of a great man and his influence on Hardin County.

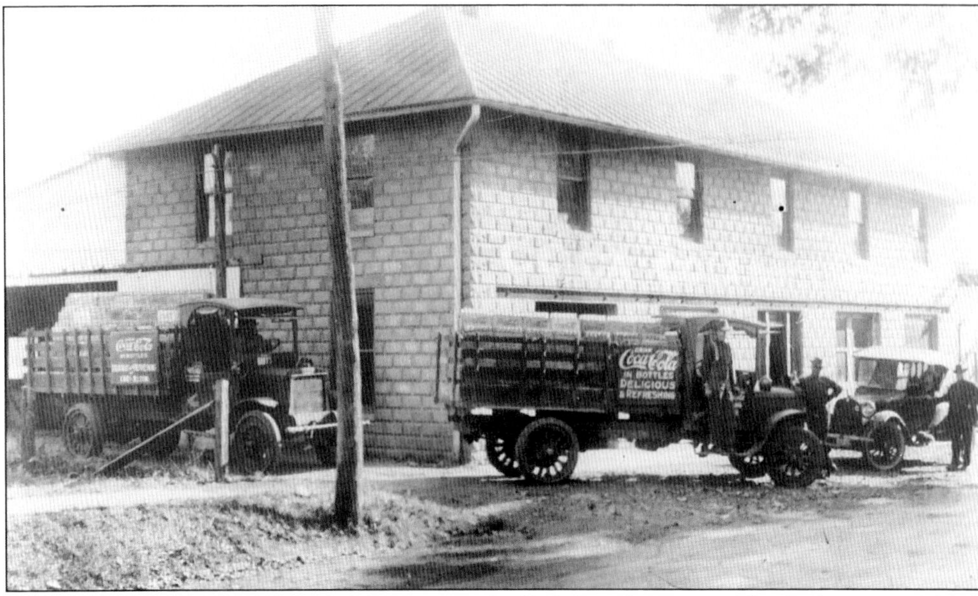

THE COCA COLA BOTTLING WORKS, 1920. Luke B. Schmidt came to Elizabethtown in March of 1920 and opened the Elizabethtown Coca Cola bottling works in the old Economy Garage building on North Mulberry Street. His staff of four employees and two delivery trucks serviced Hardin, Bullitt, Meade, Nelson, Larue, and Breckinridge Counties. By 1933, the business had outgrown the building, and a new plant was built on South Main Street (the present site of the board of education).

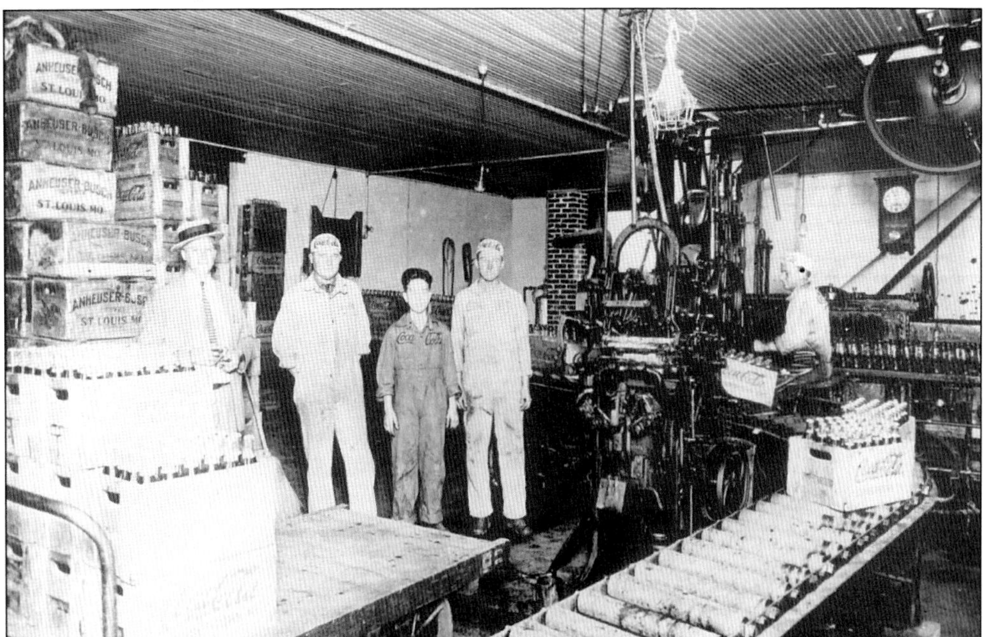

INSIDE THE COCA COLA PLANT, 1920. This is an inside view of the first Coca Cola bottling plant on North Mulberry Street, shortly after opening in March of 1920. Pictured, from left to right, are Luke Schmidt (owner), Clarence Bethel, Fairley Albert, Earl Skillman, and Jim Bethel.

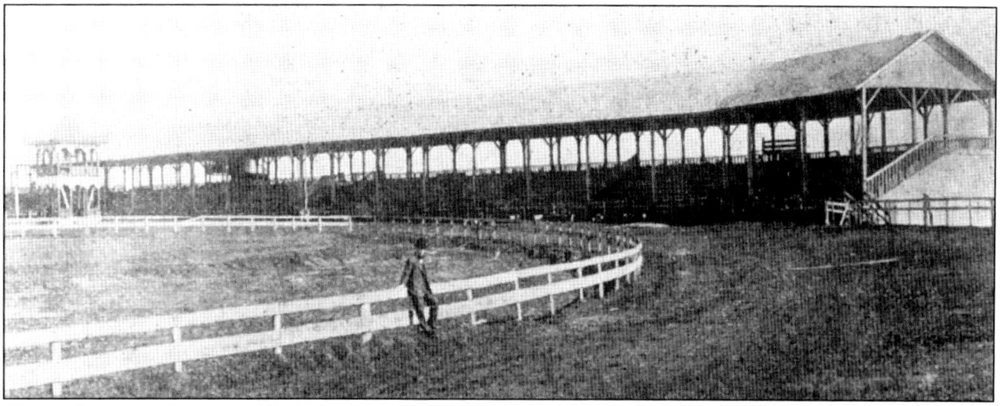

THE HARDIN COUNTY FAIR GRANDSTAND AND TRACK, 1906. The Hardin County Fair Association was organized in 1885 by a group of local farmers and businessmen. The fairgrounds, consisting of 17 acres, were located on the corner of Maple and Helm Streets, just outside the city limits at that time. An amphitheater, stables, fences, and a half-mile racetrack were built before the first fair opened in September 1885. Each year, the annual four-day event (usually running Monday–Friday during the second week of September) grew both in size and popularity. The competitive spirit of the fair motivated local farmers to improve the blood lines of their livestock. For many years, Hardin was number one in the state for its poultry breeds. Fair admission was 25¢, and ladies were admitted free on the first day. Horse racing was a popular attraction, and by 1894, the grandstand was enlarged to hold seven thousand people. Noted bands from all over the state entertained throughout the day, and mule races kept audiences laughing. Thirty-three consecutive fairs were held before the property was sold, and the buildings torn down, in 1919.

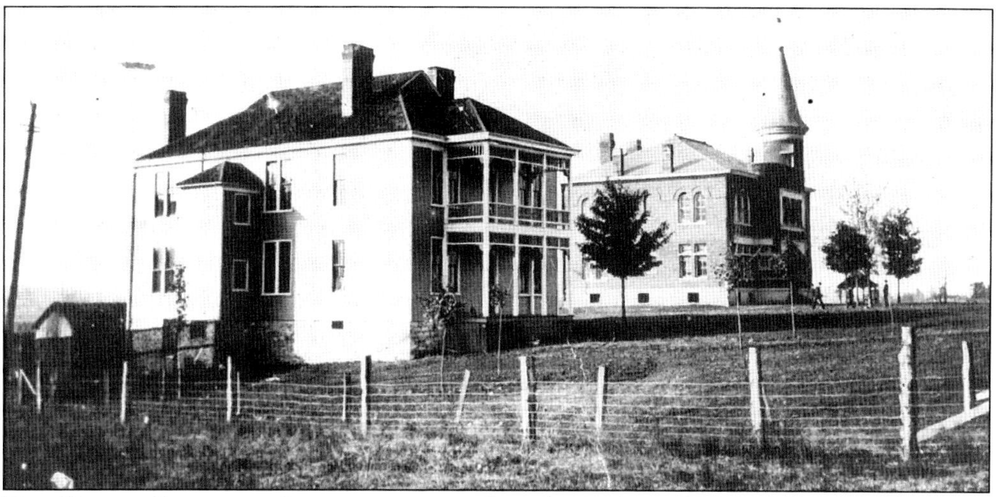

THE HARDIN COLLEGIATE INSTITUTE, 1900. Once located on what is now known as College Street, this elaborate building was the "pride of Elizabethtown" when it opened in 1893. The school's dormitory (left) and main school building (right) are pictured as they appeared in 1900. In 1911, the building was purchased as a joint venture between Hardin County and the City of Elizabethtown, and converted into a high school. When the new city high school opened in 1915, the college building and surrounding property were sold at auction. The Elizabethtown Knights of Columbus purchased the building in 1916 and used it for their meeting hall and other social functions until 1937, when it was torn down and the land was subdivided for housing.

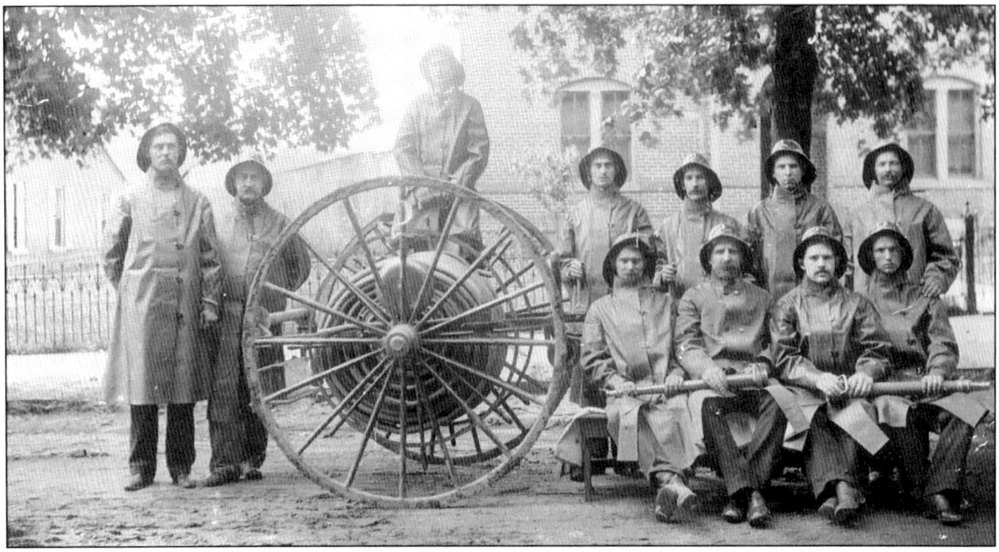

ELIZABETHTOWN FIRE DEPARTMENT HOSE COMPANY NUMBER TWO, 1896. Several times during its history the city of Elizabethtown has been devastated by fire. Undoubtedly, the worst of these disasters took place on August 7, 1869, when a small flame, assisted by a brisk wind, grew to engulf most of the business district. By the end of 1895, the city had installed 35 fire hydrants throughout town to help prevent such catastrophes. Here, members of Volunteer Hose Company Number Two pose with their equipment on North Main Street in front of the old county jail. Identified are Charles Richerson and Fritz Woelpert (seated second and fourth from left). Other men listed as being in the same company, and probably shown here, include T.C. Crawford, Ben Goldnamer, Henry Goranflo, Frank Gault, Will Cotton, Charles Huntsberry, and John Joplin.

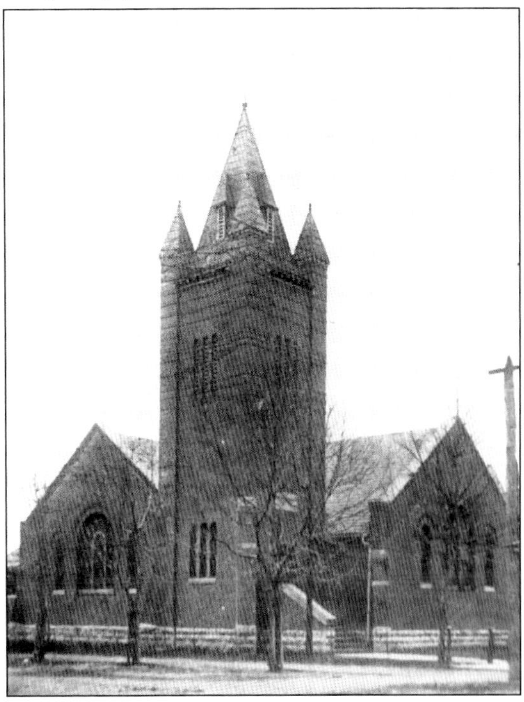

THE SEVERNS VALLEY BAPTIST CHURCH, 1908. The Severns Valley Baptist Church is the oldest Protestant organization west of the Allegheny Mountains still in existence. It was organized June 17, 1781, under a green sugar tree near Hynes Fort, with 18 charter members, all of whom had migrated here from Virginia. In 1804, the congregation began building a log structure on North Main Street (it was never completed). In 1807, Samuel Haycraft Sr. donated a parcel of land near the city cemetery, and a church was built there. In 1834, John Y. Hill was hired to construct a brick church on West Poplar Street, which was used until 1896, when the church (pictured here) was erected on the corner of South Mulberry and West Dixie. Several additions were made to this building before the congregation moved to its present site on Poplar Street in 1955.

THE FIRST NATIONAL BANK, 1906. Constructed around 1870, this building housed three of Elizabethtown's earliest financial institutions. It first opened as Thomas, Polk, and Company, being a private enterprise, with the city's wealthiest man, Samuel B. Thomas, as one of the owners. Upon Thomas's death in 1874, Philip Arnold bought into the firm. In 1886, Arnold's widow sold the building to the First National Bank, which had been operating out of the Depp building since its establishment on October 1, 1883. First National remained there until July 1, 1911, when it merged with Hardin National Bank and became the First Hardin National Bank. The building later became the home of the Hardin County Telephone Company for many years, as well as other businesses. Today, part of the building remains as the Old Vault Deli.

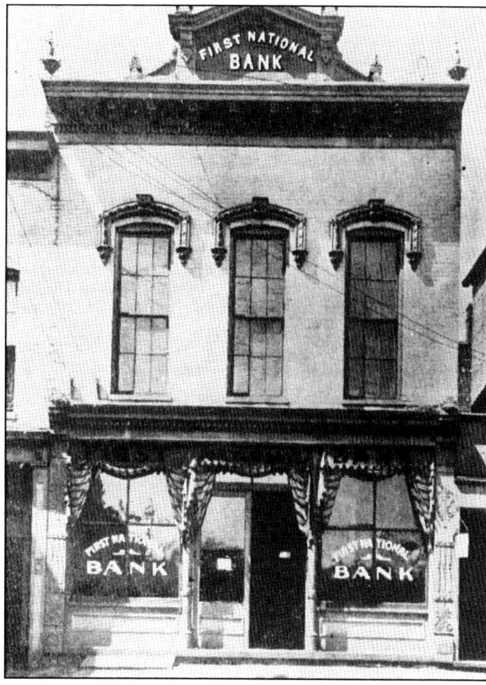

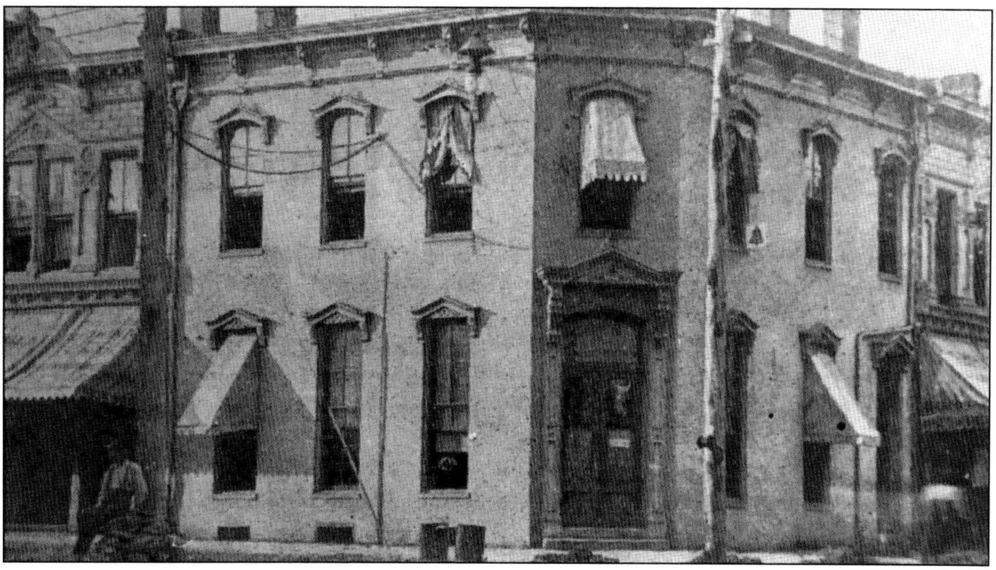

THE BANK OF ELIZABETHTOWN, 1900. Opening on April 19, 1883, the Bank of Elizabethtown was the first "publicly owned" bank in the county, operating out of a building at 123 West Dixie. In 1886, A.B. Montgomery (president of the bank) and G.M. Cresap purchased the old Depp Building on the northeast corner of the public square, shortly after the First National Bank had moved out. The building burned later that year, and a new bank (shown here) was erected on the site and opened in 1887. In 1901, the bank's name was changed to Hardin National Bank. On July 1, 1911, it merged with First National Bank, forming the First Hardin National Bank, which continued to operate on the same corner until 1922, when a new and modern structure was built across the street. Later, the building became Lex's Drug Store, and it has housed many other businesses since that time.

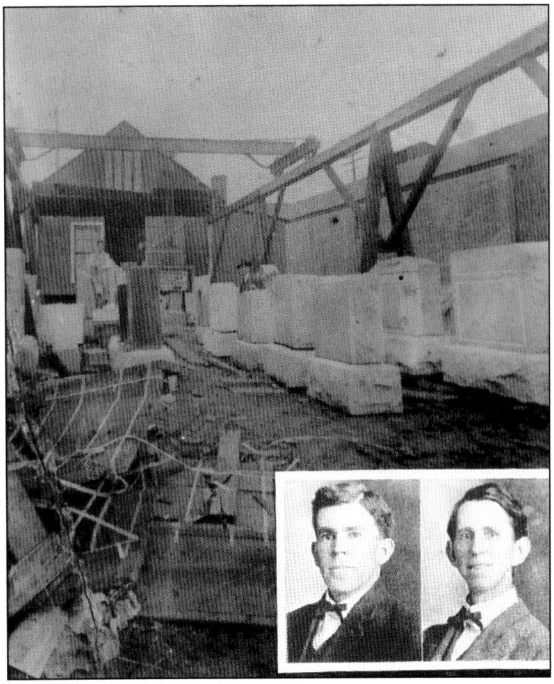

The Keith Monument Company, 1910. The Keith Monument Company was started by John E. Keith, of Cloverport, Kentucky, in 1867. In 1901, his sons, Clarence Edwin Keith and John Proctor Keith (photos inset), came to Elizabethtown and opened a branch office south of the courthouse on East Dixie Avenue. The Keith brothers were skilled in their craft, and nearly every cemetery in the county contains at least one example of their talents. Later, C.E. Keith's son Lon joined the firm, and the name was changed to C.E. Keith and Son. Lon's three sons, Clarence M. "Buddy," Roy, and John, purchased the business and moved the main plant to its present location on North Dixie. It is Hardin County's oldest family-owned business.

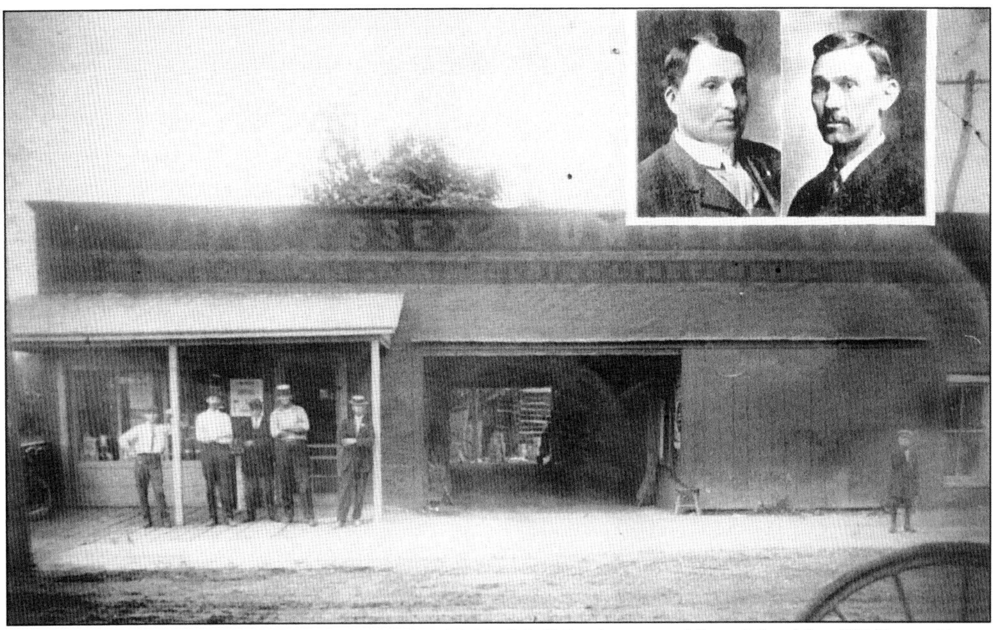

The Jenkins Essex Company, 1904. In 1904, Neff Jenkins and local builder William Essex (photos inset) formed a partnership and established the Jenkins-Essex Lumber and Hardware Company in the old F.M. Joplin building, near the Valley Creek Bridge, in Elizabethtown. The company, which was incorporated in 1914, soon acquired an implement dealership and purchased the Glendale, Vine Grove, and Stithton Lumber Companies. The implement business closed in 1926, and the company's emphasis was then focused on design and construction of commercial and residential buildings. The old building was torn down a few years ago, but the business continues to be operated by Neff's grandsons, Jay and Bert Jenkins.

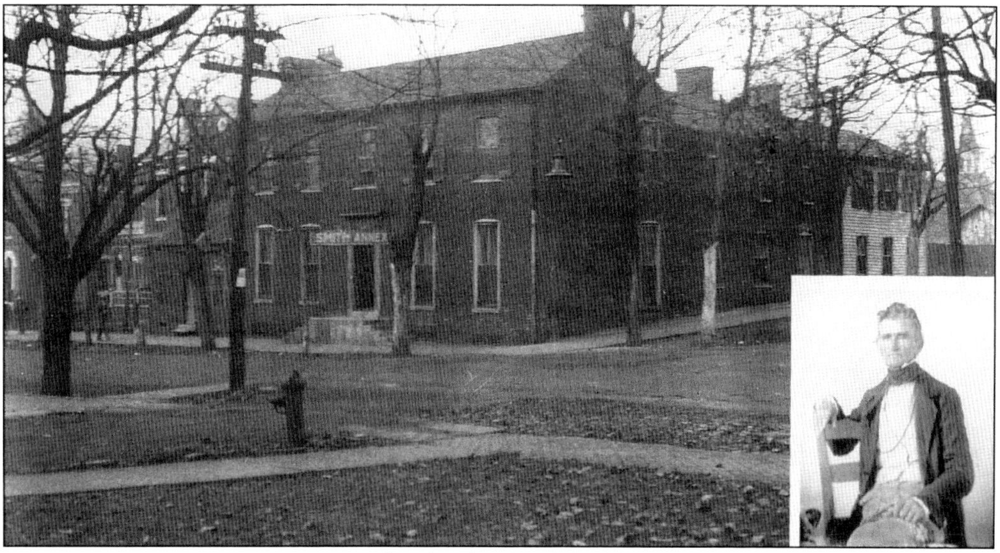

The Smith Hotel Annex, 1920. This familiar brick building, located on the corner of Poplar and Main Streets in Elizabethtown, was built by John Y. Hill (inset) in 1825. Hill and his wife, "Aunt Beck," operated a boarding house here for many years known as the "Hill House." It was from the steps of this building, on April 5, 1851, that world-famous soprano opera singer Jenny Lind (fondly known as the "Swedish Nightingale") sang to a thrilled audience of Elizabethtown residents while en route from Nashville to Louisville. Lind was accompanied on her United States tour by her even-more-famous manager, P.T. Barnum. General George Armstrong Custer (stationed in Elizabethtown from 1871 to 1873) had his headquarters in one of the brick outbuildings behind the house. Upon Aunt Beck's death in 1882, the house was sold by her step-son, Dr. James H. Hill, to Alex D. McCann, who operated it as McCann's House until 1913. A.J. Bush operated the boarding house until 1919, when it was sold to J.M. Smith, who operated it as an annex to his hotel on the square. Doctors William A. and Brown Pusey purchased the building in 1922 and gave it to the city as a community house and library, which it has remained since that time.

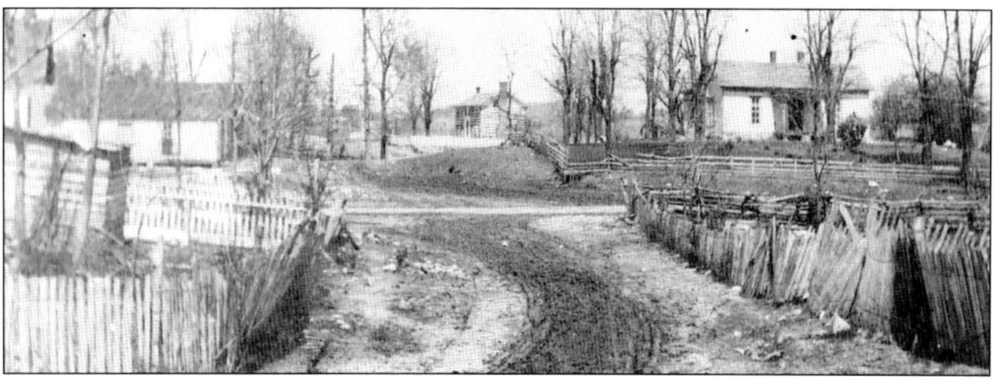

A Franklin Crossroads Street Scene, 1910. This scene, captured on an old postcard dated 1910, reflects the crude and rugged dirt roads that were common throughout Hardin County. Here, at Franklin Crossroads, two major roads leading from Cecilia to Howevalley (Kentucky Highway 86) and from Rineyville to Stephensburg (Kentucky Highway 1375) intersected. Several stores, a gristmill, and a school were located here for many years, and benefitted from the busy intersection. A post office was established here on November 17, 1857, with Samuel Franklin as postmaster. It closed in 1905.

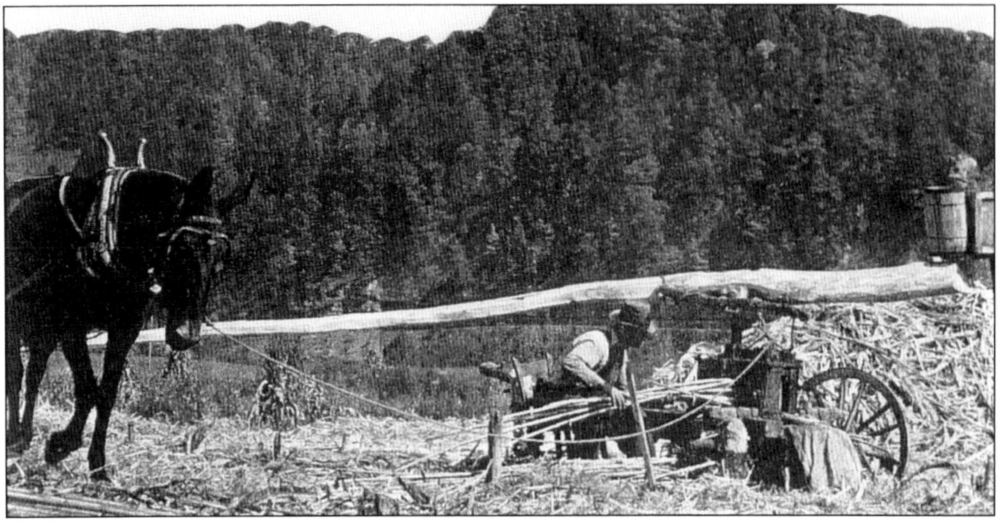

MAKING SORGHUM MOLASSES, C. 1925. A common occurrence for many LaRue County farmers, this was a time when neighbors gathered at the edge of the cane field to help with the stir-off. The golden molasses, which resulted from boiling down the sweet cane juice, was a favorite staple in almost every farmer's home. This image, taken in either Gleanings or Attilla, shows a farmer feeding the grinding jaws of the press while his trusty mule makes yet another trip around the sorghum mill.

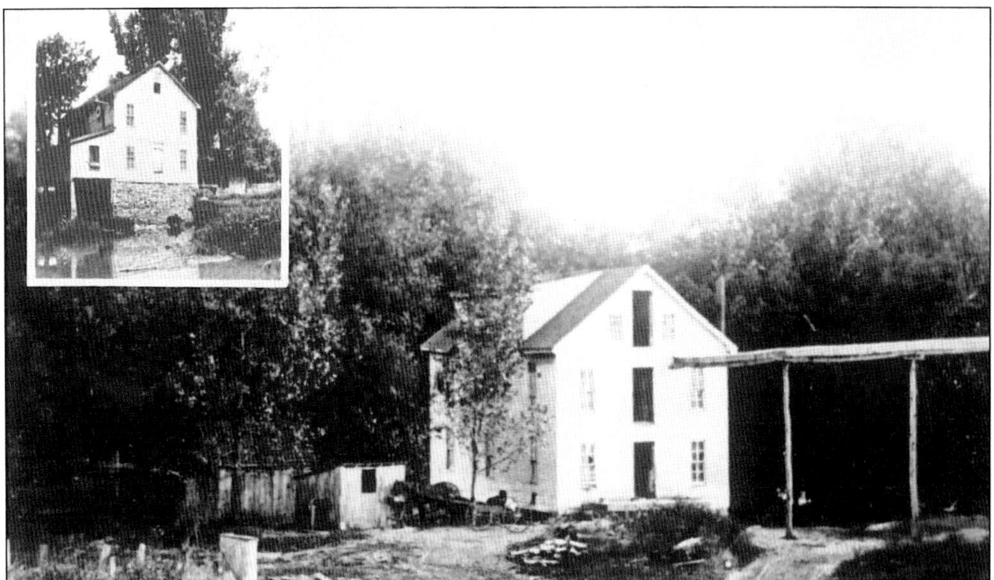

SMITH'S MILL, 1928. In 1866, George Washington Smith moved his family from the Mill Creek area of Hardin County to a 1,500-acre farm near Glendale. He also purchased a mill on Valley Creek, which had been known as Milburn's Mill. Smith, a skilled carpenter and furniture maker, soon achieved great wealth and respect. He later built fine brick homes for three of his children on the original farm. Through the years, the mill was a favorite recreational site for local residents. It was last operated by his son, George Robert Smith, who accidentally drowned there in 1934. It remained vacant for many years and finally collapsed into the creek in 1956.

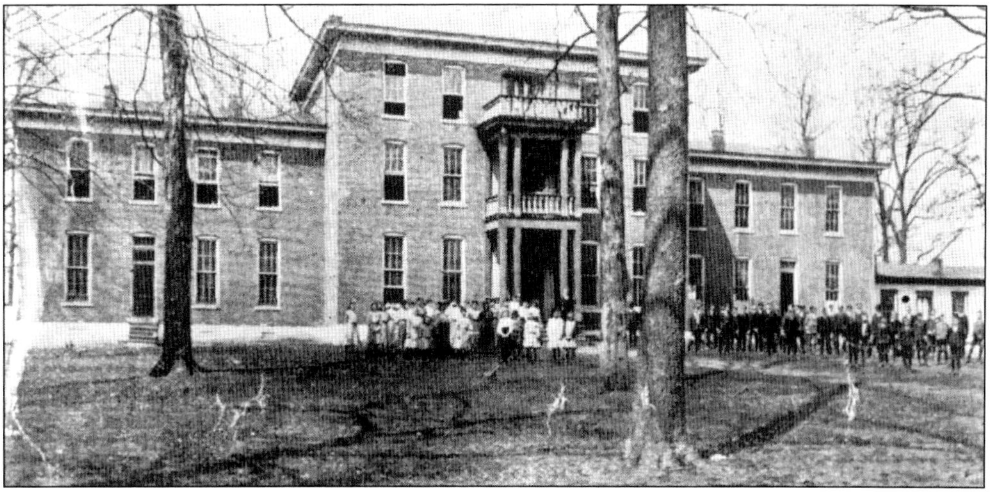

LYNNLAND COLLEGE, 1900. Located adjacent to the L&N Railroad on Gilead Church Road near Glendale, Lynnland Institute opened in September of 1867 as a boarding school for young men and women. From 1870 to 1875, it was operated as Lynnland Military Institute. In 1876, it resumed as a coed school. From 1879 to 1888, it was used as the private residence of the Samuel Sprigg family. In the fall of 1888, it reopened as Lynnland Female College. From 1895 to 1905, it was operated as Lynnland Male and Female Institute. That year, it was purchased by the Severns Valley Baptist Association, which operated the school for 10 years. On June 23, 1915, the Severns Valley Orphans Society converted the campus into the Kentucky Baptist Children's Home, which continues on the site today.

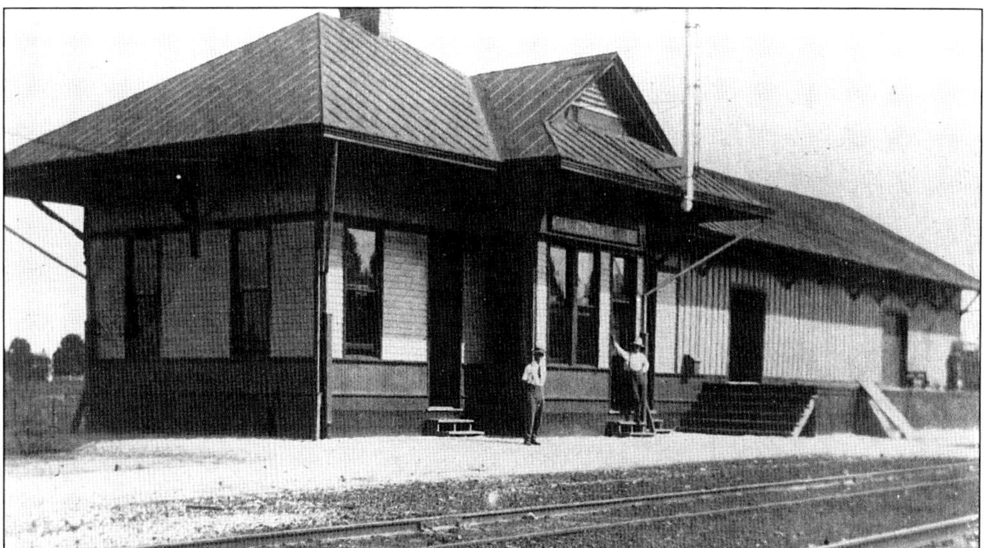

GLENDALE DEPOT, 1919. When the L&N Railroad made its way through the present-day town of Glendale in 1859, the settlement was first known as "Walker's Station." A post office was established here on March 2, 1859, with Lewis B. Walker as postmaster. The train depot, located along the L&N Railroad tracks in Glendale, was built in 1864. In 1905, it was remodeled into a "combination station," and the old station was converted into a freight room, with the addition of two waiting rooms for passengers and an office for the local agent. It was torn down in the late 1930s.

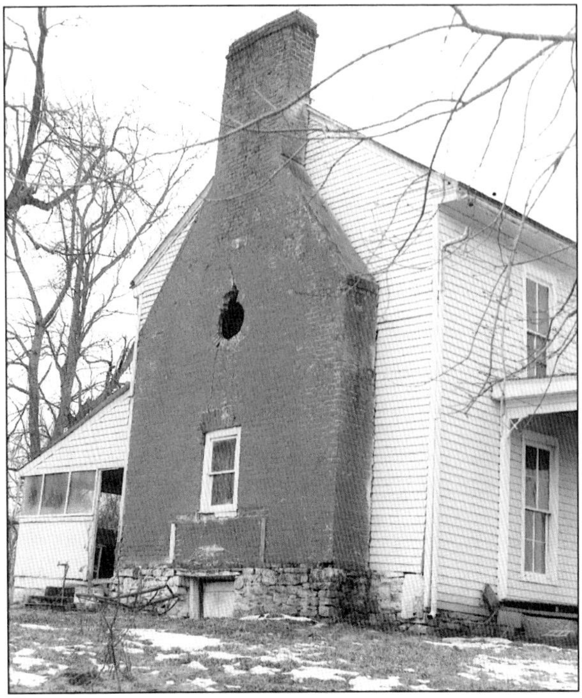

THE CAPTAIN JACOB VAN METER HOUSE, 1930. Revolutionary War veteran Captain Jacob Van Meter built this log home on the banks of Bacon Creek, near Glendale, in the late 1790s. The wide logs were hand-hewn and cut from timber on the property. The most distinct feature of the home was the 17-foot-wide chimney, equipped with a porthole which served as a lookout for possible attacks by hostile tribes. It is not known if the Van Meters ever utilized the porthole, but the danger of attack must have been great enough to warrant the need for its presence. Van Meter also built a mill near his home, which earned him the nickname "Miller Jake." The home was a popular landmark in the area until a few years ago, when it was torn down due to advanced decay.

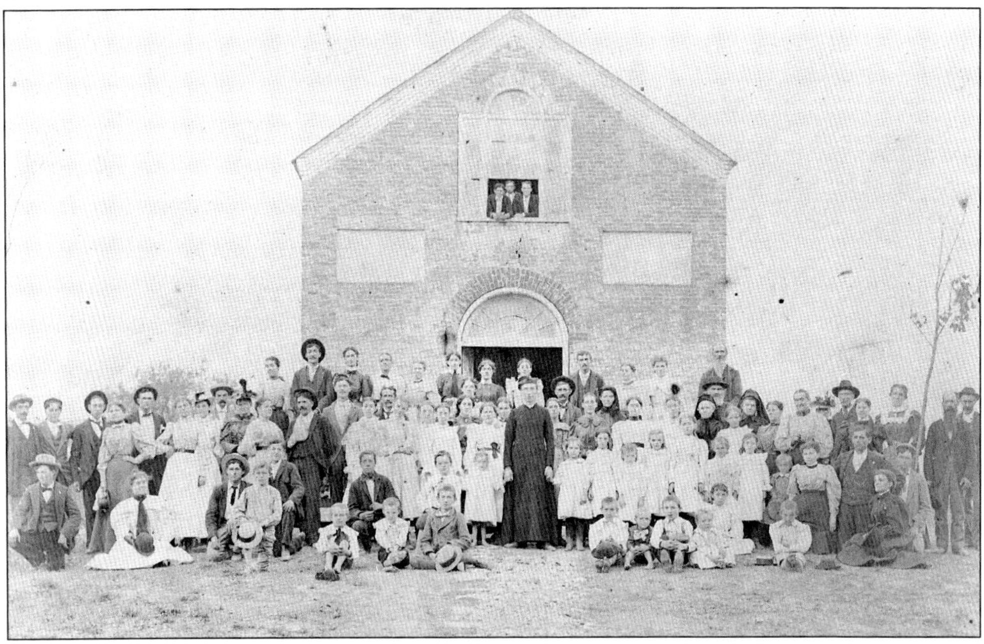

THE CONGREGATION AND CHURCH OF ST. IGNATIUS, 1896. This church once stood where the old St. Ignatius Cemetery is presently located, on Jerome Peerce Road, near Harcourt. It was constructed at a cost of $1,000 in 1842, and dedicated to the patronage of St. Ignatius on October 16 of that year. Made of brick, it measured 24 feet by 38 feet. In 1902, 6 acres of ground were purchased along present Kentucky Highway 84. The old brick church was torn down in 1903, and many of the bricks were used in the foundation and chimneys of the new frame church, which was completed in early 1905. This building is still in use today.

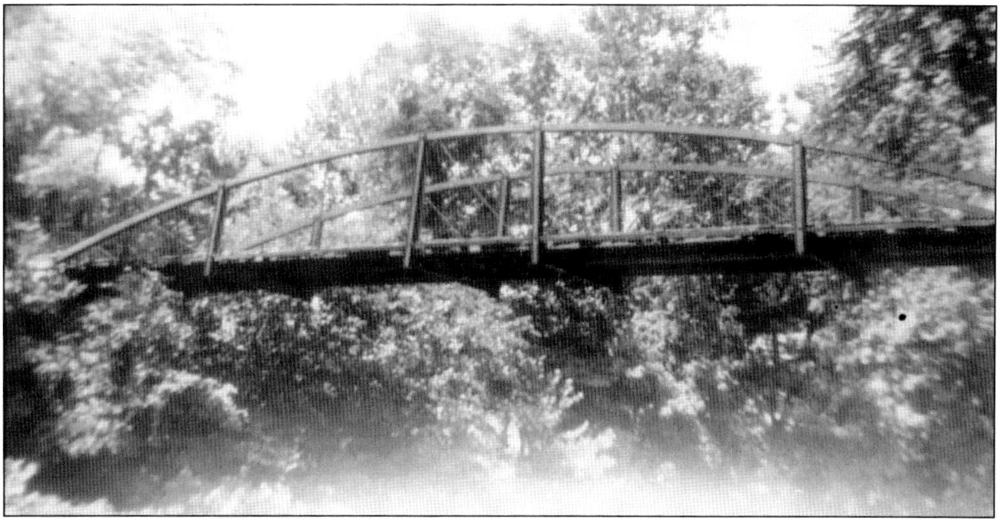

HARCOURT BRIDGE, 1920s. This old bridge, in the Harcourt community of southwestern Hardin County, was the first iron bridge to span the Nolin River. It was built in the 1880s by the King Iron Bridge Company of Cleveland, Ohio. It joined the upper and lower sides of the town of Harcourt, which grew up around Buckles Mill in the late 1800s. The town consisted of the mill, two stores, a blacksmith shop, and several residences. A post office existed there from 1893 to 1907. It was condemned and closed in June 1984, and washed away in the flood of March 1997.

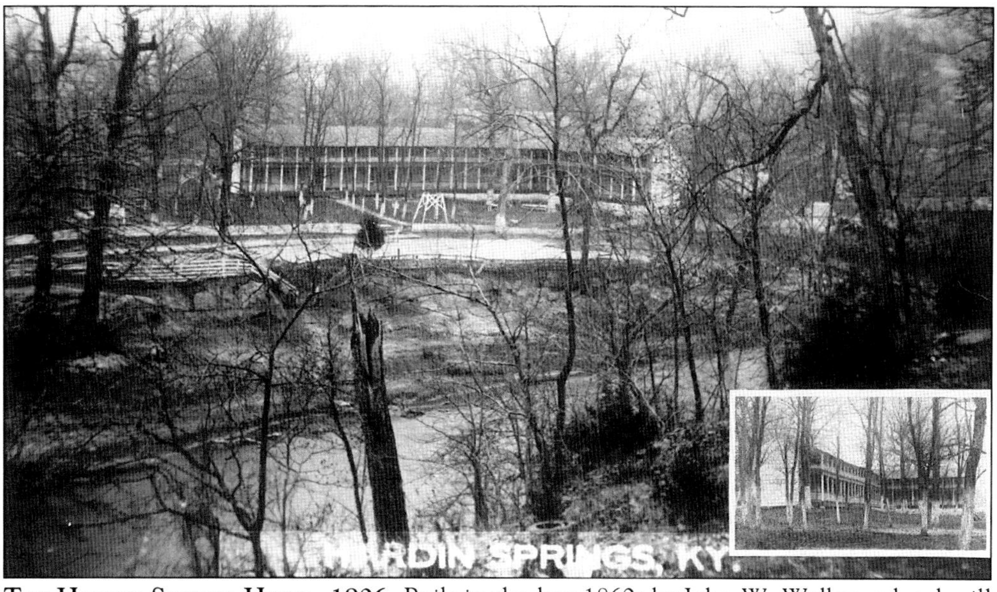

THE HARDIN SPRINGS HOTEL, 1906. Built in the late 1860s by John W. Walker, a local mill operator, the "L"-shaped hotel was situated along the banks of Rough River, in Hardin Springs, on the Hardin and Breckinridge County line. The two-story frame hotel consisted of 29 guest rooms, an office, a dining room, a dance hall, and living quarters for the owners. The hotel's season usually started on Memorial Day and continued until Labor Day. Henry Gotthardt purchased the hotel in 1903 and operated it as a family enterprise until his death, at which time his son Will took it over. Business declined as automobile travel became popular, and the building was torn down in 1955.

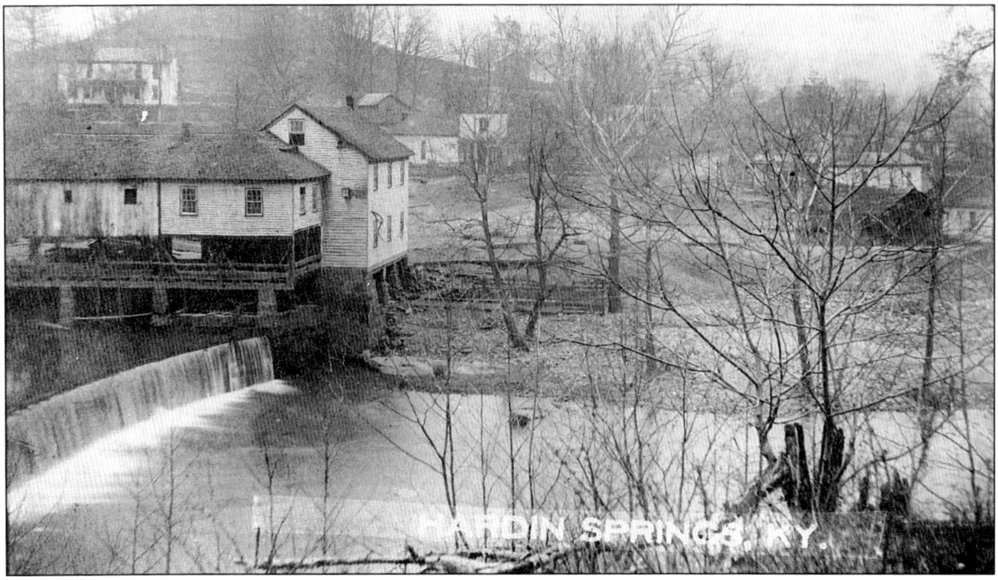

A View of Hardin Springs, 1908. The community of Hardin Springs (once known as McRaven Springs) grew up around the mill that was built by John W. Walker in 1866. Located near the mill were three mineral springs that attracted many visitors to the area who sought medical cures that were attributed to the water. To capitalize on the tourists to the area, Walker also built a hotel near the springs, renaming them "Hardin Springs," to distinguish the county they were located in. Walker's Mill stands at left in this photograph, and his home can be seen on the hill. Ezra Stone's general store can also be seen in the center background. Businesses on the right include J.W. Quiggins' store and the blacksmith shop. Clarence Payton was the last to own the mill before it was torn down in 1958.

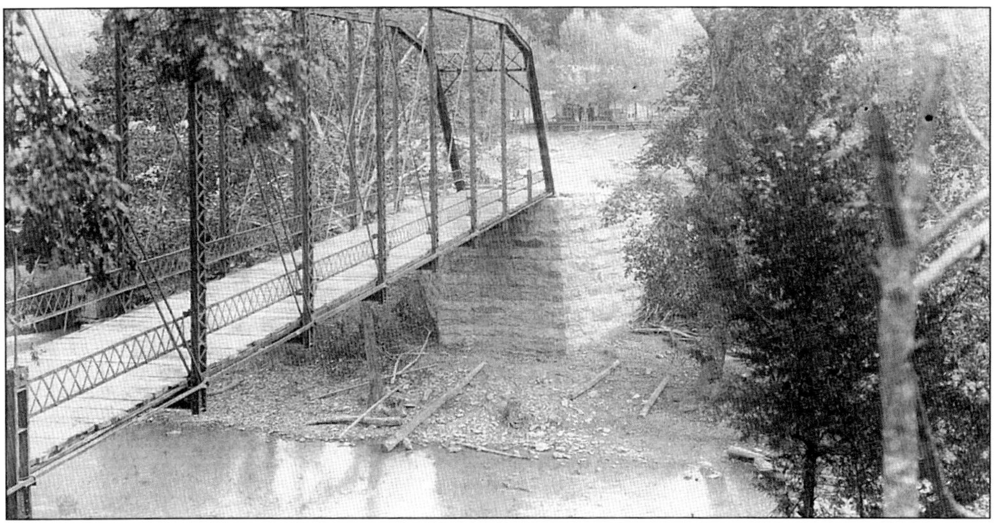

Hardin Springs Bridge, 1911. The old iron bridge across Rough River, in the town of Hardin Springs, was built in 1911. Prior to its construction, travelers had to ford the river to reach the Breckinridge County side. The bridge added to the tranquil surroundings of the small village until March 26, 1970, when a tractor trailer pulling a heavy tanker tried to cross. It collapsed into the river below, taking the hearts of many Hardin Springs residents with it. A modern concrete bridge has taken its place.

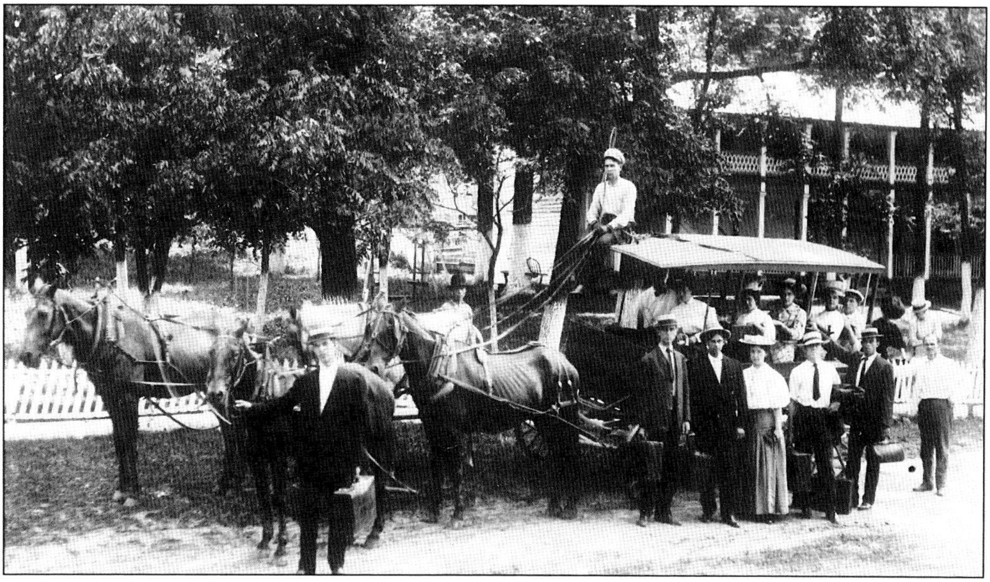

A HARDIN SPRINGS HOTEL GUEST COACH, 1910. Here, a group of guests arrive in front of the Hardin Springs Hotel. The coach, pulled by four horses, would travel to the East View Train Station and transport vacationers back to the hotel. While there, they were treated to three delicious, home-cooked meals a day. Activities included bowling, tennis, swimming, fishing, boating, hiking, hunting, and horseback riding. During the peak summer season, guests were willing to sleep on the hotel's upper and lower porches, rather than be turned away. Many Louisville residents returned each year to spend a week or two in the quaint little valley that was noted for its natural mineral springs, which were believed to have medicinal qualities.

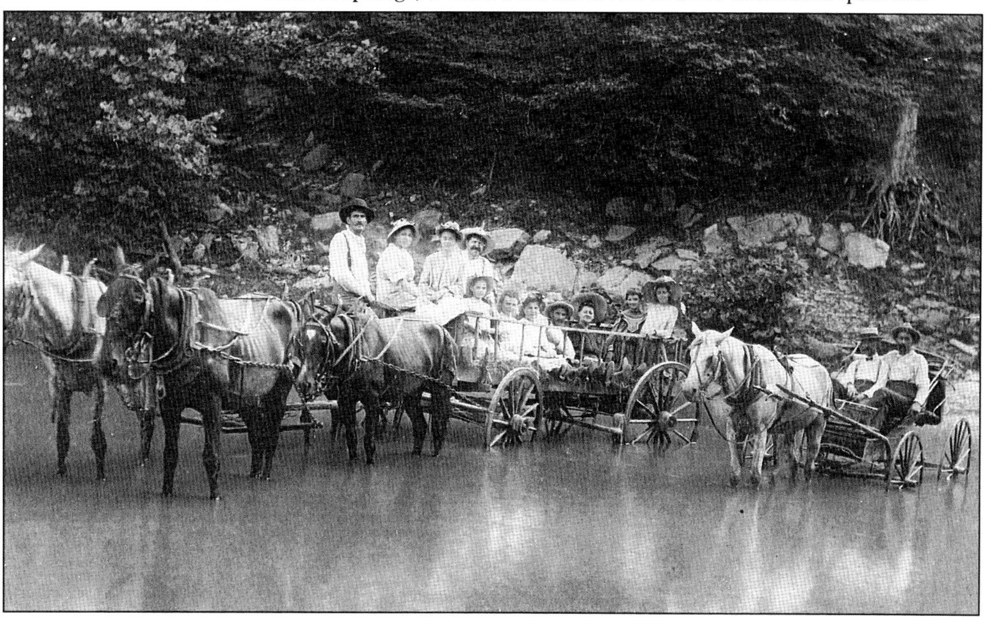

FORDING ROUGH RIVER AT HARDIN SPRINGS, 1905. A group of hotel guests are treated to a wagon ride across Rough River at Hardin Springs. "Jim Bill" Quiggins, a local merchant, operated a stable where visitors could rent horses for trail rides, or wagons and buggies for group rides. Quiggins usually played tour guide for these expeditions.

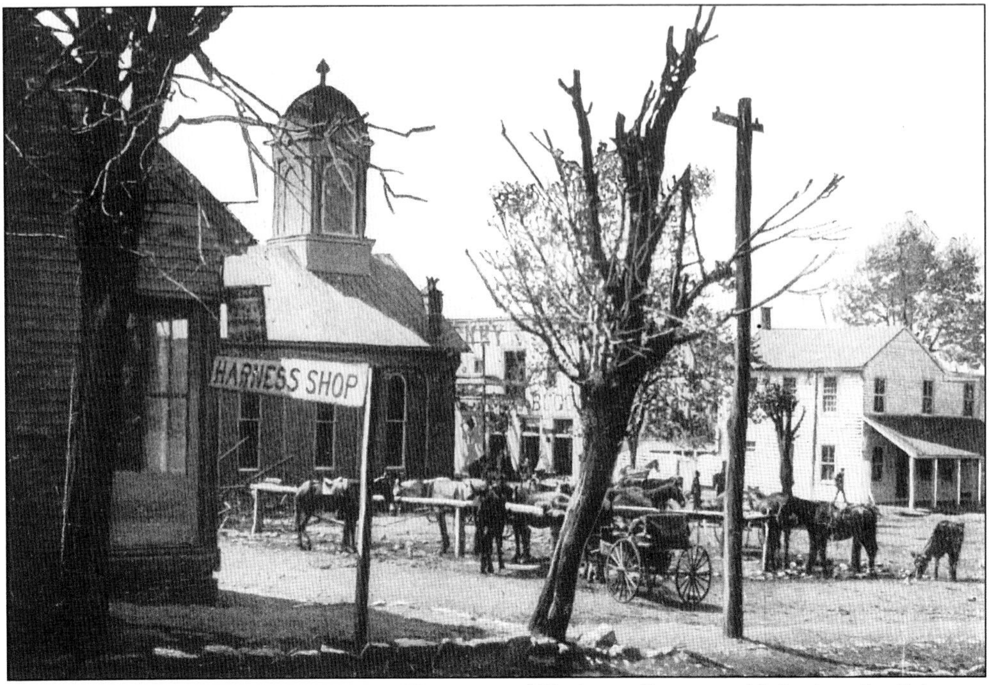

HODGENVILLE TOWN SQUARE, 1902. This view of Hodgenville was published in the February 1903 issue of *Woman's Home Companion* magazine. The Hodgenville Christian Church is the only building still standing. The frame building on the right is the Matthis and O'Bryan Saloon and Billiard Parlor. In the building behind the saloon, Henry E. Lewis sold surreys, buggies, hardware, and blacksmith items. Buggy and saddle horses were tethered at the hitching rack, while cows often roamed freely in the streets.

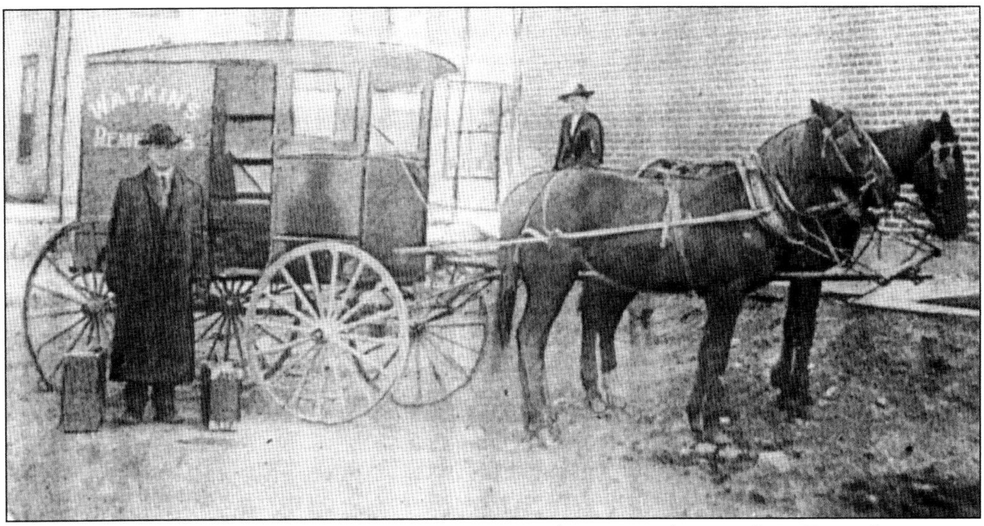

THE WATKINS MAN, C. 1900. Hallie Wilkins stands next to his Watkins Remedies wagon in downtown Hodgenville. "The Watkins Man" regularly delivered aspirin, cough syrup, ointments, and other medications as well as seasonings, extracts, and various household aides to rural LaRue County families who lived too far from town for easy access to stores. The advent of the automobile and better roads made "The Watkins Man" a thing of the past.

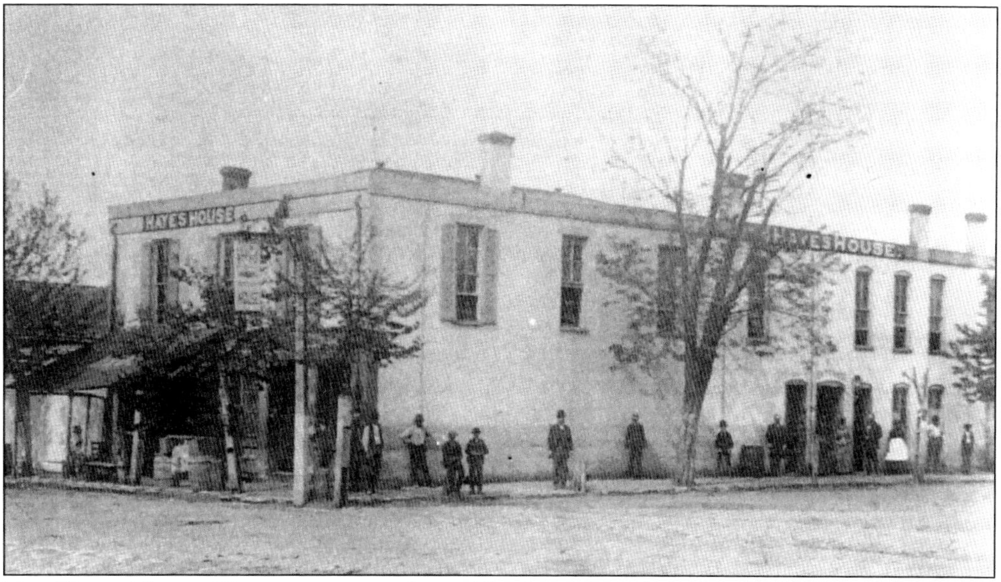

The Hayes House Hotel, c. 1885. Owned by J.R. Hayes from 1877 to 1913, this hotel was located on the square in Hodgenville where the Lincoln National Bank now stands. A saloon and dry good store were on the main floor fronting on Main Street (now Lincoln Boulevard). Barrels filled with water in case of fire were near the front doors. The main entrance to the hotel was at right, near where the employees of the hotel are standing. The Farmers National Bank purchased the property in 1913, the year the hotel was dismantled.

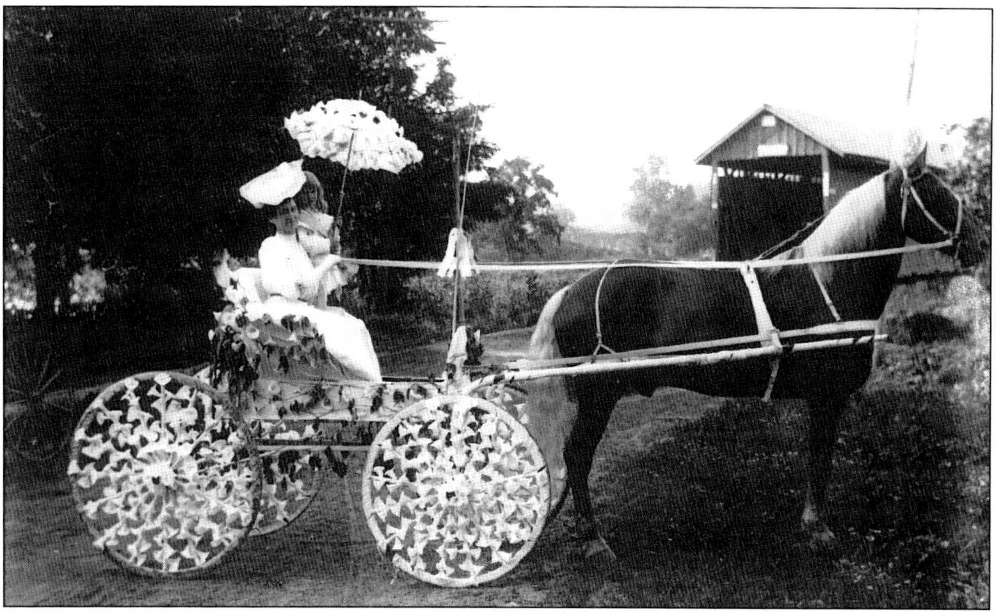

A Horse, Wagon, and Covered Bridge, 1908. Mrs. E.B. (Jessie) Ludwick is holding the reins with her right hand and a little girl with her left arm, in front of the John Burba residence and the covered bridge in Hodgenville. LaRue Countians often decorated their carriages and wore their "Sunday finest" on holidays, anniversaries, and other special occasions during the latter part of the 19th century and early part of the 20th century.

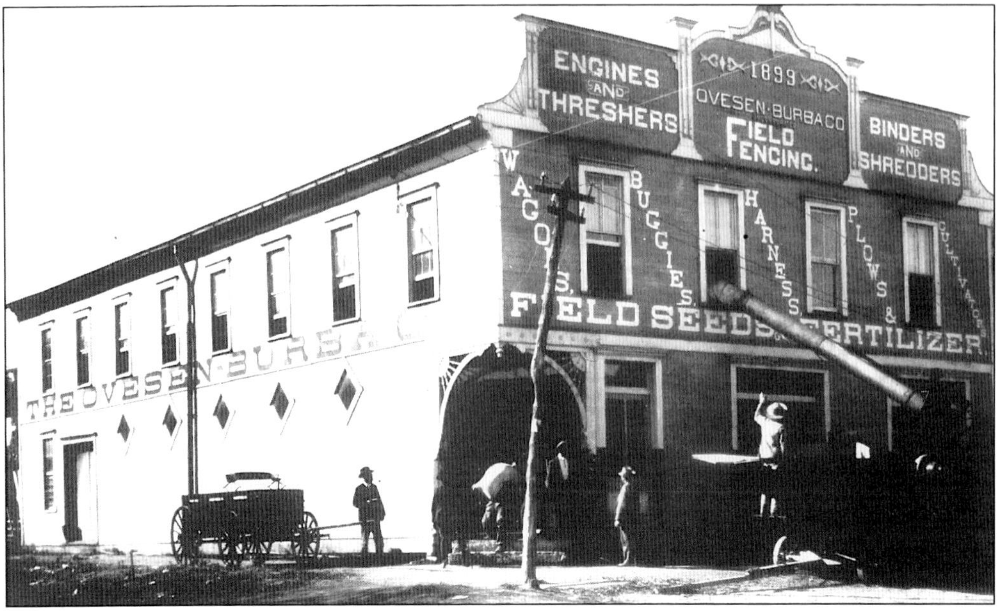

THE OVESEN-BURBA COMPANY, c. 1920. This company was a machinery and farm supply store located on the southwest corner of Greensburg Street and East Main Street in Hodgenville. The store had its beginnings in 1894, when it was primarily a hardware business. This photograph shows seed being augered into the second floor of the store building. German immigrant August Ovesen and John Henry Burba were the proprietors at this time. The building was dismantled around 1925, and a large garage was built in its place.

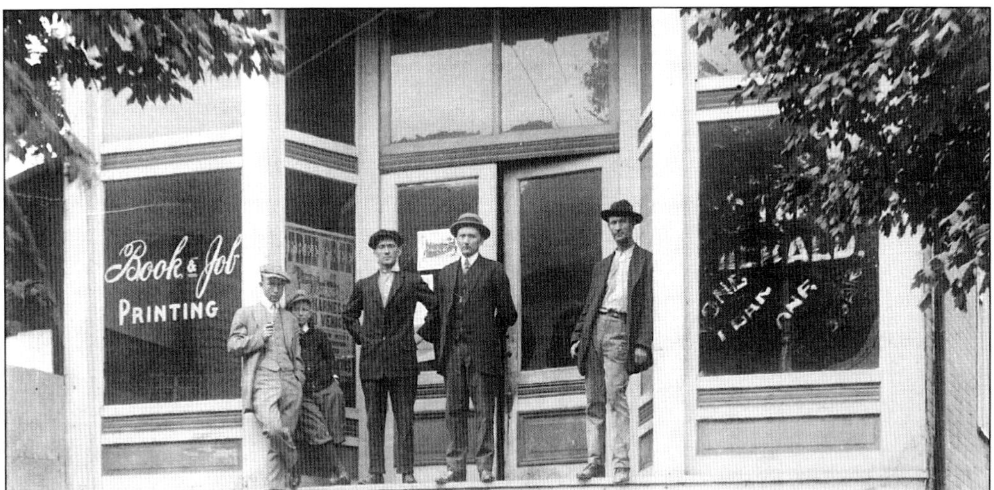

THE LARUE COUNTY HERALD OFFICE, c. 1910. The *LaRue County Herald* occupied this building in Hodgenville, which stood where the Woman's Club building is now located. After the 1914 fire, the *Herald* moved into a newly constructed building at 114 North Lincoln Boulevard. In 1919, the *LaRue County News* occupied the above building until it merged with the *LaRue County Herald* in 1921. Pictured, from left to right, are Charles Creal, Tyler Munford, Roscoe G. O'Brian, Roy Munford, and Dick Kirkpatrick. The *LaRue County Herald* archives (now on microfilm) provide the major source of information as to the county's early history, people, and happenings.

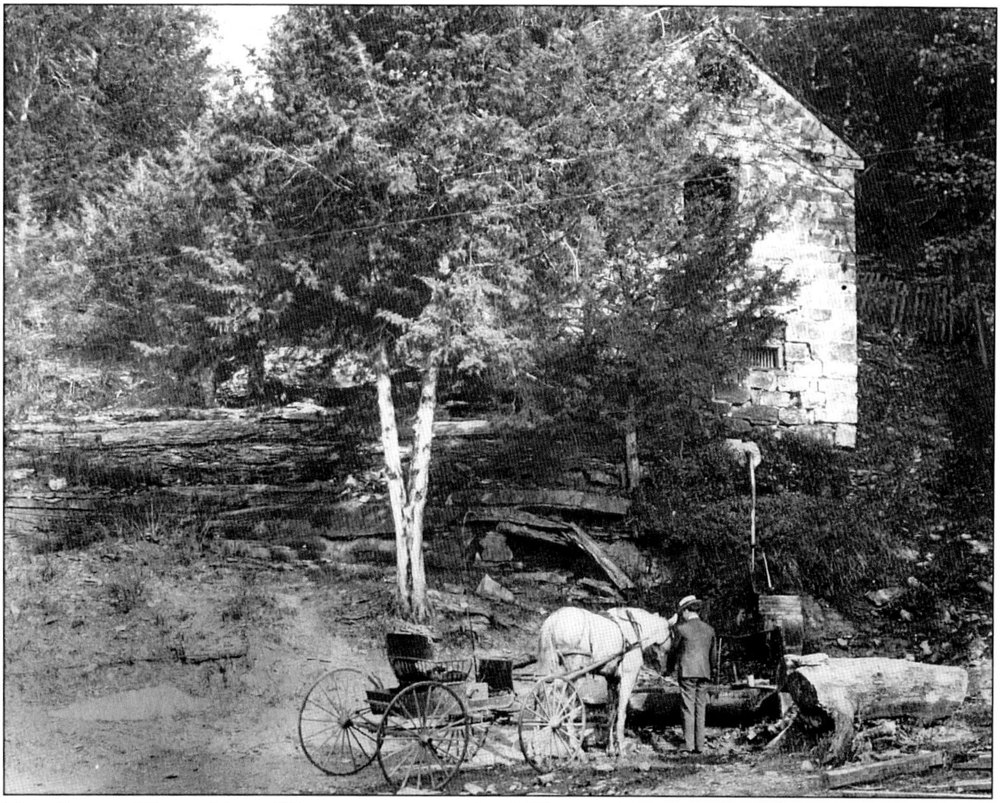

The Spring House Near Hodgenville, c. 1905. This structure was built by Joseph Kirkpatrick in the 1790s on the north side of the Bardstown Road. Its stone walls were built thick enough so the house could be used as a fortification. Inside, milk and butter were kept cool in the spring, and for many years it was used as a school. Travelers who passed by in the early 1900s often stopped for a refreshing drink of cool spring water for themselves and their horses.

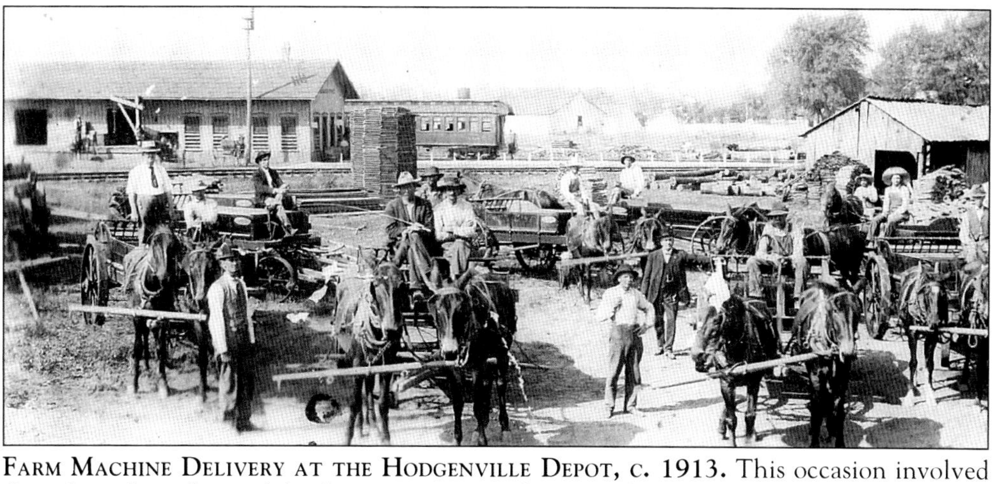

Farm Machine Delivery at the Hodgenville Depot, c. 1913. This occasion involved the sale and purchase of the first manure spreaders ever delivered to LaRue County. Most of the people were there to pick up their equipment but took time to pose for the camera. The teams of horses and wagons are hitched to the farm machinery as the farmers prepare to leave the depot.

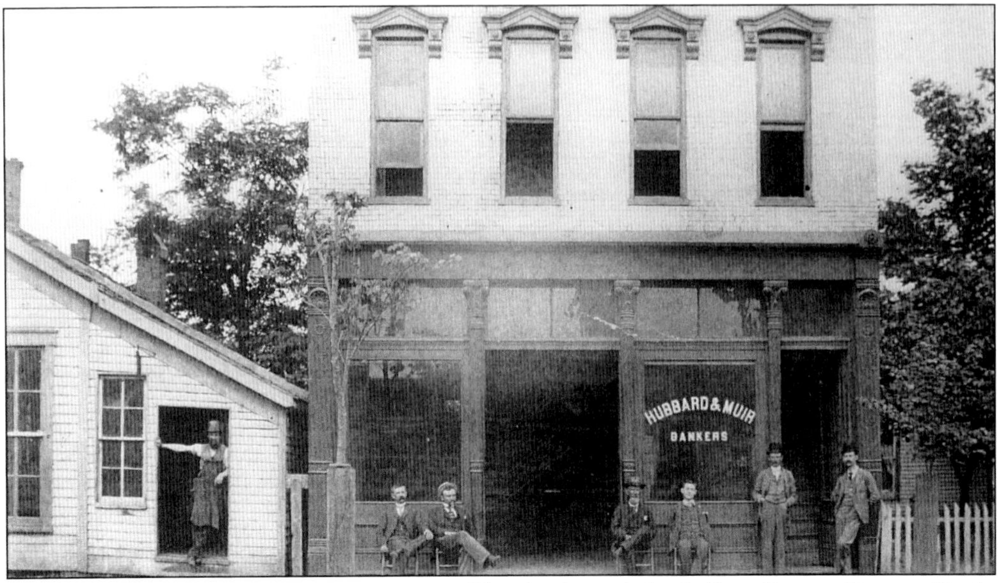

THE HUBBARD AND MUIR BANK, C. 1904. This bank, and the LaRue County Deposit Bank, were the first two banks in Hodgenville. Both were organized in the 1880s and were later consolidated under the latter's name. This picture shows, from left to right, Mr. Reed, a shoemaker (in the doorway of his cobbler's shop), J.W. Muir, Frank Sympson, Jacob Hubbard, Charles Jacob Hubbard, and attorneys David H. Smith and Murray Rodman Hubbard.

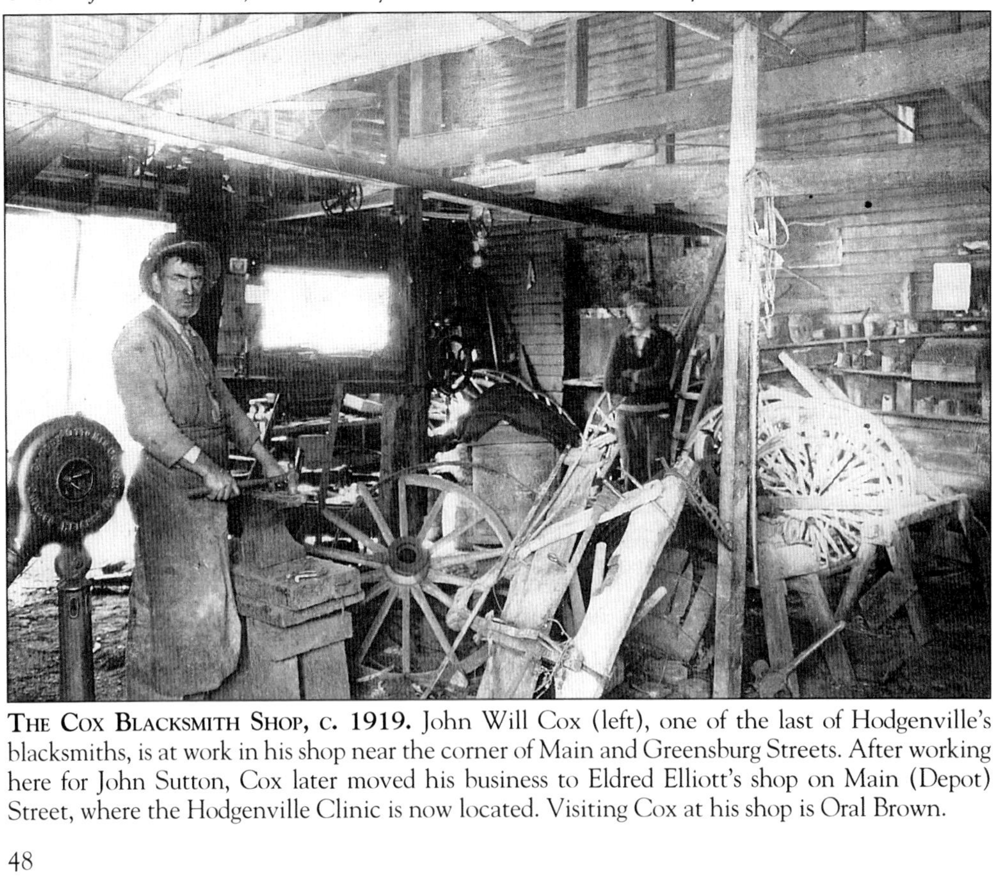

THE COX BLACKSMITH SHOP, C. 1919. John Will Cox (left), one of the last of Hodgenville's blacksmiths, is at work in his shop near the corner of Main and Greensburg Streets. After working here for John Sutton, Cox later moved his business to Eldred Elliott's shop on Main (Depot) Street, where the Hodgenville Clinic is now located. Visiting Cox at his shop is Oral Brown.

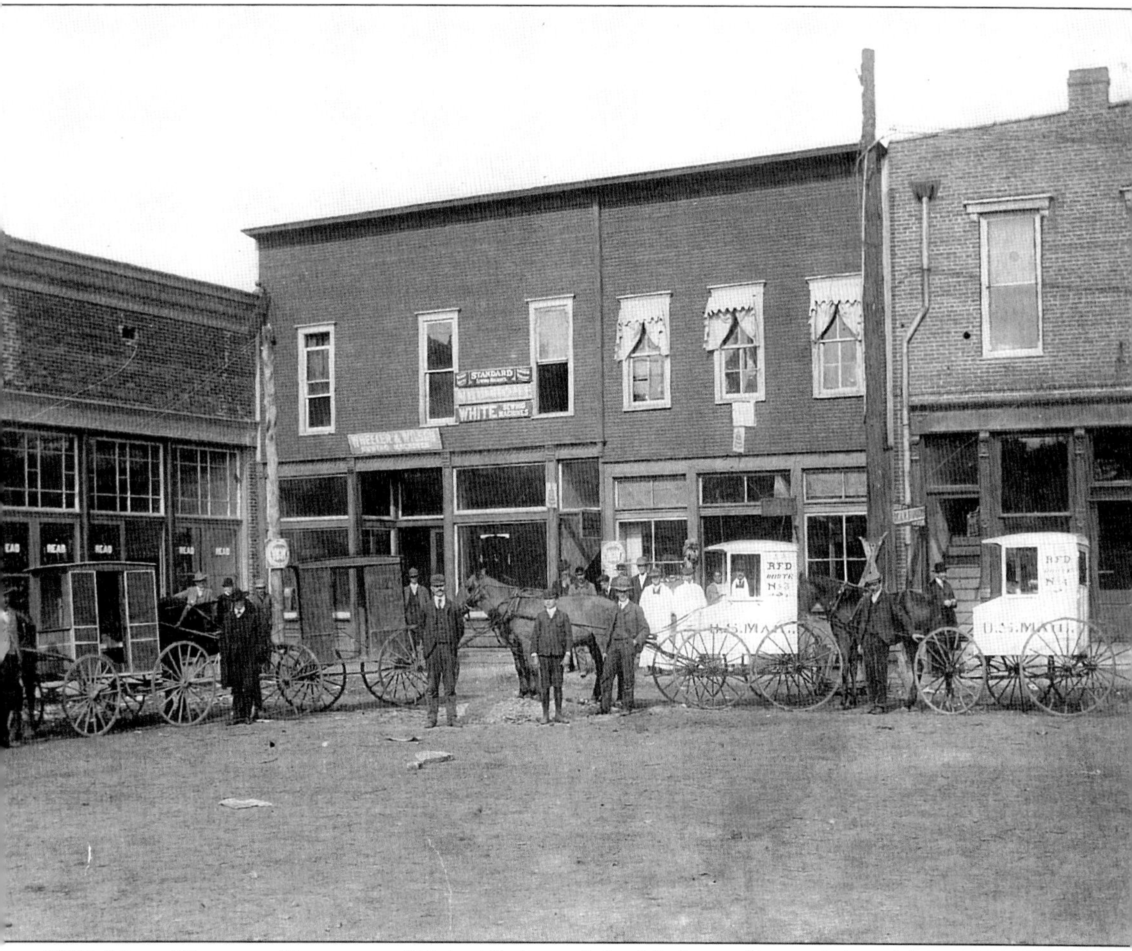

RFD Mail Wagons, December 1904. All four of the Hodgenville rural free delivery mail carriers and their mail wagons are lined up on the square in Hodgenville. The occasion marked the beginning of official mail service to the rural areas of LaRue County. Butler Brown is the mail carrier for RFD route number one, Bill Durham for RFD route number two, Roy Hargan for RFD route number three, and "Pegeye" O'Bryant for RFD route number four. Hargan and O'Bryant have been provided with new Harrington light runner mail wagons for their routes.

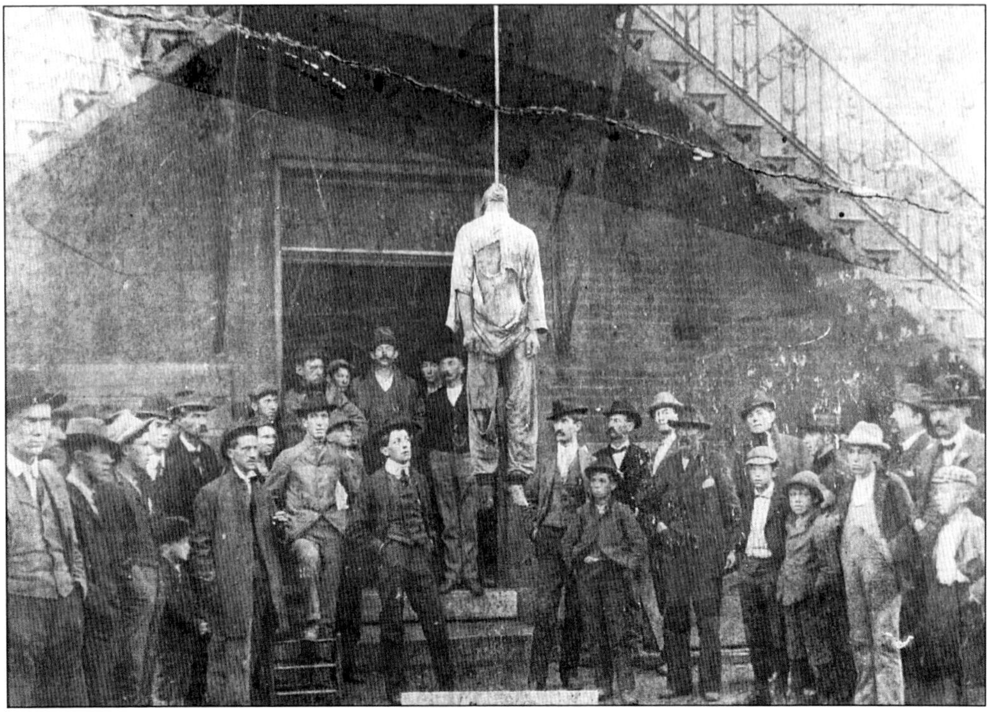

COURTHOUSE LYNCHING, OCTOBER 30, 1901. Silas Easter, a black man, was accused of molesting a young white boy and briefly lodged in the Hodgenville jail. A large mob, which included the boy and his father, forcibly took him from the jail to the LaRue County Courthouse, where he was hanged. Taken the following morning, this photograph depicts the aftermath of the only known incident in LaRue County in which a lynch mob mentality was allowed to get the upper hand over justice and due process.

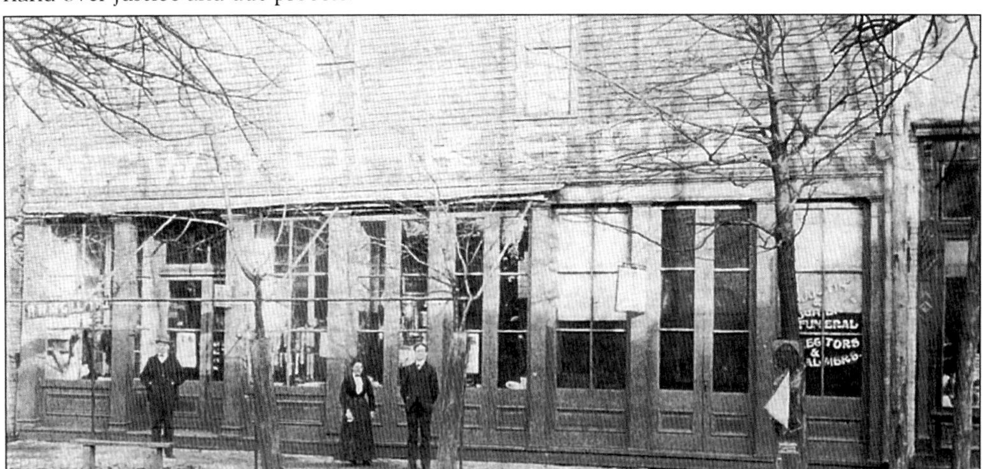

THE NEW YORK STORE, C. 1895. This building was located north of the Hayes House Hotel in Hodgenville. "R.W. McGill and Brothers," printed on the left window, identifies the proprietors of this prominent men's and women's clothing store. An 1896 *LaRue County Herald* advertisement for the store states, "If we can't fit you, we will make you a suit from 10,000 samples to select from." Martin and Daugherty, Funeral Directors and Embalmers, were located next door.

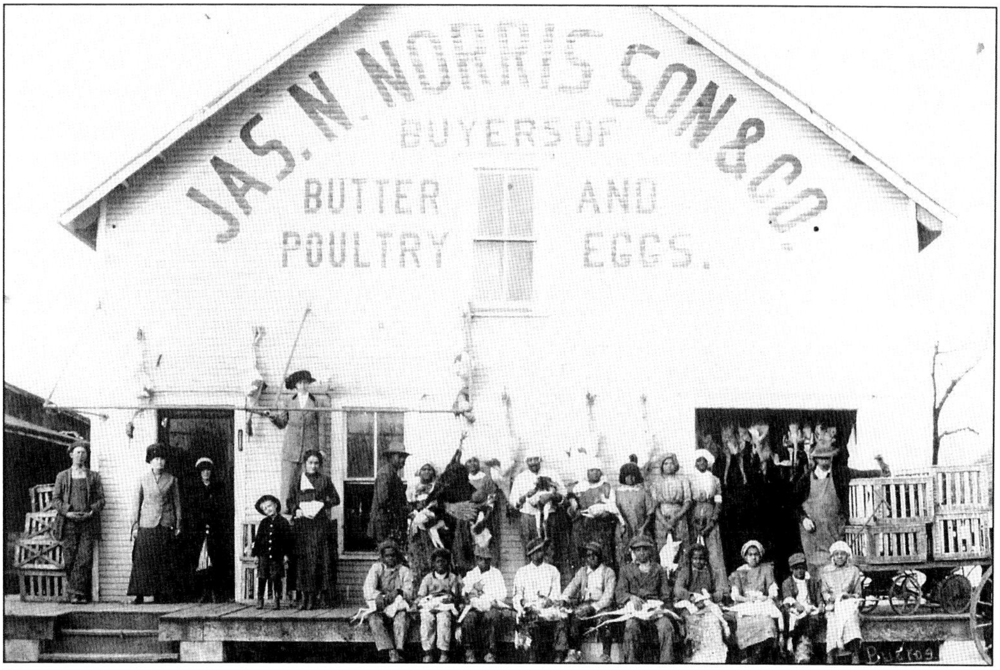

The Jas. N. Norris Son and Company Store, c. 1925. This building was located at the west end of Water Street, next to the R.B. Hayes and Company building. The business was also owned and operated by R.B. Hayes, and the "Norris" name was the same as the Louisville-based firm for which Hayes bought produce. Each of the young boys who worked there was given a chicken and paid 50¢ for a day's work.

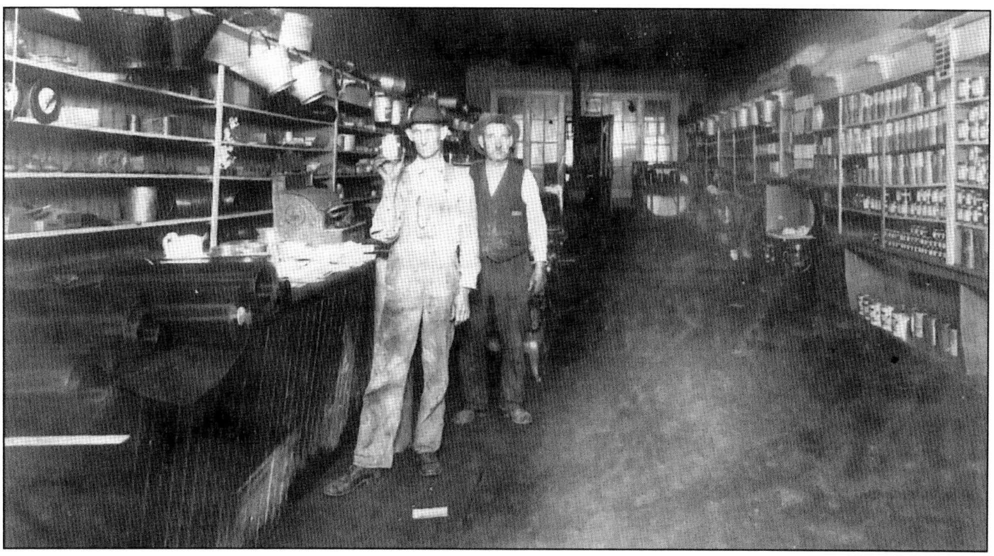

The Interior of Kinsey's Tin Shop, c. 1925. Hodgenville tinsmith Frank Kinsey stands behind his son, Herman Kinsey, as they pose for the camera. Shelves of stove pipe, galvanized coal buckets, 5-gallon cans, a machine used for the prefabrication of stove pipes, an old stove, cans of paint, and rolls of tin used to make stove pipe for heating stoves that burned coal and wood can be seen. Frank Kinsey, an expert tinsmith, operated his shop for many years in the square in Hodgenville.

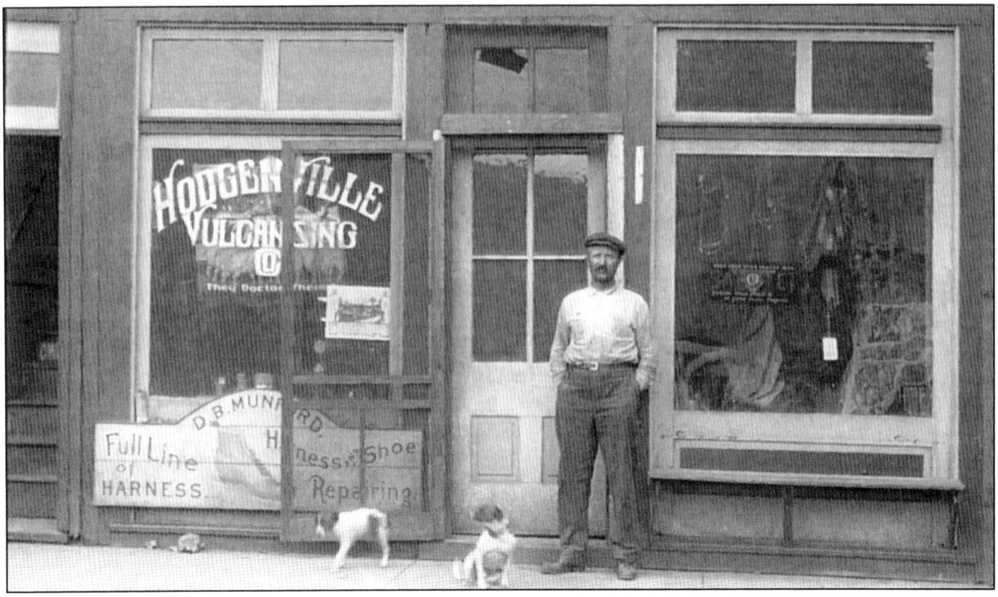

The Hodgenville Vulcanizing Company, c. 1912. D.B. Munford, the owner and proprietor of this business known primarily as a harness shop, stands with his dogs, waiting for a customer. Munford repaired harnesses, shoes, boots, saddles, and various other leather goods at this shop. It was in the rear section of this building that the fire originated which destroyed approximately 26 businesses located primarily in the northwest quadrant of the town square on the night of April 28, 1914.

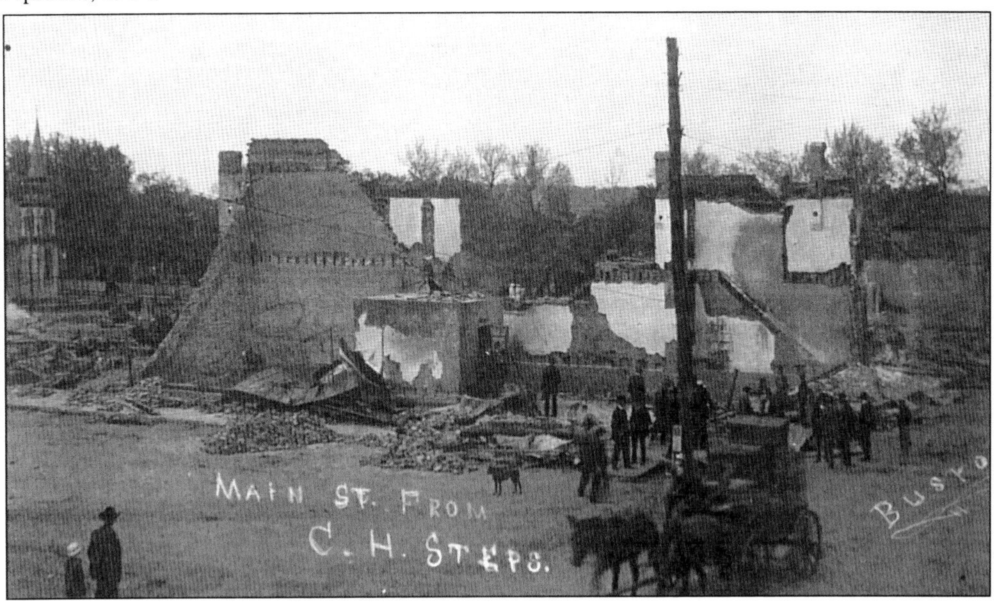

The Fire in Downtown Hodgenville, April 28, 1914. Standing on the courthouse steps, Hodgenville photographer D.P. Busroe captured the devastation caused by the fire. The LaRue National Bank vault (left center foreground) is all that remains of the bank that previously stood on the northwest corner of the town square. The fire did not reach the Hodgenville Methodist Church (far left), located at the west corner of North Walters Avenue and West Water Street.

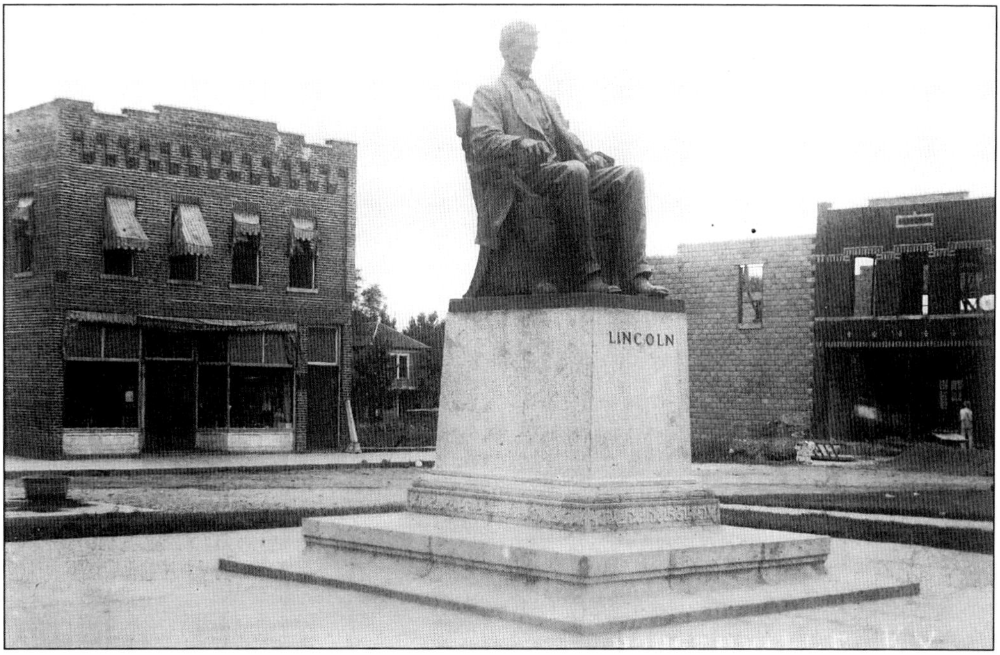

THE RECONSTRUCTION OF DOWNTOWN HODGENVILLE, 1916. This picture, also taken by D.P. Busroe, reflects the work that had been done to reconstruct part of the northwest quadrant of the square. Between the newly constructed building at left and the Lincoln statue, the Bean house on Walters Avenue can be seen in the distance. The Busroe family also lived on Walters Avenue, between the Catholic church and the Jake Walters residence.

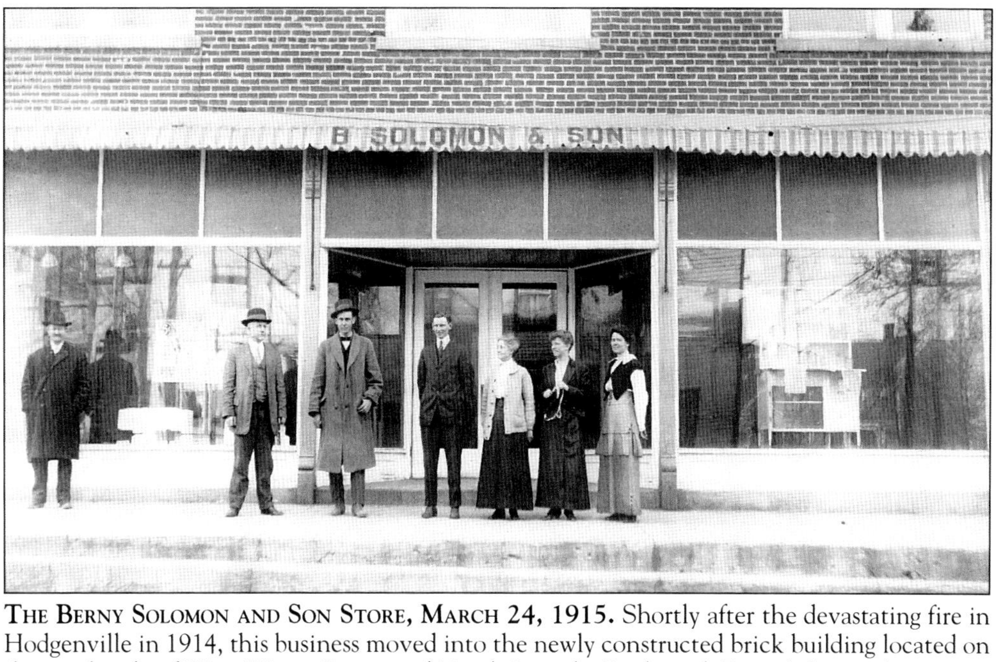

THE BERNY SOLOMON AND SON STORE, MARCH 24, 1915. Shortly after the devastating fire in Hodgenville in 1914, this business moved into the newly constructed brick building located on the south side of West Water Street and North Lincoln Boulevard. From left to right are Mr. Smith, Warfield McGill, Cad P. Thurman, Berny Solomon, Katie Hargan, Florida Hayes, and Ms. Walters.

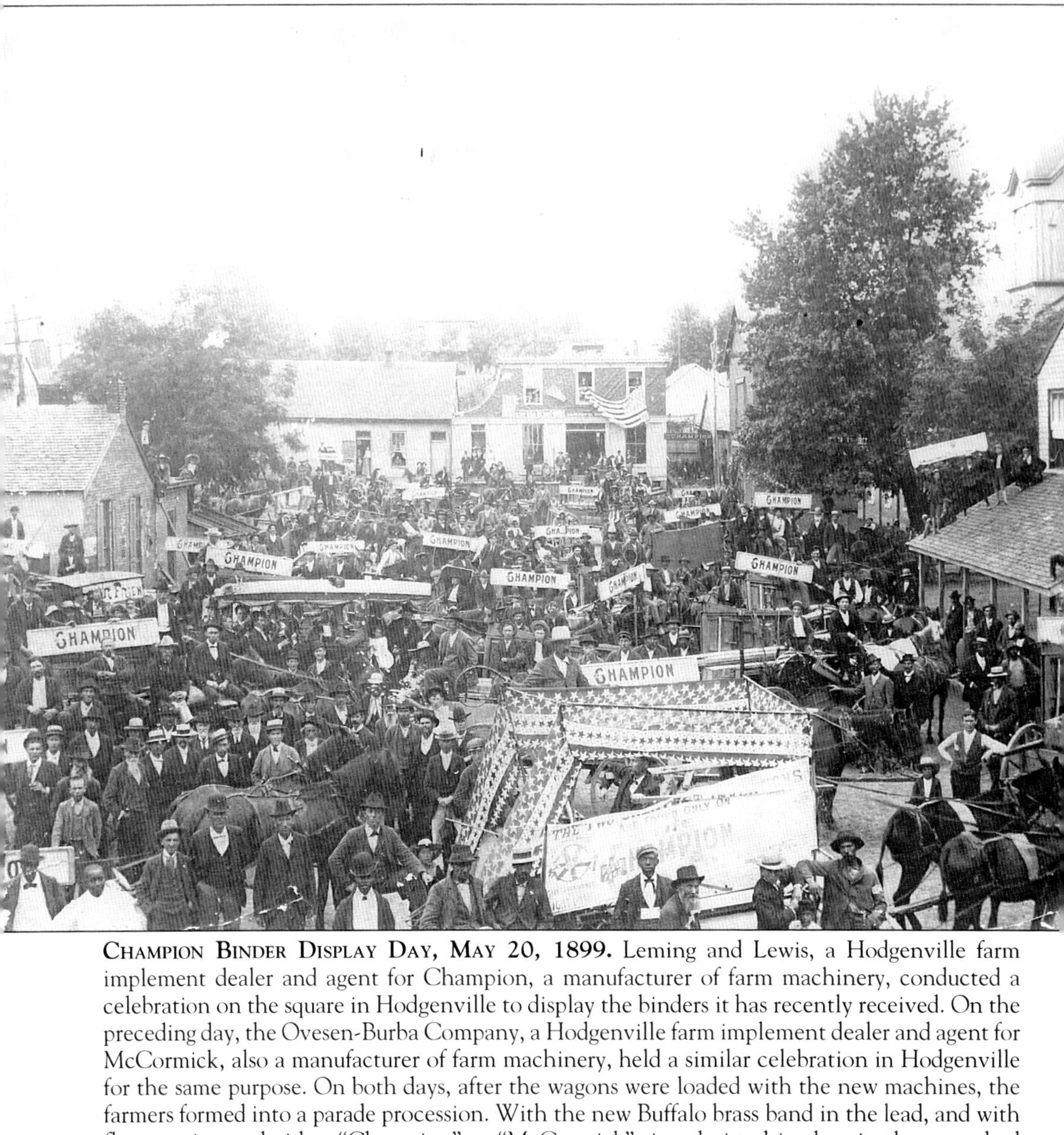

CHAMPION BINDER DISPLAY DAY, MAY 20, 1899. Leming and Lewis, a Hodgenville farm implement dealer and agent for Champion, a manufacturer of farm machinery, conducted a celebration on the square in Hodgenville to display the binders it has recently received. On the preceding day, the Ovesen-Burba Company, a Hodgenville farm implement dealer and agent for McCormick, also a manufacturer of farm machinery, held a similar celebration in Hodgenville for the same purpose. On both days, after the wagons were loaded with the new machines, the farmers formed into a parade procession. With the new Buffalo brass band in the lead, and with flags waving and either "Champion" or "McCormick" signs hoisted in the air, they marched through the streets to the tune of "What Shall the Harvest Be?" Hodgenville photographer D.P. Busroe was on hand on both occasions to take pictures of the celebrations. Although the two displays were conducted by competing dealers, the *LaRue County Herald* reported on May 28, 1899, that they engaged in the exercises with the utmost friendly feeling and, together with several agents of both machine companies, had as much fun as could be had at a picnic. The *Herald* also stated that the dealers impressed upon the public that Hodgenville was one of the largest markets for farm implements in the state.

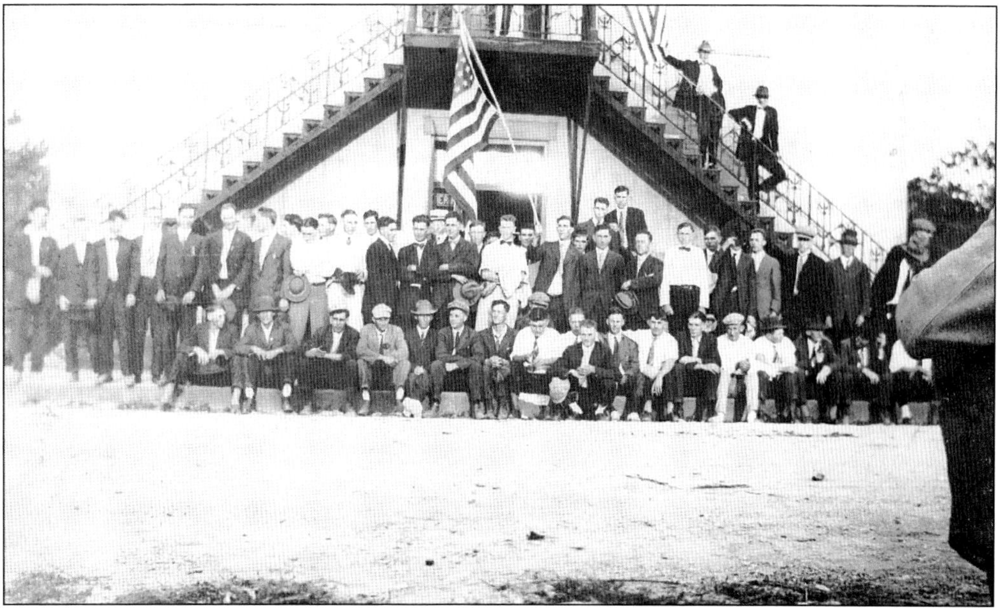

World War I Draft, September 18, 1917. LaRue County's draft quota for the Army has assembled in front of the courthouse in Hodgenville. More than five hundred people, including school students and bands from Buffalo and Hodgenville, cheered the young men as they prepared to depart for Camp Zachary Taylor. The 60 future World War I soldiers at the assembly heard many patriotic speeches, songs, and well wishes. Of these 60 men, 9 died in France. Their names are recorded on a marble monument in the southeast corner of Lincoln Square.

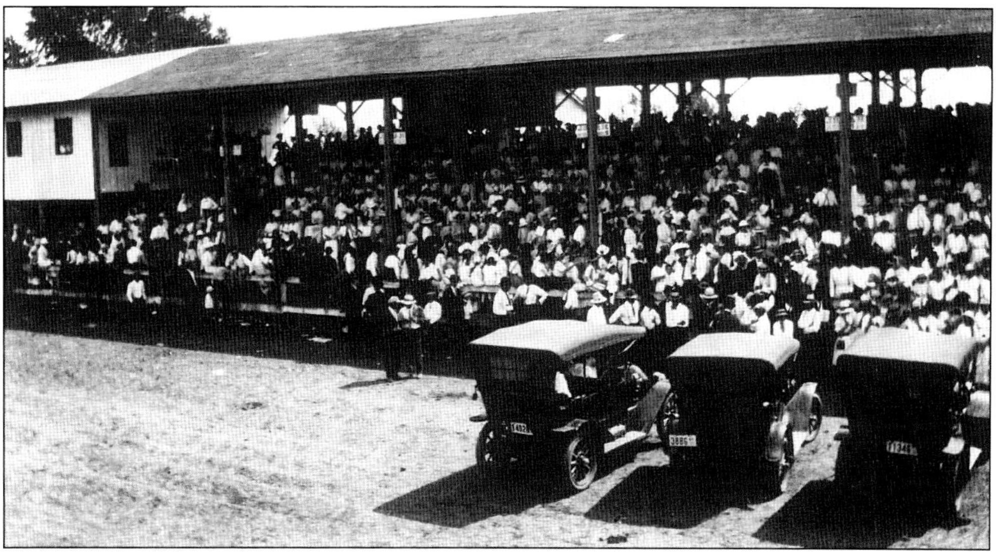

The LaRue County Fair, 1909. In September 1906, the Hodgenville Commercial Club met to consider organizing a LaRue County fair. A board of directors was soon chosen, 30 acres of land was purchased, and stock was sold. Equine stables and a floral hall were constructed. James Daugherty built the grandstand, and the first of many highly successful LaRue County fairs occurred on September 10–12, 1907. This picture of the floral hall (left) and grandstand was taken during the 1909 fair.

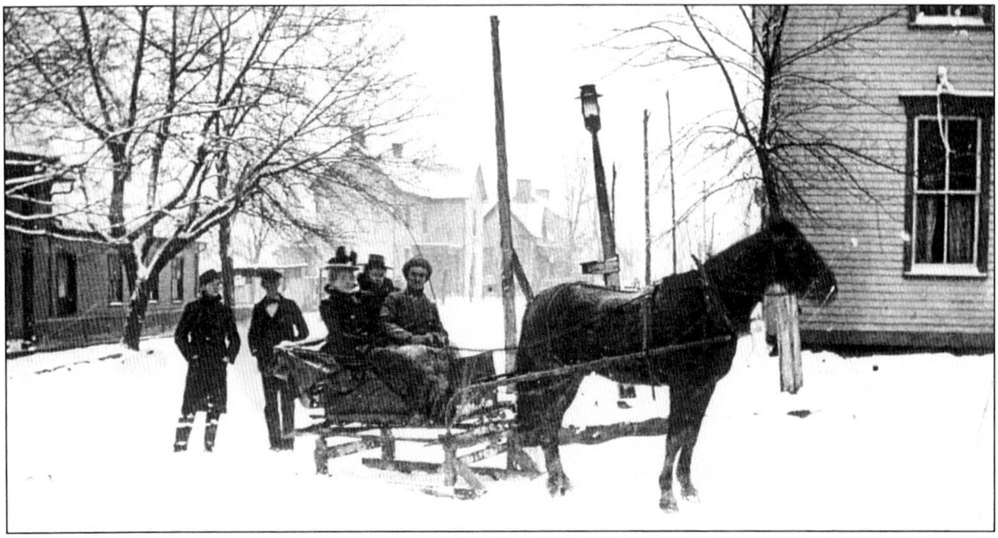

A One-Horse Open Sleigh, c. 1899. Beavin Hamilton holds the reins while seated in his hand-made sleigh at the intersection of present-day North Lincoln Boulevard and East Water Street in Hodgenville. The residence of the town's founder, Robert Hodgen, built about 1789, is in the far center background. The Ford Hotel, formerly the Tarpley Hotel, is at right. Telegraph lines along Water Street and a street lantern are also visible in this beautiful snow scene. The first electric street lights in Hodgenville were installed by the Hodgenville Light and Water Company in 1900.

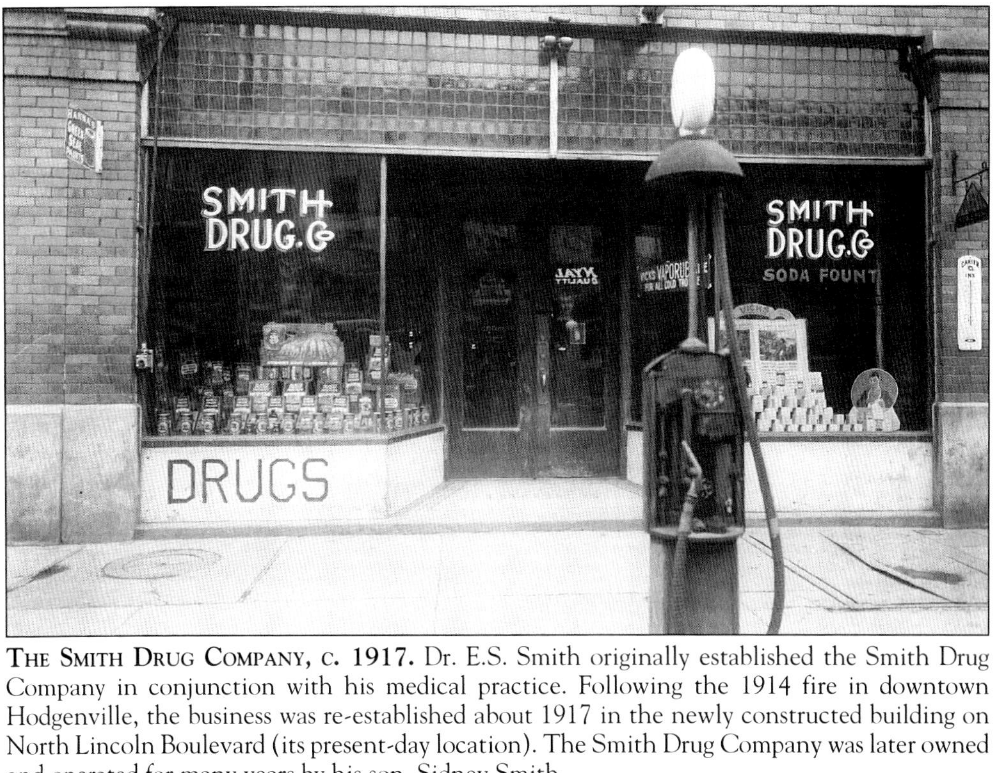

The Smith Drug Company, c. 1917. Dr. E.S. Smith originally established the Smith Drug Company in conjunction with his medical practice. Following the 1914 fire in downtown Hodgenville, the business was re-established about 1917 in the newly constructed building on North Lincoln Boulevard (its present-day location). The Smith Drug Company was later owned and operated for many years by his son, Sidney Smith.

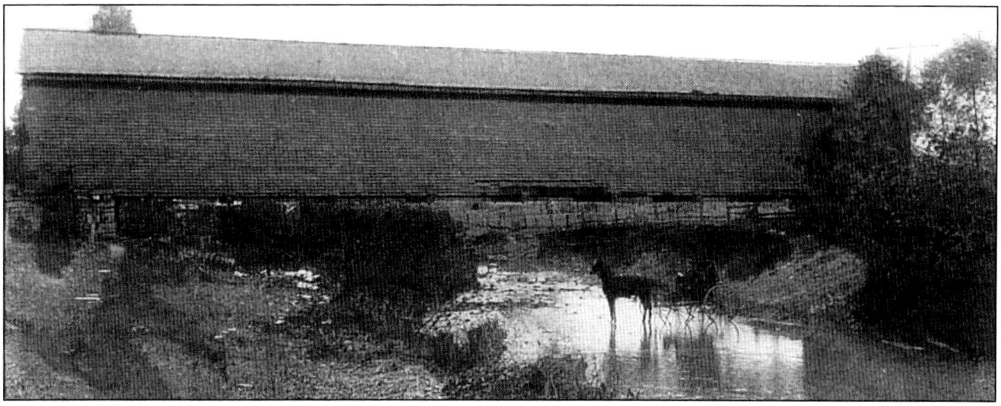

The Hodgenville Covered Bridge, c. 1908. This one-lane wooden, covered bridge along Lincoln Boulevard, just north of Water Street, was built about 1880 by Hodgenville carpenter and undertaker John Robert Nantz. It remained in use until it was replaced about 1920 by a modern, two-lane, steel bridge. This postcard image of the bridge over Nolin River was made by Cincinnati photographer Albert Kraemer. Many of Kraemer's early Kentucky postcards typically depict bridges, railroad depots, courthouses, churches, river scenes, etc., and are now highly collectible and often historically significant.

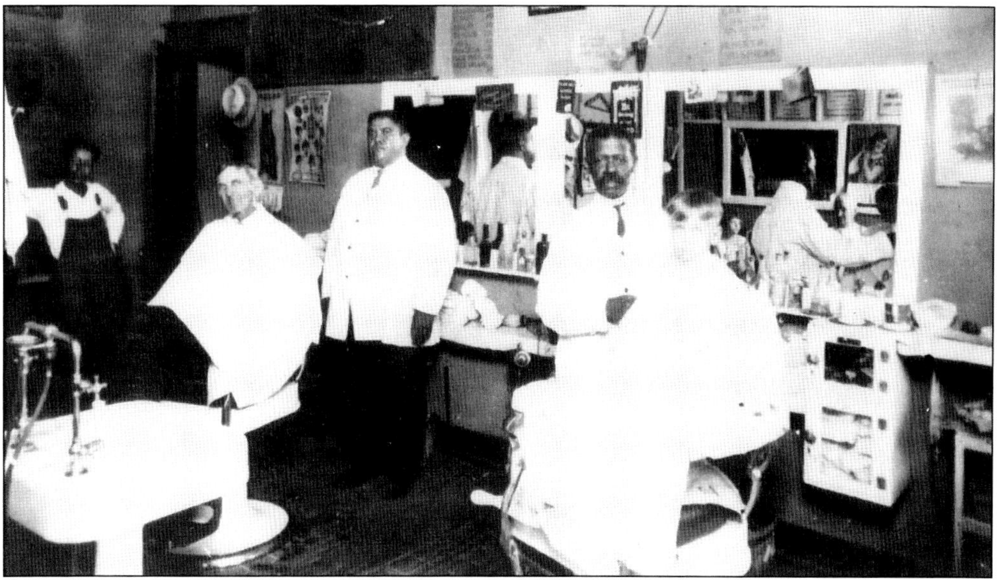

The Quinn and Price Barber Shop, c. 1925. Woodrow Price (left) and Jesse R. Quinn (right) pose in their barber shop on the square in Hodgenville. The sign in the upper right reads, "No Swearing or Vulgar Talk in This Shop." Quinn, whose parents were born in LaRue County as slaves, began working as a shoe-shine boy at the age of 13 in May 1885, in the Hodgenville barber shop of "Uncle Bob" Price. He started a four-year apprenticeship as a barber under "Uncle Bob," who had learned barbering as a slave. He later worked with "Uncle Bob's" son, Dude Price, and finally opened his own shop. He saw all five Presidents who visited Hodgenville during the first six decades of this century, but Woodrow Wilson was the only president he ever met personally. "Brother Quinn," as he was called, was very religious and could quote Biblical scriptures by memory with amazing recall and accuracy. Woodrow Price was an accomplished barber who served many patrons for several decades in Hodgenville and always took a leading part in all activities of his church.

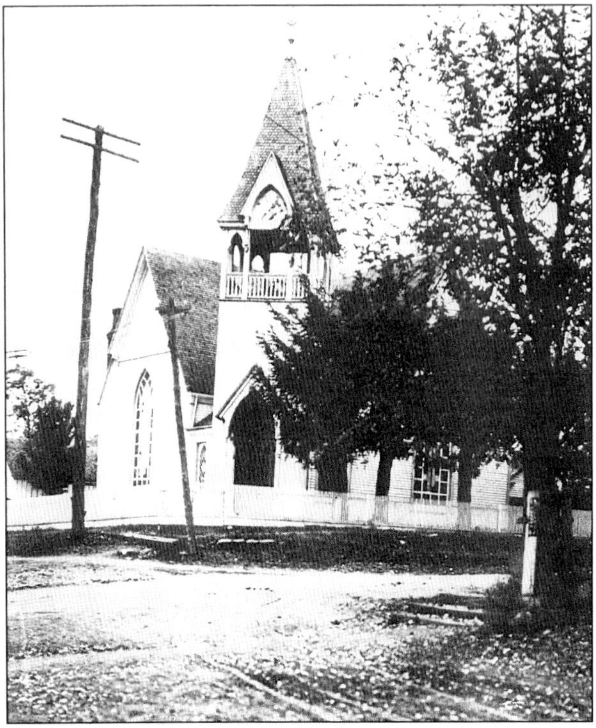

THE HODGENVILLE PRESBYTERIAN CHURCH, C. 1898. Woodrow Wilson, once a Princeton University professor, lectured a large and appreciative audience in the Hodgenville Presbyterian Church on June 23, 1898. The subject of his speech, "Patriotism," was an especially timely topic considering that the Spanish-American War was then in progress. Dr. William Foster, also a professor at Princeton University, was responsible for securing Wilson's appearance under the auspices of Hodgenville's Kenyon College. The church was constructed in 1893 on the site where the LaRue County Public Library now stands. The previous Presbyterian church, one of Hodgenville's first houses of worship, was built on the same lot in 1838.

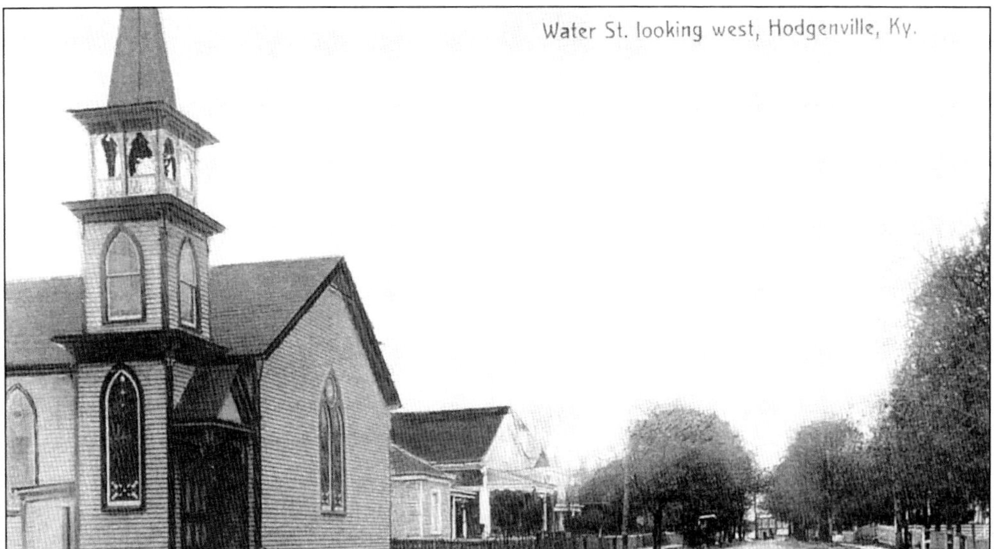

THE HODGENVILLE UNITED METHODIST CHURCH, C. 1908. This postcard image of the church and other residences along West Water Street was made by Albert Kraemer. Construction of the church building was completed in early January 1890. Dedicatory services were conducted by Rev. J.J. Tigert and assisted by the pastor, Rev. W.C. Hayes, on Sunday, January 26. The church remained at this location until 1941, when the building was sold for $1,700 to the LaRue County Certified Seed Association. Many luxurious two-story residences were constructed in the late 1800s along Water Street, which for many years was known as "Quality Street."

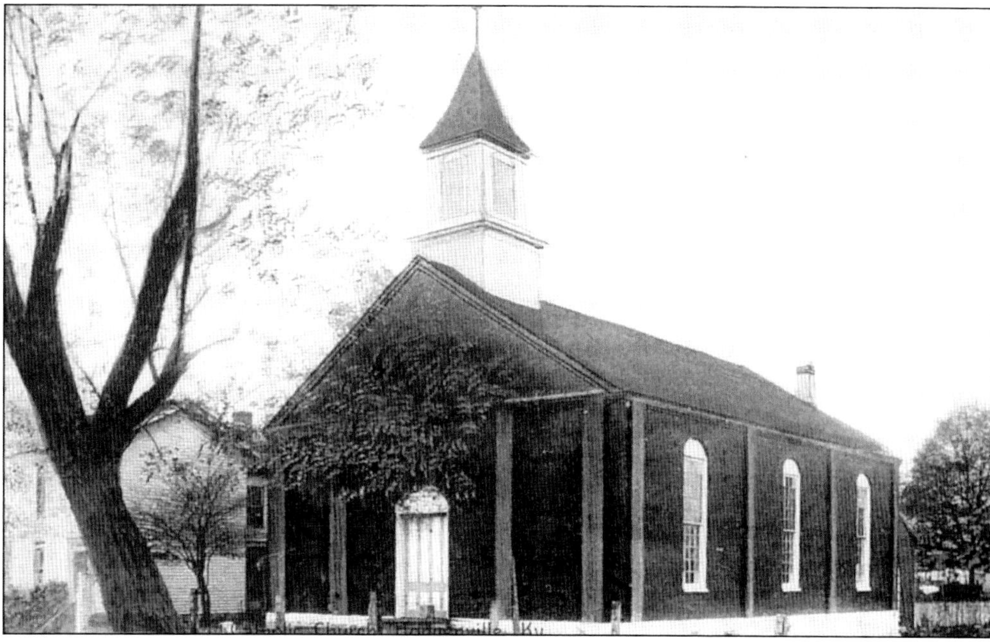

OUR LADY OF MERCY CATHOLIC CHURCH, C. 1908. This church was built on the southwest corner of Walters Avenue and High Street in Hodgenville in 1858. The postcard image was made by the Kraemer Art Company. Father Anthony Reinhart's pastorate lasted from 1878 to 1906. Rev. G.A. Vantroostenberghe then attended to the needs of the parish until February 1915. He was succeeded by Rev. Engelbert Schmitt, who was the last resident pastor of the church.

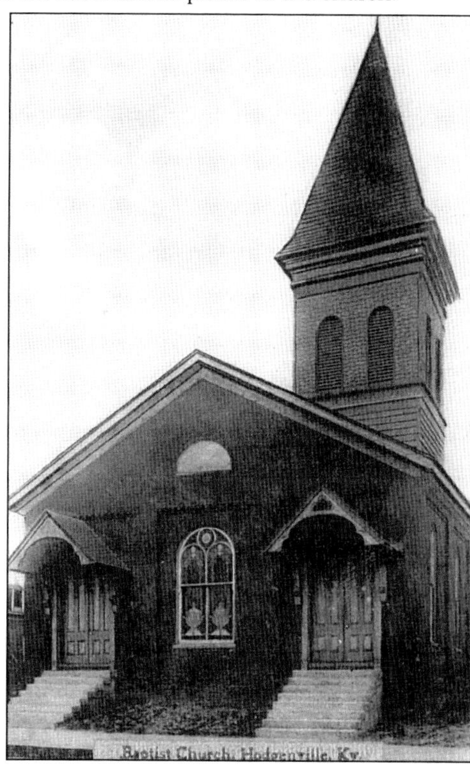

THE HODGENVILLE FIRST BAPTIST CHURCH, C. 1908. According to Spencer's *History of Kentucky Baptists*, the first Hodgenville Baptist Church was admitted to membership in the Salem Association on September 30, 1838. Located on East Main Street, the pictured church building was constructed in 1878. At revival meetings in the 1920s, many people could not gain admittance. For this reason, and due to the increase in the size of the church's congregation, it was vacated in 1926. This Albert Kraemer postcard image also reveals picturesque stained-glass windows and a steeple, which were removed many years ago. From 1880 to 1930, the pastors were, in the order named, I.W. Bruner, W.T. Underwood, R.N. Barrett, B.J. Hagan, C.C. Marshall, J.S. Detweiler, E.A. Cottrell, W.E. Mitchell, and E.H. Blakeman.

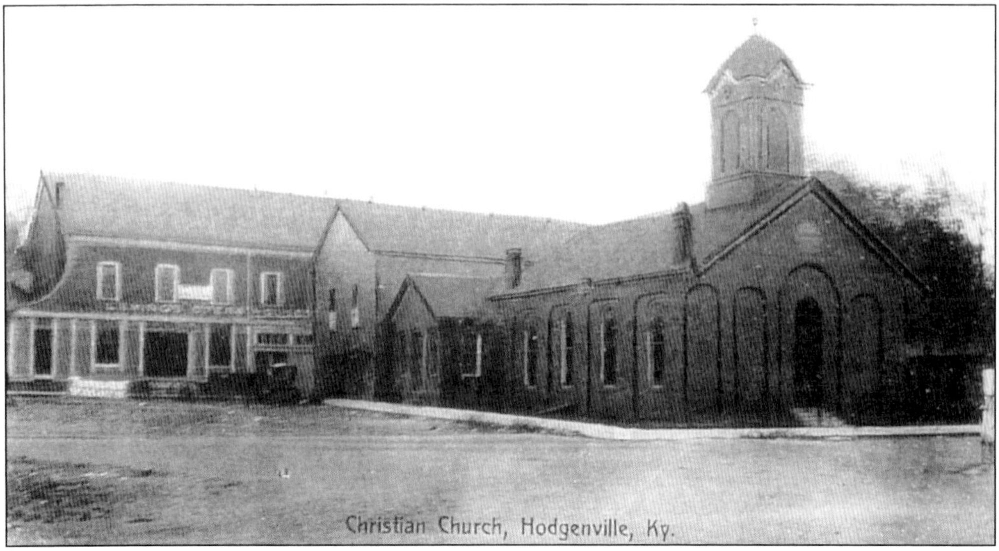

CHRISTIAN CHURCH, THE BURBA HARDWARE STORE, AND LEMING'S OPERA HOUSE, C. 1908. The Hodgenville Christian Church, built in 1877, is on the right, next to the Burba Hardware store, in this Kraemer Art Company postcard scene. William Leming's Opera House (left) had a large roller-skating rink on the second floor, which was also used for girls' basketball games and the presentation of plays and operas. The main floor was for the display and sale of farm machinery, wagons, hardware, furniture, paints, and related items.

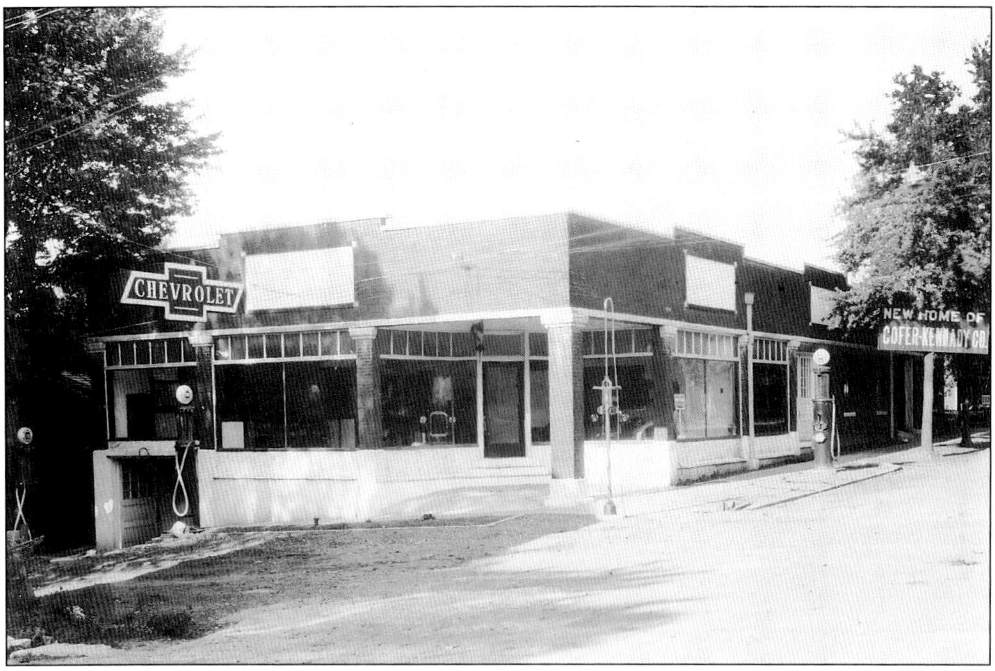

THE COFER-KENNADY COMPANY CHEVROLET AUTOMOBILE AGENCY, C. 1928. This agency and car dealership is housed in this brick building at the northeast corner of Water Street and Lincoln Boulevard. Two new model automobiles are behind the show windows, and three gas pumps and an air outlet are on the front and side of the building. In more recent years, C.D. Polley, then his son, Robert B. Polley, d/b/a Polley Auto Parts, occupied this location.

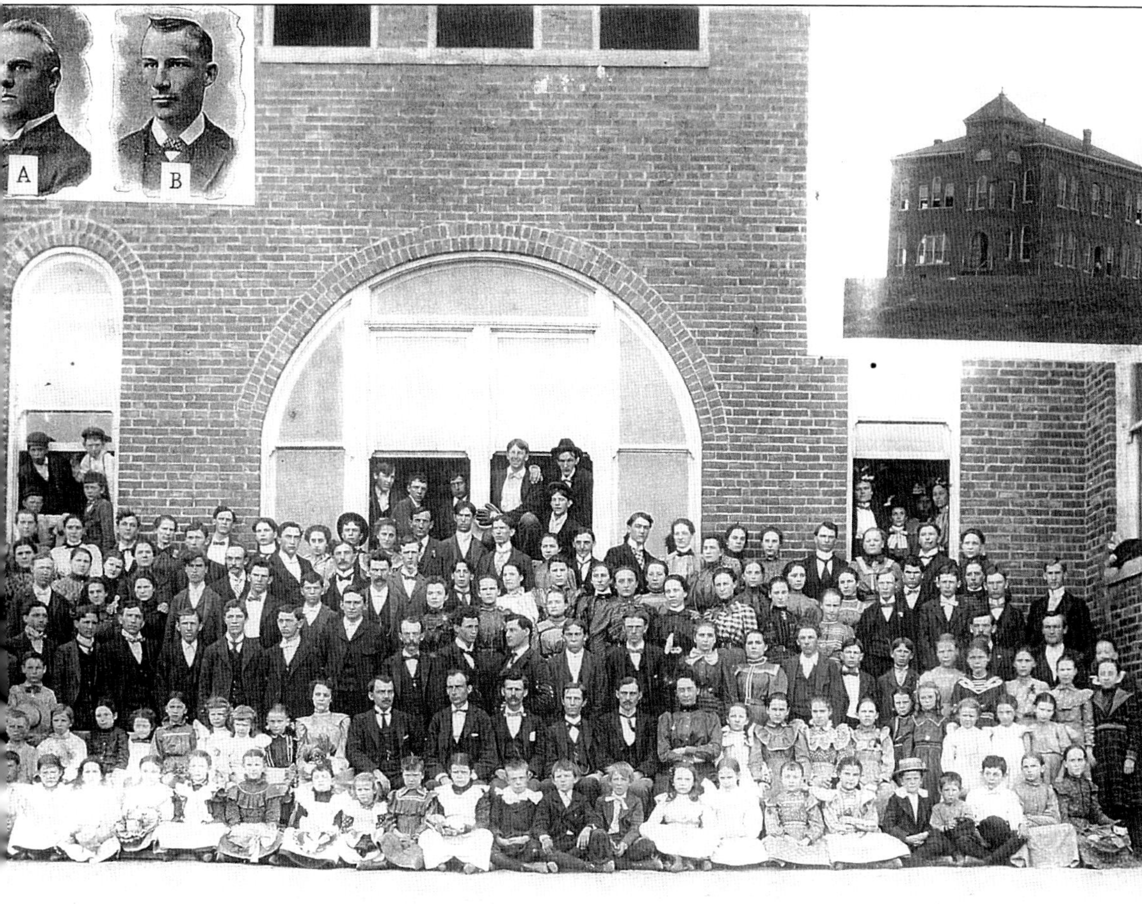

KENYON COLLEGE, C. 1900. Incorporated in November 1897, Kenyon College was located in Hodgenville, where the Hodgenville Grade School building now stands. A.I. Peterman (A), a noted educator, was superintendent of instruction at the college. John C. Pirtle (B), the principal and business manager, was arguably the foremost advocate of education from the late 1800s to 1930 in LaRue and Hardin Counties.

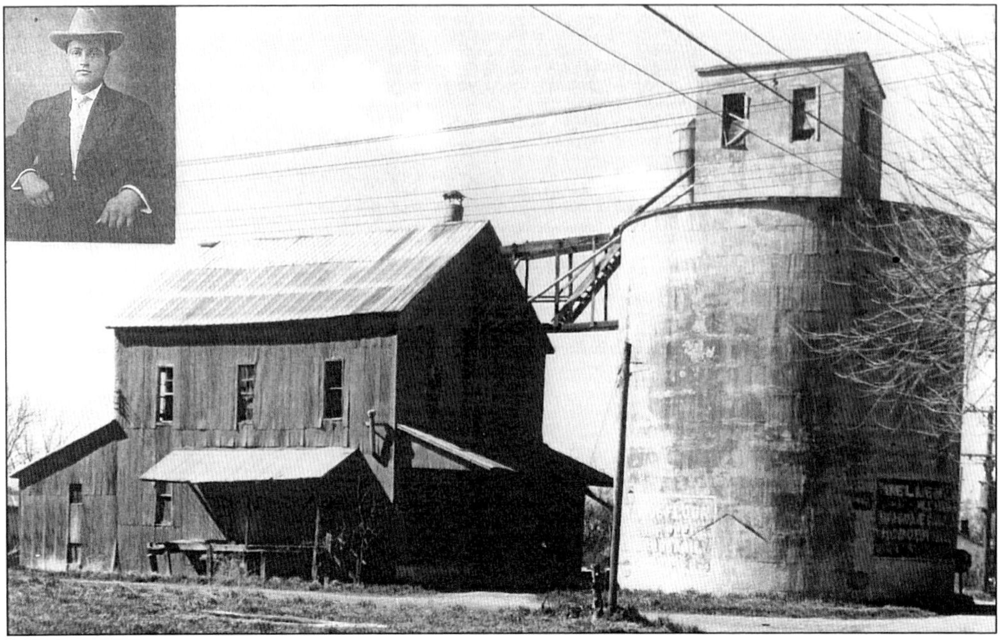

The Hodgenville Roller Mill, c. 1930. Located at the west end of Water Street near the railroad depot, the Hodgenville Roller Mill was in operation throughout the late 1800s until the early 1950s. It was owned and operated by S.T. Boyd and A.T. Boyd from 1912 until 1919. J.M. "Mace" Howell briefly ran the mill after he purchased it in 1919. Shortly thereafter, he turned over the Mill's day-to-day management to his son, James R. Howell (inset), who purchased it in 1928 and operated the mill for nearly 25 years. The mill's best-selling brands of flour were "Belle of LaRue" and "Old Kentucky Home." The large, cylindrical grain elevator still stands, although the mill was dismantled in the late 1950s.

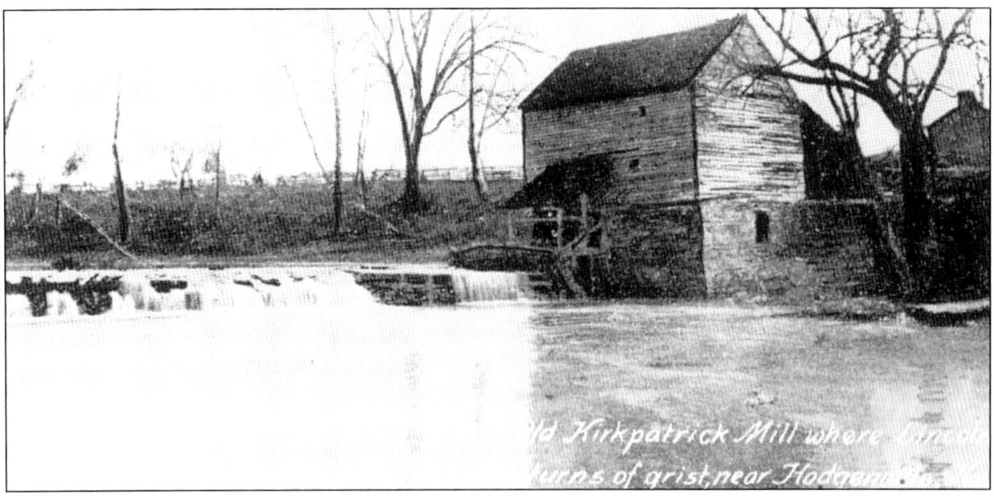

The Kirkpatrick Mill, c. 1909. This mill was established by Gabriel Kirkpatrick, the son of early Phillips Fort settlers Joseph Kirkpatrick and Eleanor Friend Kirkpatrick. It later became known as Mather's Mill, taking that name from Cary W. Mather, Joseph's son-in-law, who succeeded in its management and ownership. Located about 2 miles from Lincoln's Birthplace, on the south fork of Nolin River, the gristmill is believed to have been patronized by Thomas Lincoln and young Abraham.

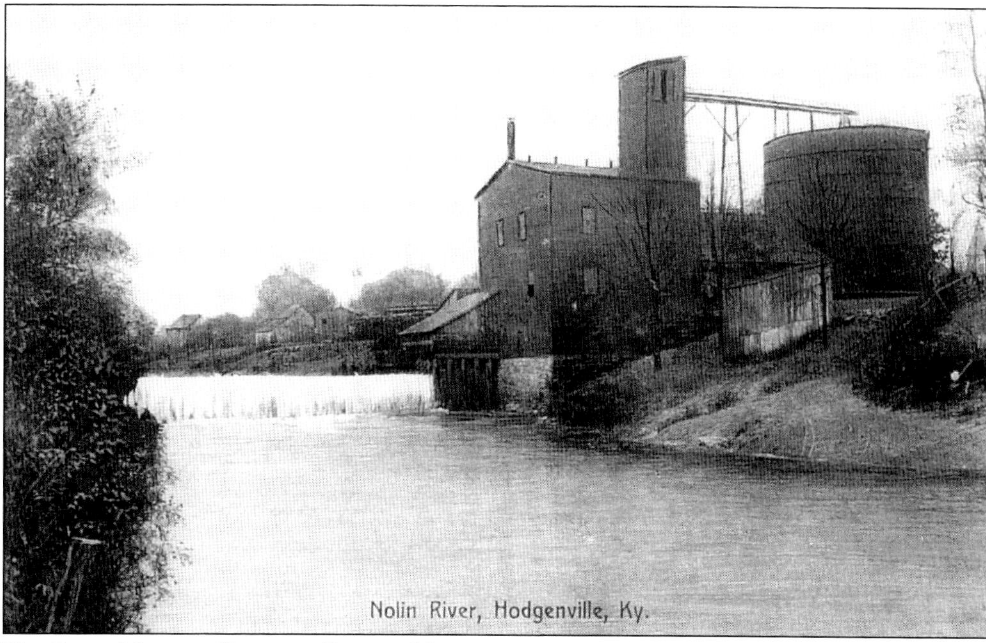

THE LYNN MILLING COMPANY ROLLER MILLS, C. 1908. This mill, also known as the Lynn Mills, was located in Hodgenville at the original site of Robert Hodgens' Mill—the first mill ever established on Nolin River. This postcard by Albert Kraemer shows Nolin River and the entire milling operation. From 1900 to the early 1920s, the Lynn Mills was owned and operated by Oscar Morrison, A.W. Pickerill, E.A. Ferree, W.G. DeZarn, and G.W. Baird. During this time, "Golden Plume" and "White Lily" were the mill's best selling brands of flour. The mill was run most of the year by water power, but also had an excellent steam engine which was used during a portion of each year. The accompanying picture shows two local belles posing in front of the grain elevator, about 1920.

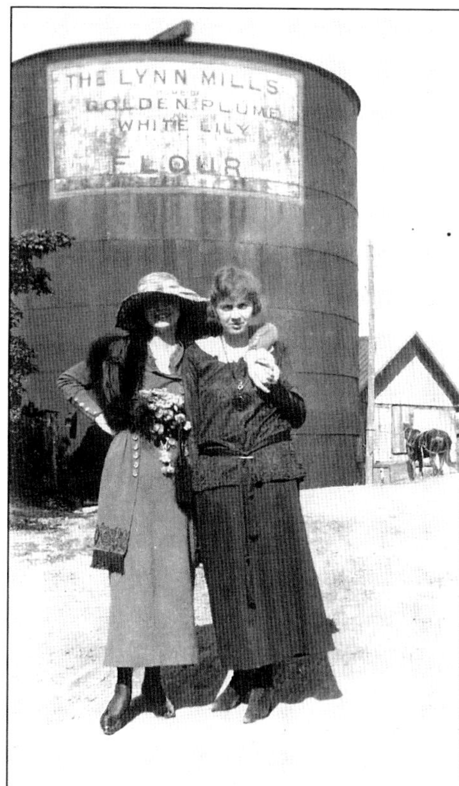

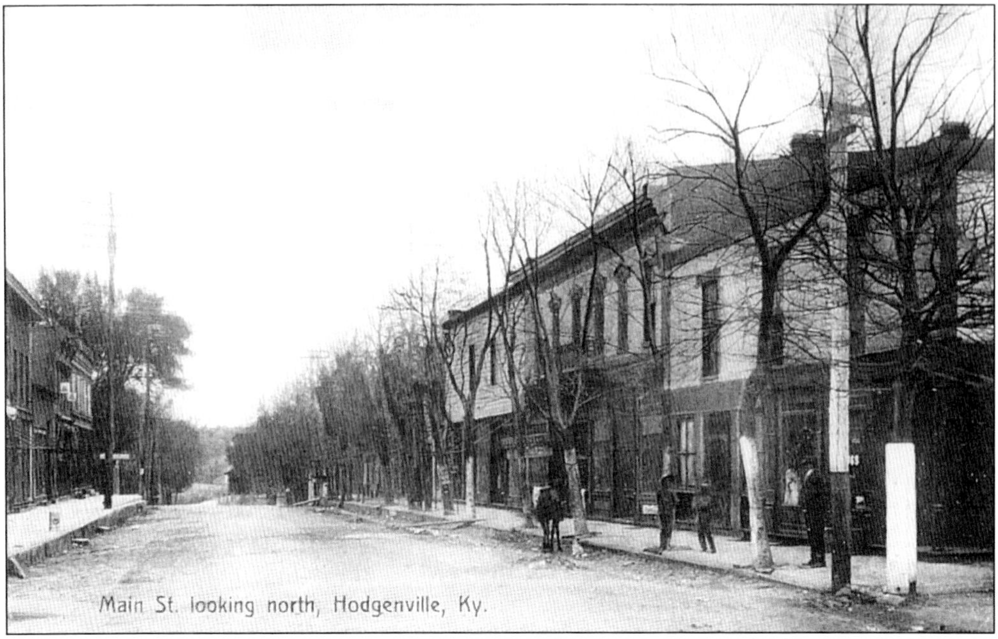

A North Hodgenville Street Scene, c. 1908. This postcard view, looking north from the square, was taken by Cincinnati photographer Albert Kraemer. The Hayes House, a hotel owned and operated by J.R. Hayes, and other businesses are on the right. A newly formed concrete sidewalk is at left in front of other business establishments. The south end of the covered bridge can be seen down the road (now Lincoln Boulevard) leading toward Elizabethtown.

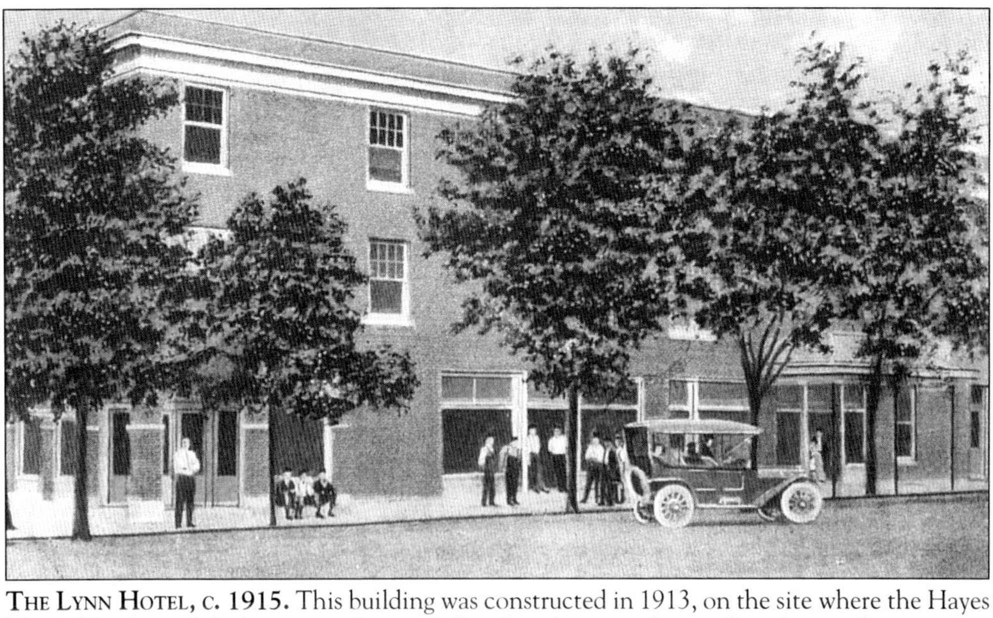

The Lynn Hotel, c. 1915. This building was constructed in 1913, on the site where the Hayes House Hotel stood, before it was dismantled earlier that year. Located on the northeast corner of the square in Hodgenville, the Farmers National Bank and a barbershop occupied a section of the first floor. An advertisement on a later postcard of the hotel boasted, "Famous for Country Ham and Fried Chicken Dinners—Modern Rooms—Innerspring Mattresses."

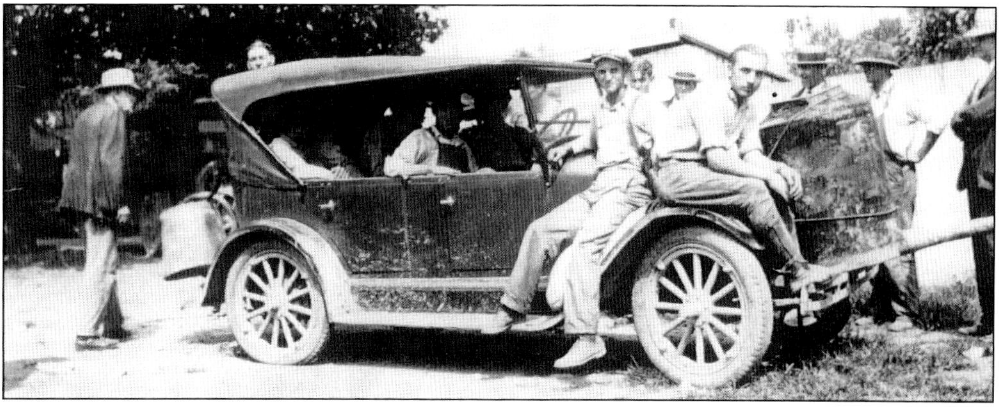

Arresting Moonshiners, c. 1929. A moonshine still raid near the LaRue County-Nelson County line near Howardstown resulted in the apprehension of four moonshiners, who are seated in this 1926 Model-T Ford touring car. The main portion of the still and drain pipe are strapped to the front of the car, and the coil and top part of the still are strapped to the rear. Bill Dever, Hadley Strange, and Perry Mather were the deputized revenue agents who made the arrests.

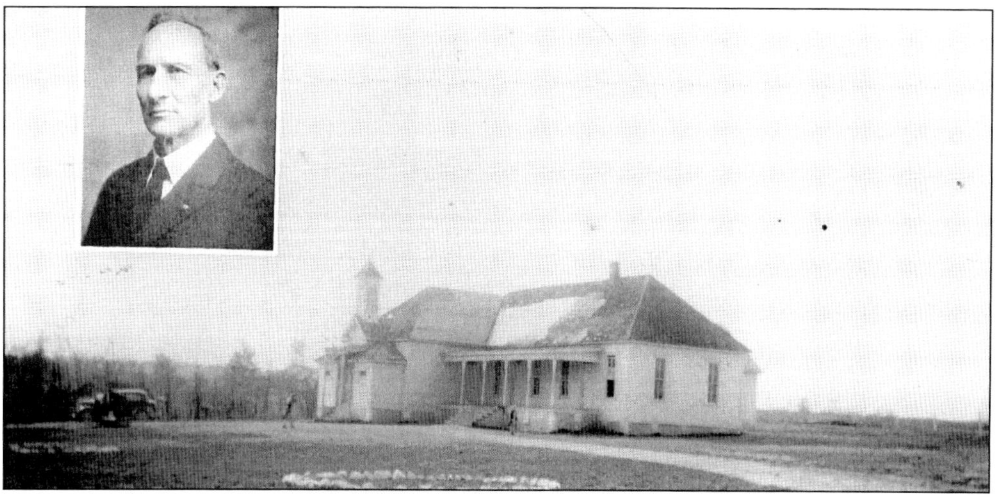

Howevalley High School, 1930. The Howevalley settlement of western Hardin County was named in honor of John and Rachell Howe, early pioneers of the area. The post office here was established on September 8, 1852. A one-room log school was built in the area about the same time by the Klinglesmith family. It was in this old school that one of the county's most famous and respected educators, John Cox Pirtle (inset), received his primary education. Upon completing college at Princeton University, Pirtle returned to Howevalley and conducted the county's first high school out of his home. His devotion to and love for teaching soon earned him the title of "Master Teacher," and his services were sought by accredited schools throughout the area. He was head of the Uptonville Institute and Normal School, in Upton, from 1890 to 1898; president of East Lynn College in Buffalo from 1895 to 1899; and president of Kenyon College in Hodgenville from 1897 to 1903, after which he returned to teaching high school at Howevalley. He was principal of the Elizabethtown City Graded and High School from 1917 to 1929. The photo here shows the old Howevalley school building, which contained four large rooms—three of which were used for the high school, the fourth of which was used for grade school. It was replaced in 1937 by a new brick building that is still in use as a primary school today.

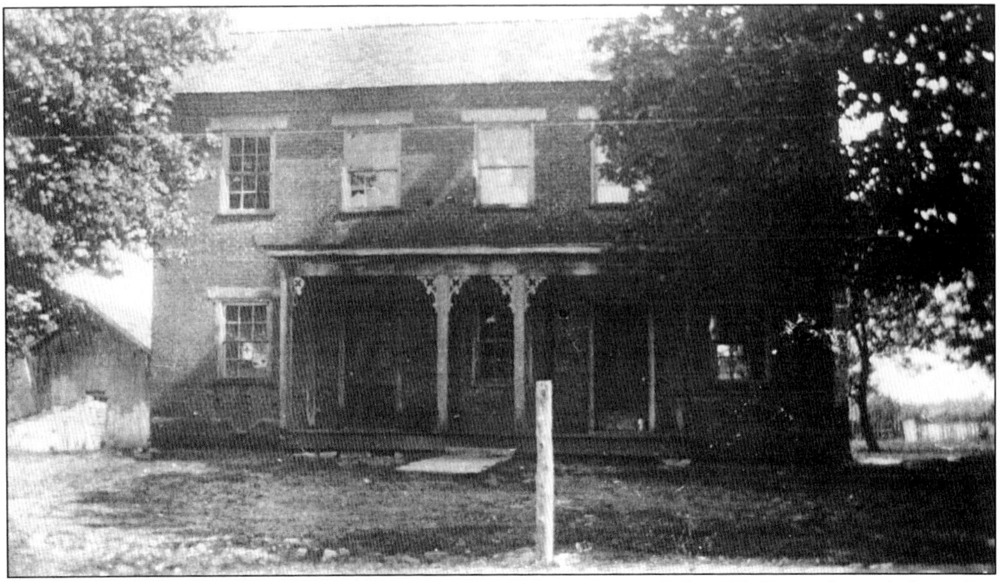

The McDougal Residence at Camp Wickliffe, c. 1880s. John McDougal resided in this brick house, near Leafdale, in LaRue County in 1861. He was the son of Alexander McDougal, the first pastor of Nolin Baptist Church when it was organized in LaRue County in 1803. During the Civil War, Brigadier General William Nelson and his Fourth Division made camp here from December 14, 1861, until February 14, 1862, and used the house as a hospital. Located near a supply depot in New Haven, the site was selected for observation purposes and named Camp Wickliffe in honor of Governor Charles A. Wickliffe. The house, located on Kentucky Highway 470 and photographed in the 1880s, was dismantled in the 1930s.

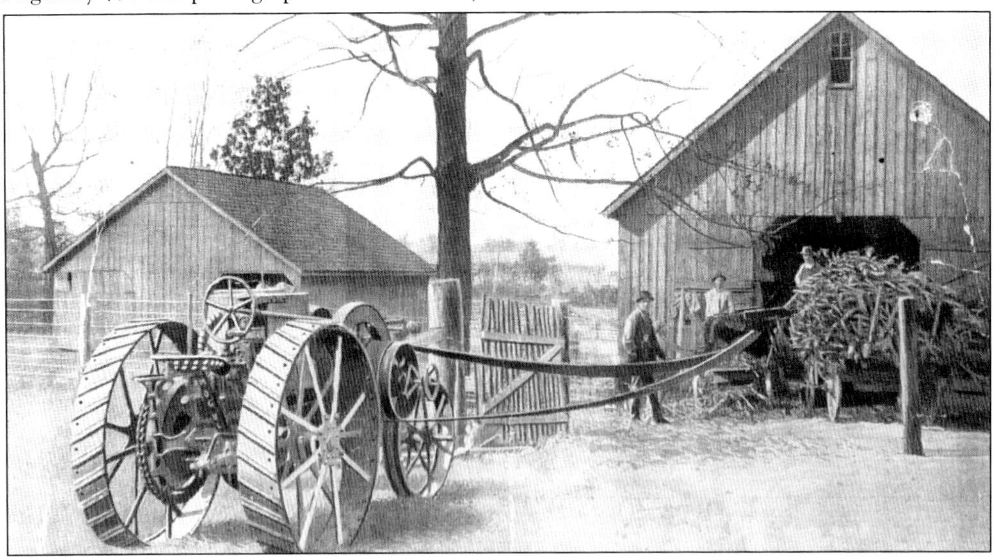

The Meers' Farm and Tractor, 1915. A tractor, believed to be the first used in LaRue County, is furnishing power to shred fodder on the Meers' farm, located in the Brooks neighborhood of the Maxine Community near Magnolia. The Meers family (father and two sons) can be seen supervising the operation. The Brooks Schoolhouse is barely visible in the distance. This photograph appeared on the front cover of the January 1916 issue of *Kentucky Farming* magazine.

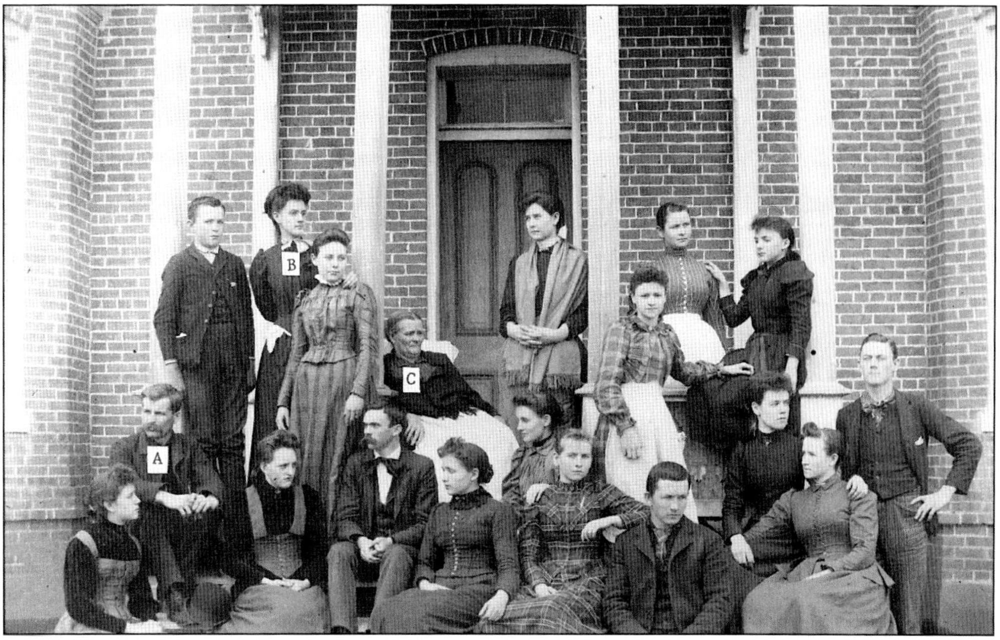

MAGNOLIA COLLEGE, 1893. Incorporated April 9, 1880, Magnolia College was located in a beautiful brick building, which burned in the spring of 1894. This 1893 photograph taken at the college includes (A) Professor S.A. Beauchamp, (B) Professor Mary Beauchamp (his wife), (C) Lizzie Lamkin (the college matron), and students. The building had a two-story porch, double-bay windows, and a chapel. It was erected at a cost of $5,000 as a result of the progressive support and financial assistance provided by B.G. Beavers of Nolin, Kentucky. After the building burned, the college was never quite the same, although a new building was constructed to take its place, as depicted in the postcard image below, *c.* 1909. The Magnolia Elementary School now stands on the site where Magnolia College was located.

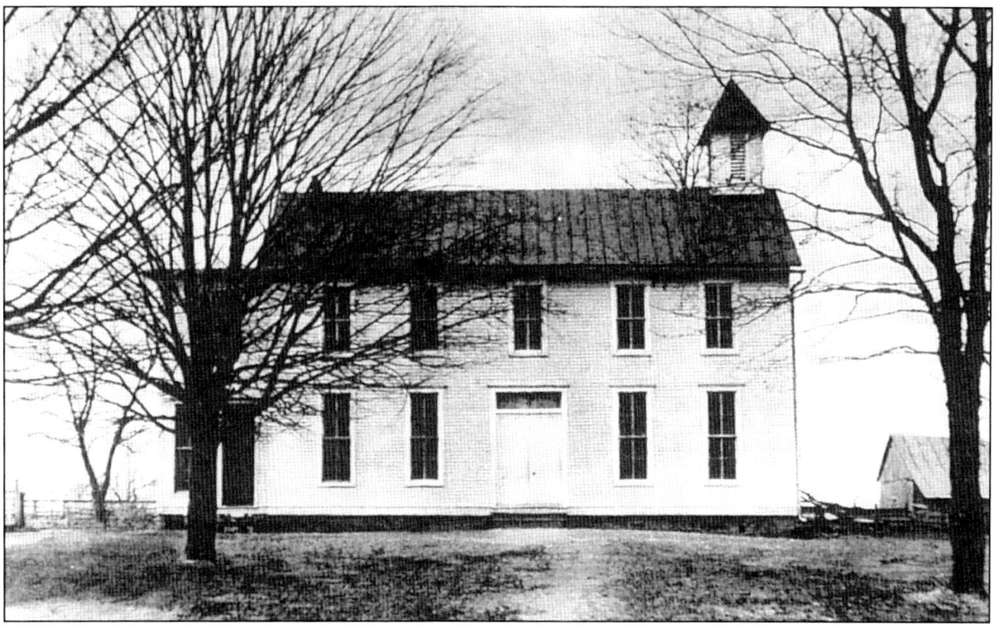

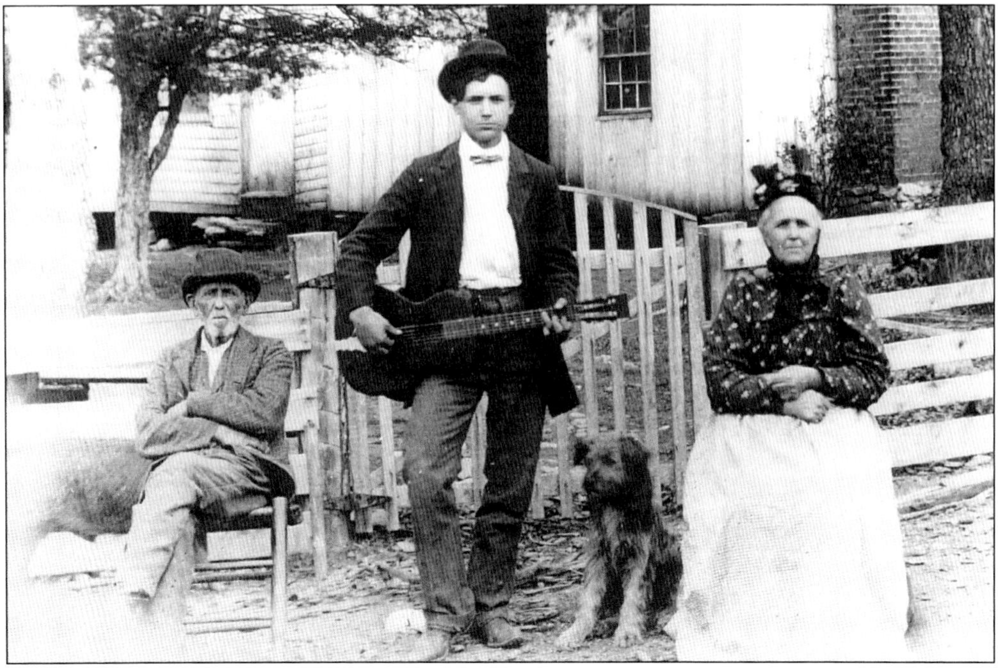

THE BROOKS FAMILY NEAR MAGNOLIA, C. 1905. Dudley Brooks (seated left) and his wife, Martha Jackson Brooks (seated right), flank their son, Wilburn Brooks, and his dog in front of their residence on what is now Highway 357. The hog at left was uncharacteristically camera shy that day. This photograph was taken by Hodgenville photographer D.P. Busroe.

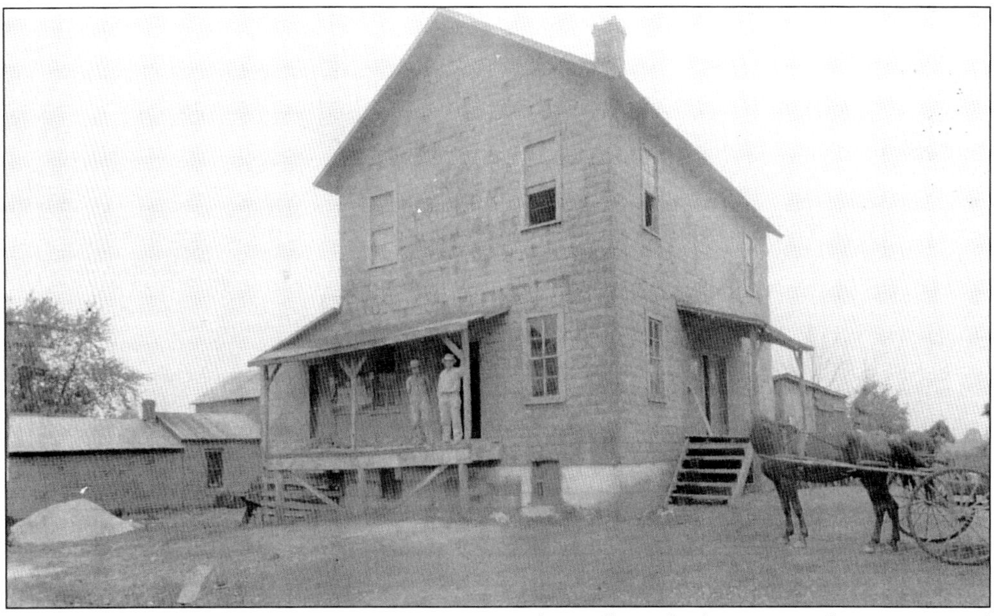

THE MAGNOLIA ROLLER MILL, NOVEMBER 1929. This mill was built in Magnolia in 1917, and continued in operation for about 40 years. Chester Miller (left) is standing on the porch with C.L. Miller, the proprietor. White "bleached" flour, made from wheat grown on nearby farms, was packaged in 24-pound bags that displayed a large Magnolia blossom (white flower) as a part of the colorful design.

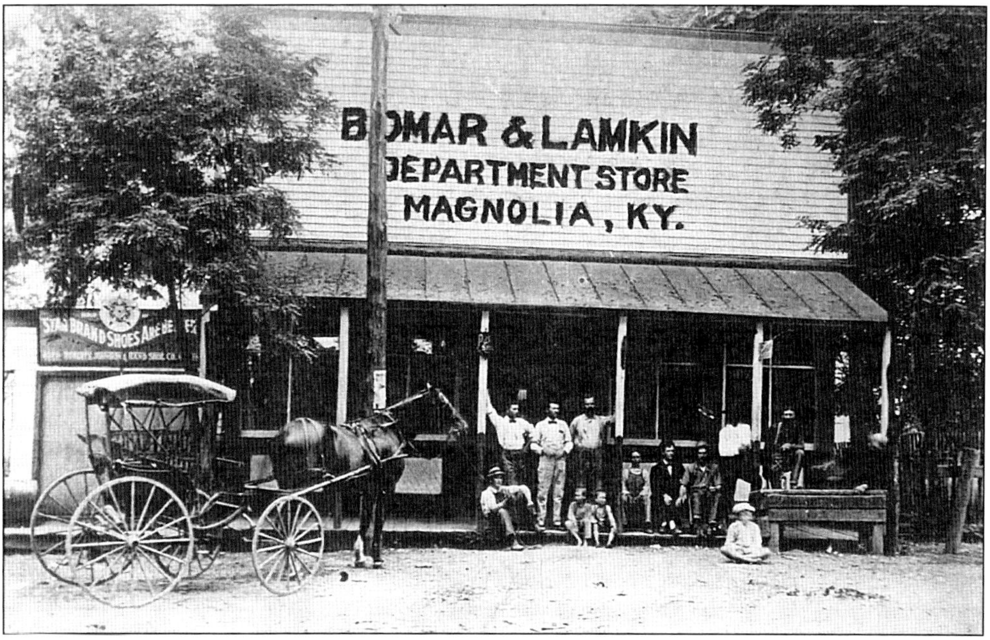

THE BOMAR AND LAMKIN DEPARTMENT STORE, C. 1905. This store was the largest and finest general merchandise business in Magnolia. It was owned and operated by its founders, Jim Bomar and Logan Lamkin. An 1898 newspaper advertisement for the store states, "Come in and see our ready made clothing; we can fit anybody, from a three year old boy up to a large-sized man."

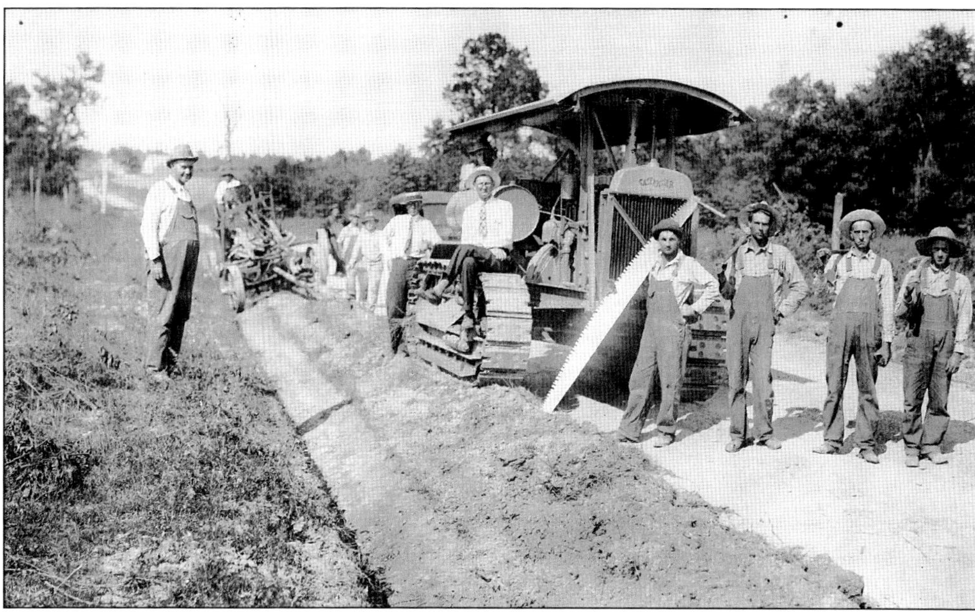

ROAD CONSTRUCTION NEAR MAGNOLIA, C. 1925. This modified, Model-80 Caterpillar Tractor is pulling a horse-drawn grader (ditch and bank-cutting machine with a grader blade) along Jackson Highway (U.S. 31 East) near Magnolia, in LaRue County. This scene signifies another stage in the passing from horse-and-buggy days into the mechanized age of travel, as roads become wider and more compact, with clearly defined and contoured ditches.

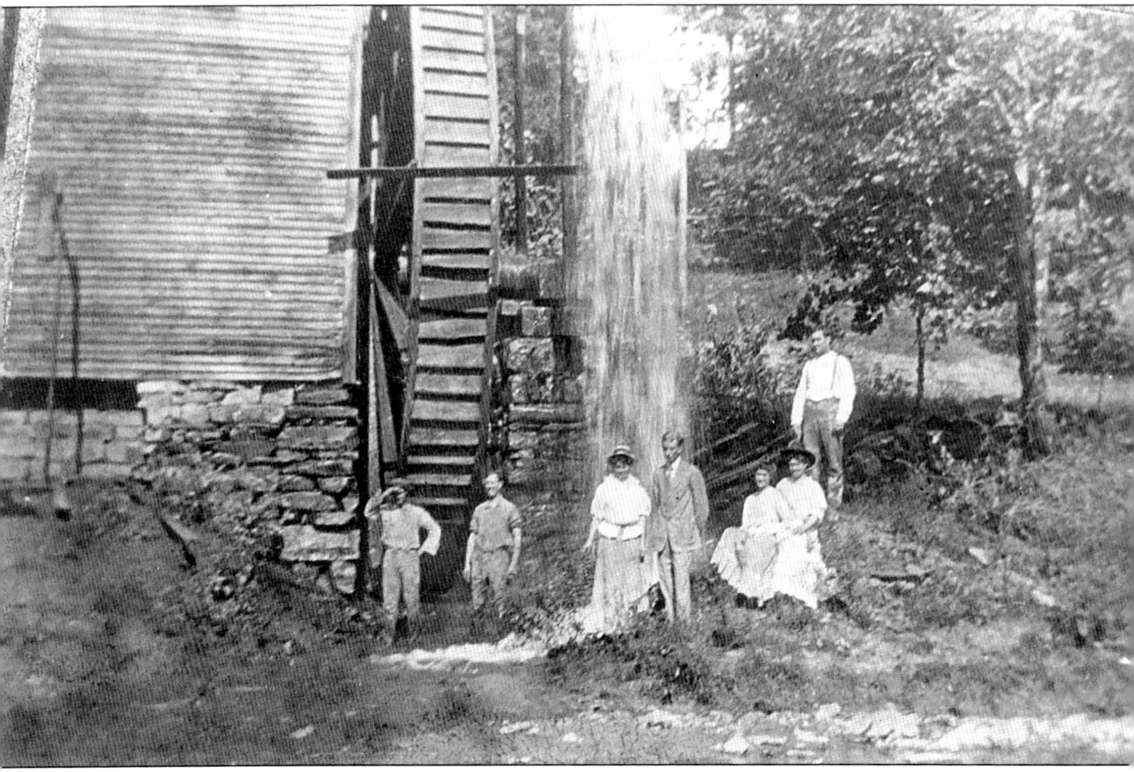

THE HOWELL MILL AT MALT, C. 1925. The Howell Mill was built in 1861, along Otter Creek at Malt, in the Ball Hollow section of LaRue County. The gigantic, wooden "overshot" water wheel was the second largest in Kentucky. The mill was powered by a large stream of water from the creek that was troughed into a man-made millrace along the hillside from an upstream waterfall. When the water reached the forebay at its hillside destination, it was channeled into a second wooden trough down to, and just beyond, the top of the wheel. Buckets were attached to the wheel, so that when water flowed over the wheel it would fill the buckets and then spill into the next ones and, slowly but surely, turn the wheel. During the late 1800s and early 1900s, the mill was operated at different times by James M. "Mace" Howell and his sons, Fred Howell and James R. Howell. The Malt Post Office and Store were located across the creek, and for many years the area was the center of activity for people residing within a large radius of this community. Many moonshine stills existed up and down the three branches of Otter Creek, both during and after Prohibition days. Otis Howell, a former resident of the Malt community in Ball Hollow, recalls his father, Fred Howell, telling him of standing atop the Howell Mill in the early 1920s and seeing smoke from as many as seven stills in operation at the same time.

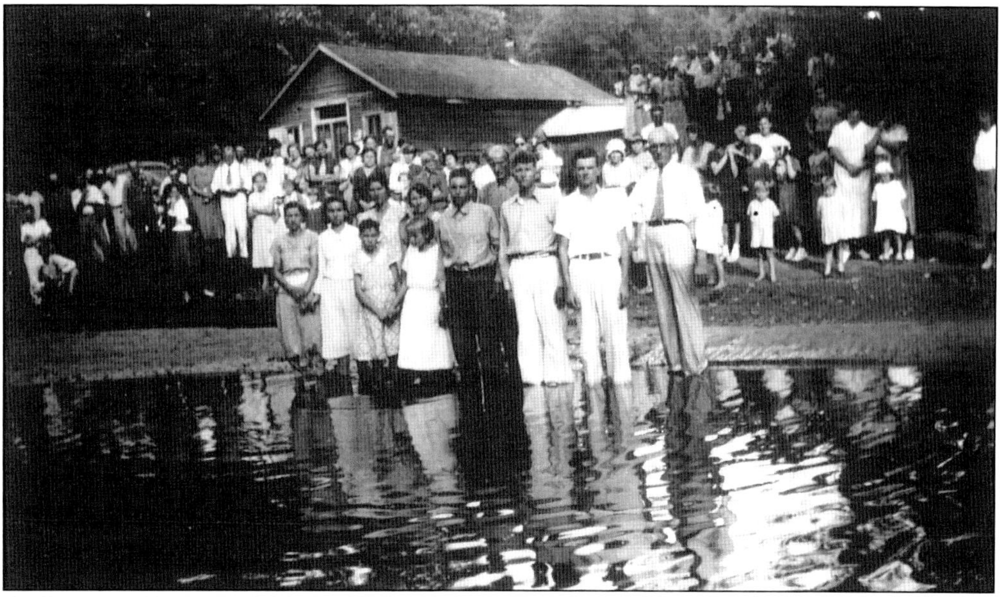

A Corinth Baptist Church Baptism, c. 1930. Candidates for baptism and Rev. L.B. Cantrell (front right) pose for this picture while standing in the west fork of Otter Creek, at Malt, in LaRue County. Located between the Malt General Store and Post Office (behind the congregation) and across from the Howell Mill, this creek site was used for baptisms for many decades by churches in the southeastern portion of the county. The ceremony usually occurred on a Sunday afternoon, following the morning church service.

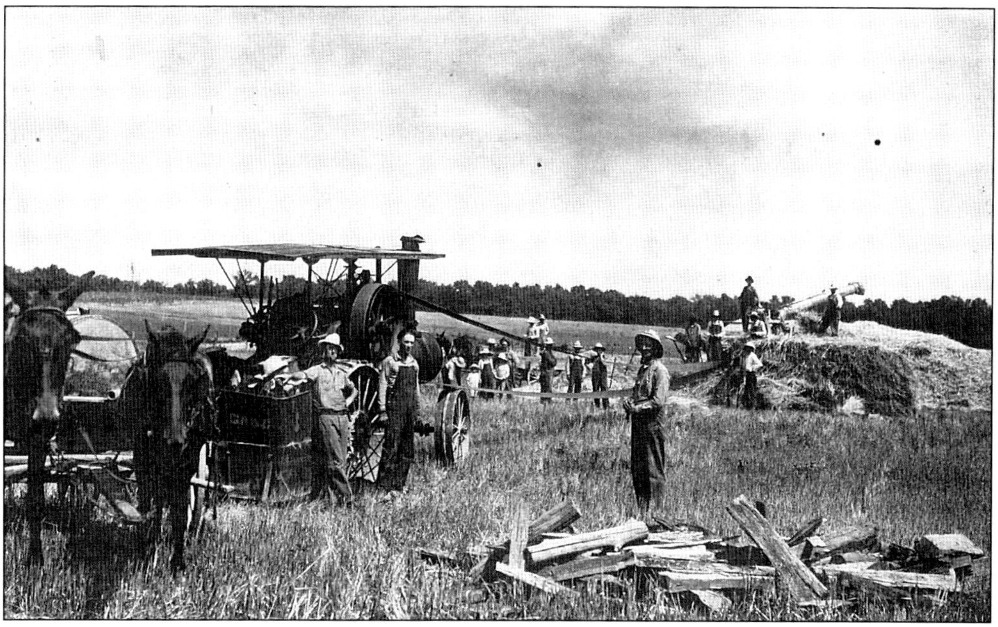

Wheat Threshing at Benningfield Farm in Mt. Sherman, c. July 1925. Family members of all ages and neighbors pitch in to assist Andy Benningfield (right center foreground), Homer Benningfield (bib overalls at left), and George Benningfield (far left wearing white hat). Neighboring farmers in this LaRue County community routinely worked together, going from one farm to another during the wheat-threshing season.

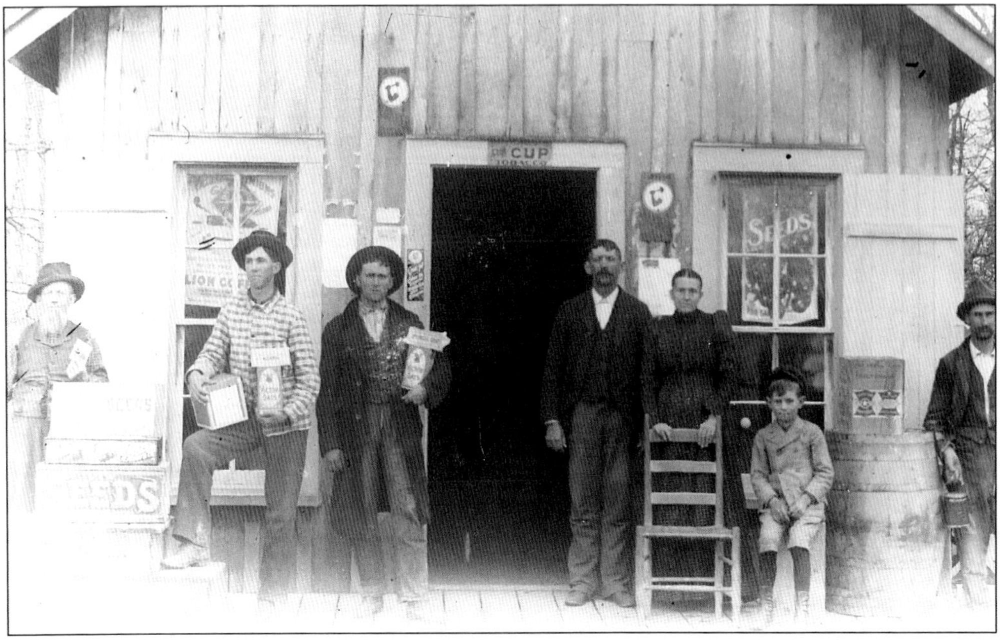

THE MT. SHERMAN GENERAL STORE, C. 1902. D.M. Ferry and Company Seeds, Lion Coffee, Castor Oil, Victor Oats, Arm and Hammer Soda, and Cup Tobacco are some of the product names visible upon close inspection. This picture was taken by Hodgenville photographer D.P. Busroe. The small LaRue County town of Mt. Sherman, located near the Green County line, had its beginnings immediately after the Civil War.

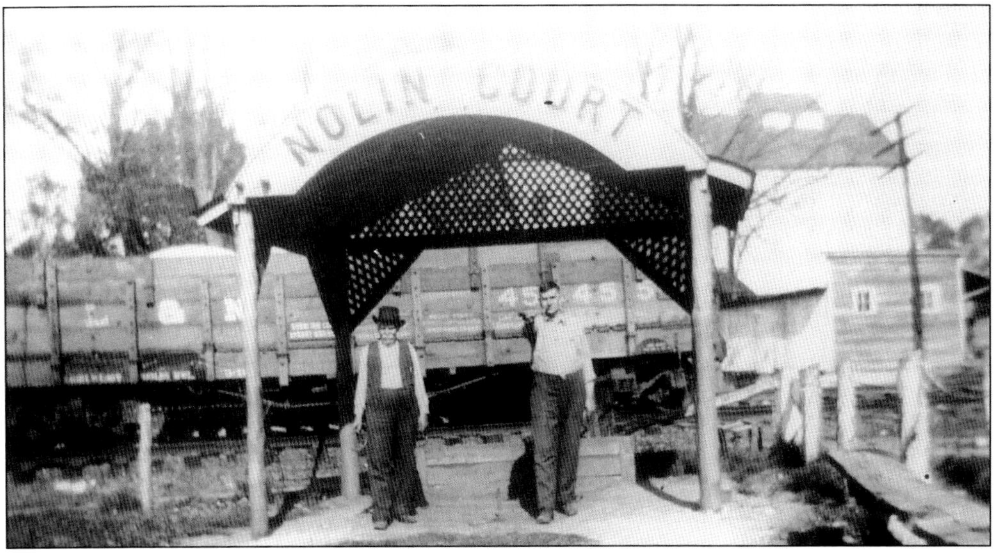

THE NOLIN HORSESHOE PITCH COURT, 1926. Passing through the town of Nolin today, one would never dream that a large mill, bank, hotel, depot, general store, hardware and farm implement dealership, and school were once in operation there. During the 1920s, a first-class horseshoe court (Nolin Court) was located here, and it attracted serious and talented competitors from everywhere. Several nationally known competitors gave exhibitions here. In this photo, taken in 1926, Powell Akers (left) and J.L. Harris square off in some friendly competition. The famed Lynnland Mill can be seen in the background at right.

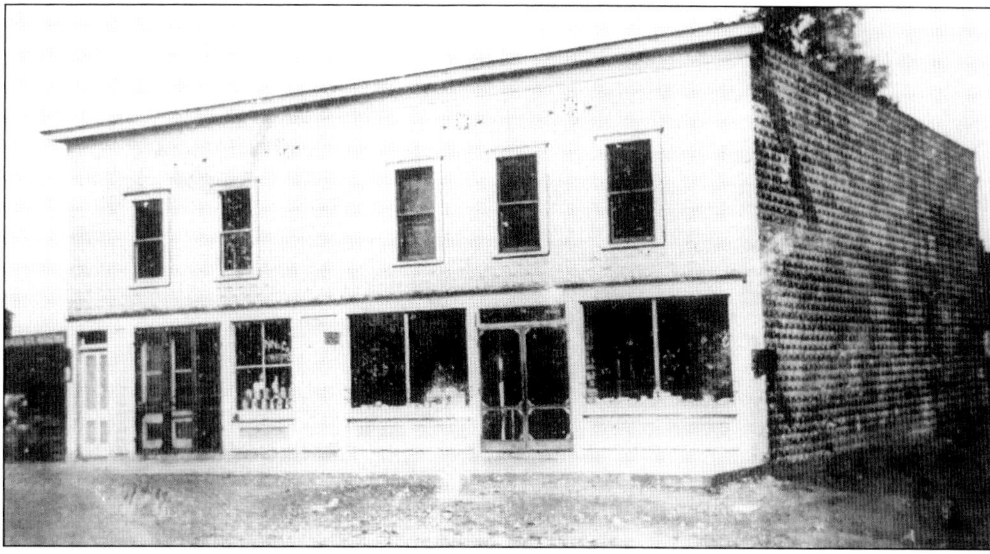

The Nolin Mercantile Company, 1908. The town of Nolin had its beginnings on the banks of the Nolin River, between Glendale and Sonora. The first post office was established in the vicinity on May 25, 1836. The L&N Railroad passed through the river community in 1854. The old mill here (Lynnland Roller Mills), built in 1874, owned by Taylor Watkins and operated by Jerome F. Albert, was one of the largest and most profitable enterprises in the county. In the 1890s, these two men also established the Nolin Mercantile Company. This large, two-story building housed a general store and hardware dealership for many years, operated by J.L. Harris. The building no longer exists.

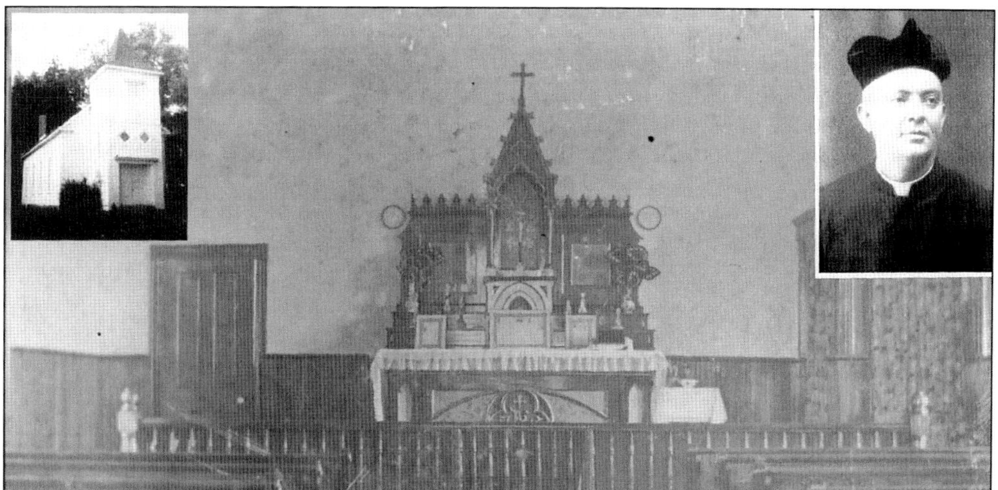

The St. Anthony Catholic Church, 1900. During the Civil War, a large Union training camp (Camp Nevin) was established near the L&N Railroad, in the Red Mills area of southern Hardin County. A Catholic church (probably a log structure) was built near the camp to serve the spiritual needs of the soldiers stationed there. Many soldiers who died while there are buried in the old cemetery near the Nolin River, which was used by Catholics and Protestants. In 1899, the Catholics of the area built a new frame church, under the direction of Rev. James P. Cronin (inset). This photo shows the inside of this church shortly after its construction. The church was closed in 1969, due to a decline in Catholic families in the area.

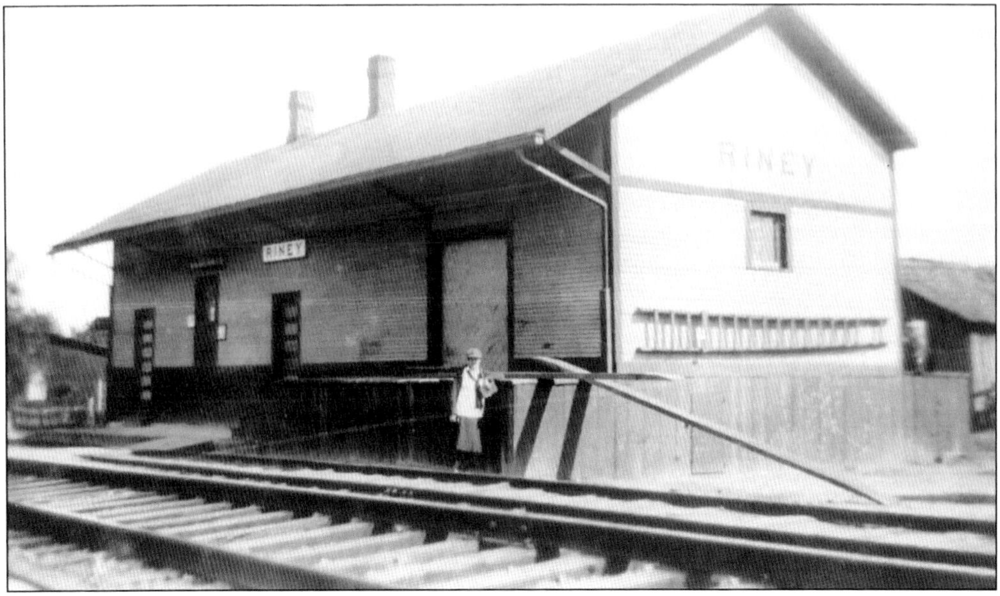

THE RINEYVILLE DEPOT, 1917. The town of Rineyville, once referred to as the "Garden Spot of the World," traces its beginnings to a small settlement on Otter Creek, where a post office was established on January 22, 1856. When the railroad came through the area in 1873, the town relocated to its present site, and took the name "Rineyville" in honor of Zachariah Riney, one of the area's first settlers. The area was famous for its large oak trees and apple orchards. The first train came through Rineyville on September 1, 1874. The depot shown here, known as Riney Station, probably dates to that period.

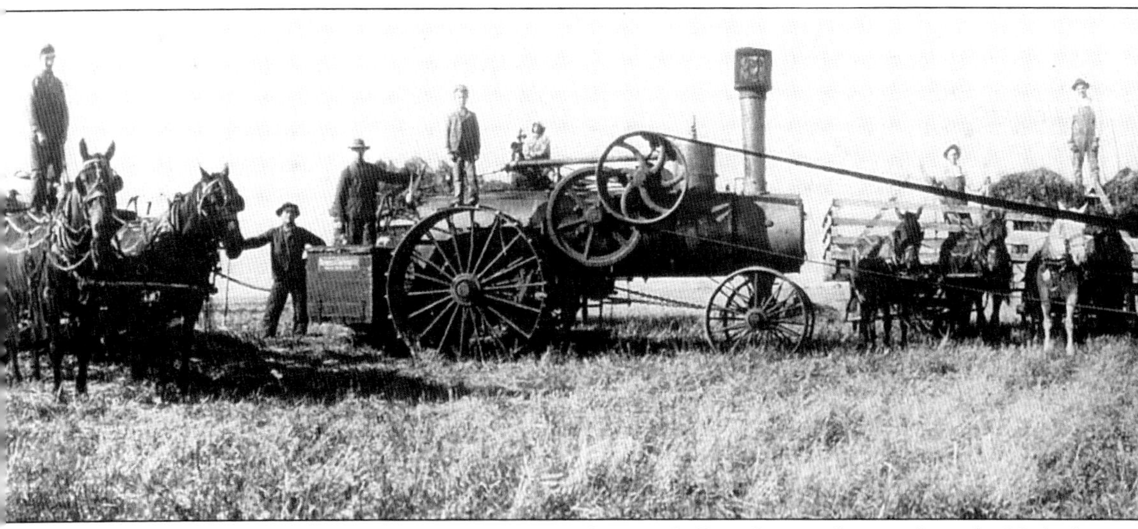

WHEAT THRESHING NEAR ROANOKE, C. 1925. Sixteen LaRue County farmers from the Nicholas and Wilkins communities pose with their horses and mules, pulling wagons loaded with bundles of wheat, at a farm near Roanoke. Water entering the Nichols and Shepard Company steam traction engine from the tanks on the wagon at left created steam which supplied the energy needed to operate the threshing machine at right. The threshing process began when the

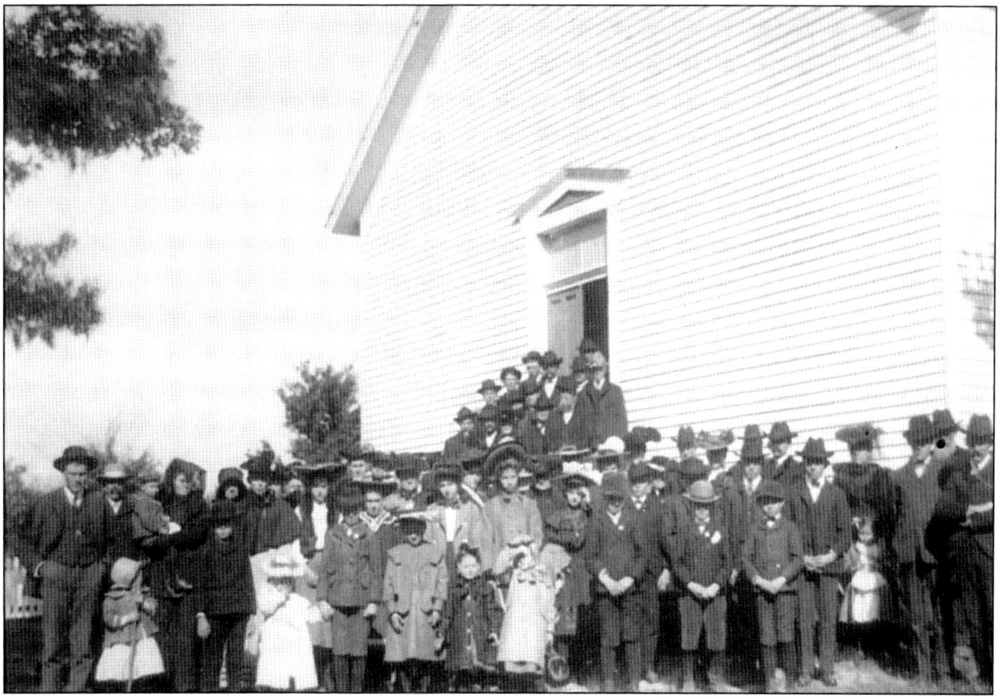

THE RIDGE SPRING METHODIST CHURCH, 1906. The congregation of the Ridge Spring Methodist Church, near Rineyville, was founded in 1882. A one-room schoolhouse, built about that time near the church, was also given the Ridge Spring name. Many ancient stones dot the cemetery adjoining the church. Residents of Rineyville worshiped here for many years before building their own church in town. The Ridge Spring School bowed to history long ago, but the church is still in use today.

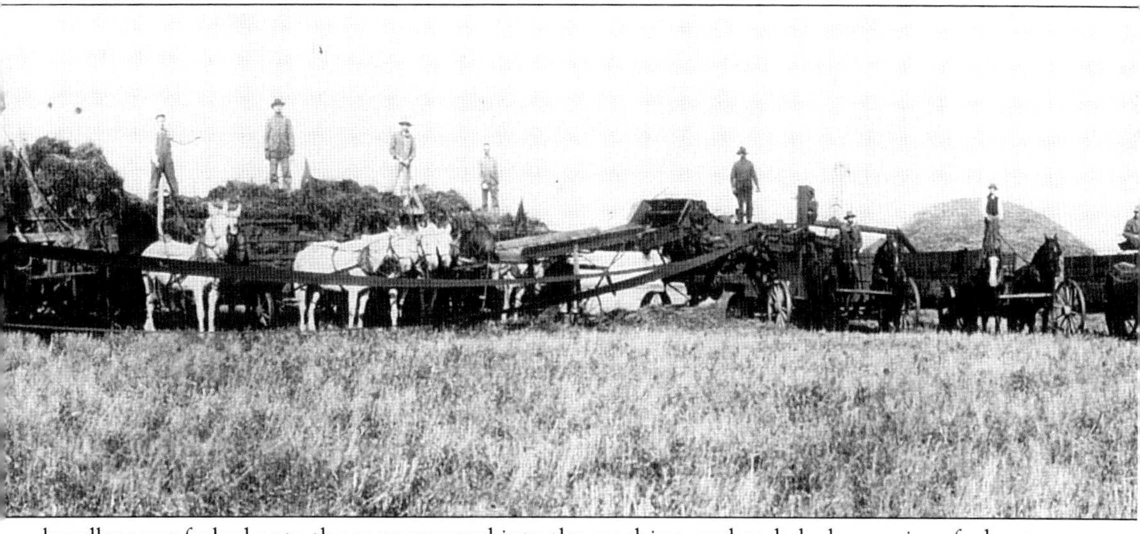

bundles were forked onto the conveyor and into the machine, and ended when grains of wheat were threshed out and the straw was blown into a stack. The wheat grains were then bagged and hauled to a granary. Cooperation, camaraderie, and an occasional libation for those so-inclined helped make the work more enjoyable.

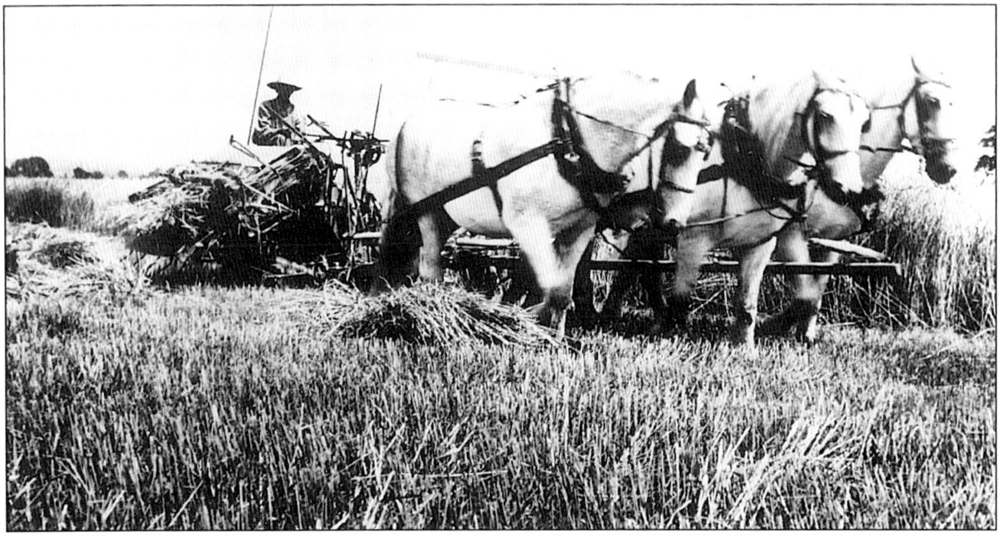

A Harvest Scene in Roanoke, c. 1927. Ben Harrison Trumbo is reaping and binding wheat with his three matched, white Percheron mares, Nellie (left), Sallie (center), and Easter, in the Roanoke community. He and his wife, Rosie Mae Trumbo, reared 12 children (9 boys and 3 girls) on this farm, located in the northern part of LaRue County. The farm is now owned by one of their sons, Burt Trumbo.

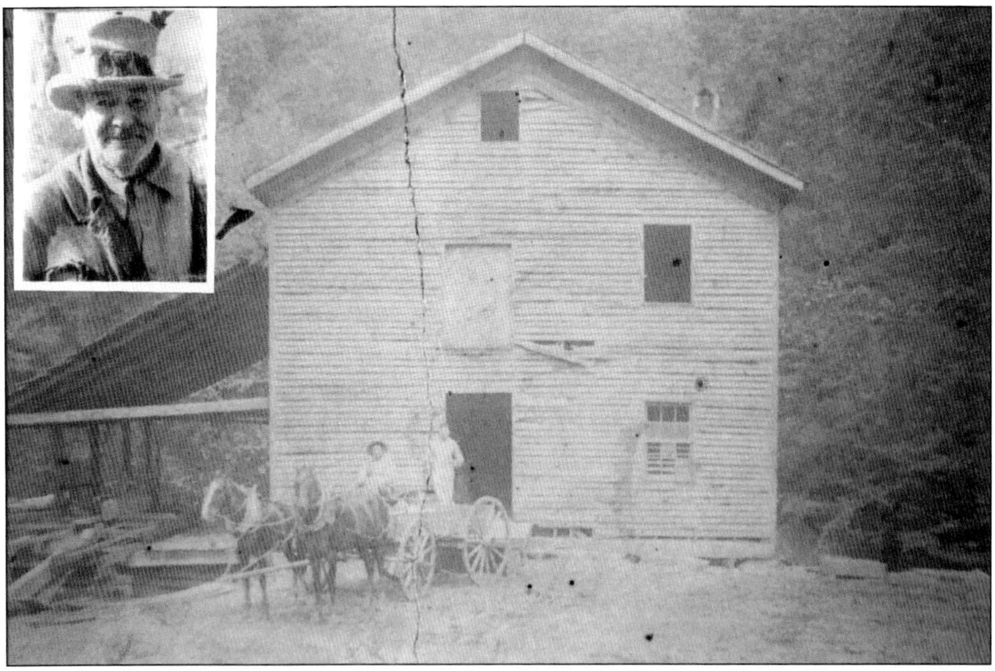

The Pierce's Mill, 1900. Built in the 1860s, S.M. "Boat" Pierce (inset) purchased this old mill on Rough Creek, near the Solway community of western Hardin County, in 1900. As payment for his services, the miller kept half of the lumber sawed, and one gallon of meal for every bushel ground. The flood of 1937 extensively damaged the building, and it was replaced with a smaller structure, which was torn down in 1951 upon his death. Former owners were known to be John Oliver, the Hill family, and the Williams family.

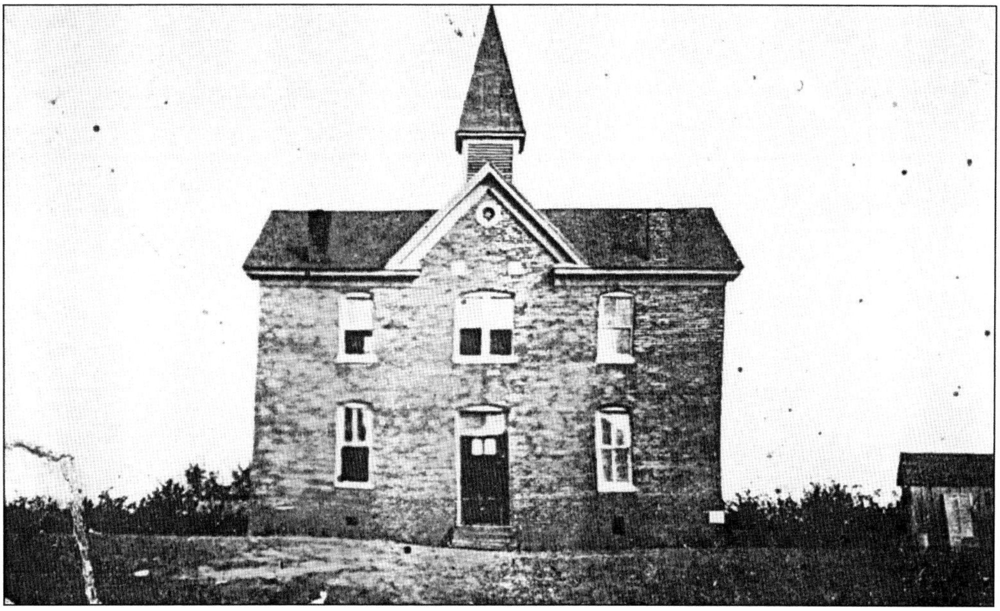

SONORA COLLEGIATE INSTITUTE, 1900. Constructed in 1894, this popular school was opened in Sonora on January 21, 1895, with W.H. Sprigg as principal. The cornerstone was laid by Misses May Spurrier and Maude Bland. Trustees were Ben Spurrier, M.C. Bogue, and W.R. Perry. Many additions were made to the original structure over the years, with a high school being added in the 1920s. It was torn down in 1951, and replaced with the present building that is still in use as Sonora Elementary.

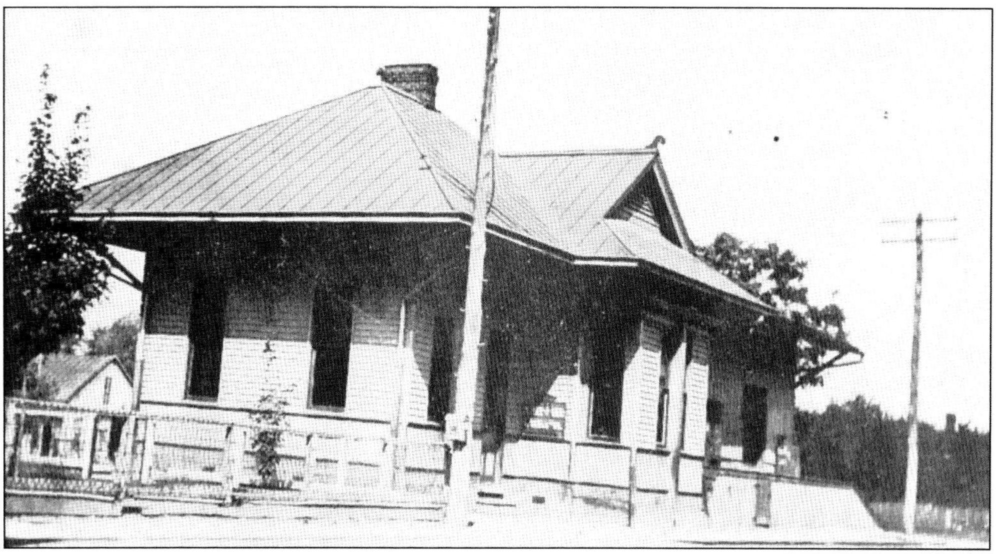

THE SONORA DEPOT, 1910. Upon the completion of the L&N Railroad through the area in the 1950s, a post office was established on August 5, 1858, and was known as Buck Snort. According to tradition, while the railroad was being built, a local resident who heard the train's whistle for the first time commented "just listen to that buck snort." Hence, it became the town's first name. It was changed to Sonora in 1859, in honor of a popular restaurant keeper. The depot here was built in 1864, and extensively remodeled in 1903. It was torn down many years ago.

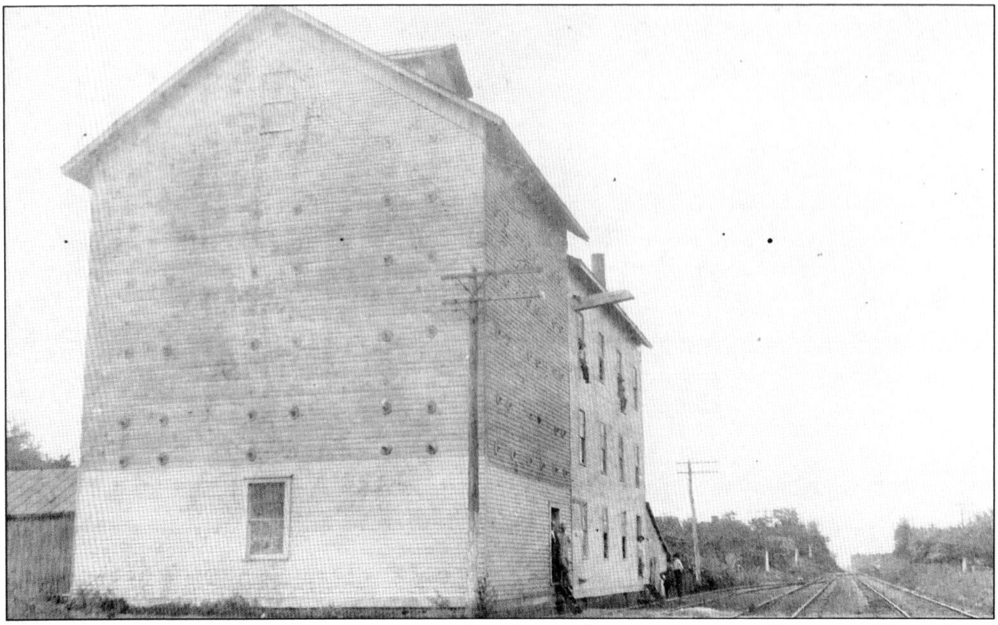

The Sonora Milling Company, 1900. This large, four-story, steam-driven mill was built by Polk Mason and Thomas Peak in 1883, and managed by a Mr. Sheehan until 1896. J.P. Summers later bought into the business and operated the mill for many years, followed by W.R. Routt. Harvey Withers, a mill employee, said that he could recall a time when 20 teams and wagons were lined up to use the mill. Grain was unloaded on the first floor and traveled by elevator to the top floor, where it was ground in a series of rollers. The product was screened and funneled down to the next floor of the mill, where it was ground again. The process continued until flour emerged on the lower floor, where it was then bagged. The old landmark was torn down in the 1960s.

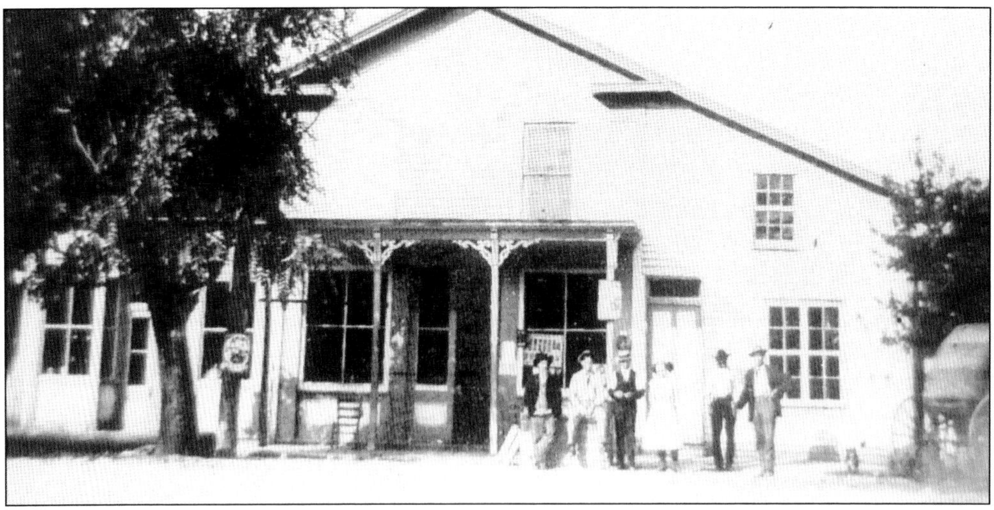

The H.A. Bading Store, 1908. In the 1890s, H.A. Bading and B.C. Spurrier operated this store, which sold hardware, staple groceries, and farm implements, on Sonora's main street. In later years, Mr. Bading acquired full interest in the store and brought his son-in-law, Bernie L. Thurman, into the business. Mr. Bading became a prominent figure in Sonora and was a member of the board of directors when the Bank of Sonora was formed.

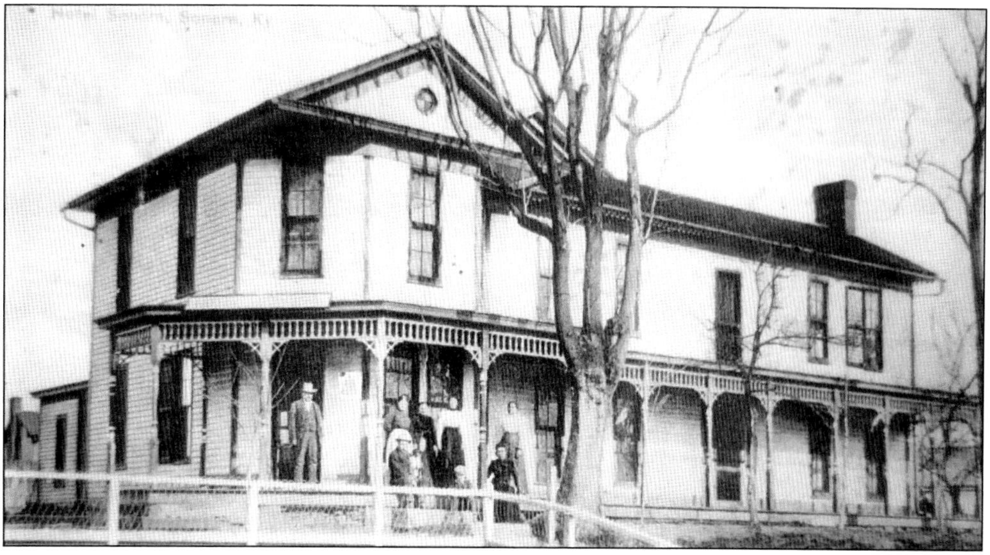

THE SONORA HOTEL, 1910. This hotel was built in the late 1800s near the L&N Railroad tracks. For many years it was managed by the Henry Nichols family. Many recall Tom Durbin cutting hair in the hotel lobby each Wednesday and Saturday for 15¢. Rooms were $1 per day, with meals costing 50¢. The railroad company maintained a small park (shown surrounded by a fence) near the hotel. In 1919, W.R. Routt purchased the hotel and operated it with his wife, Lennie, using part of the building for their living quarters. Covert H. Routt became the owner in 1932 and used it as a private residence until it was sold to R.E. Tabb in 1970 and torn down.

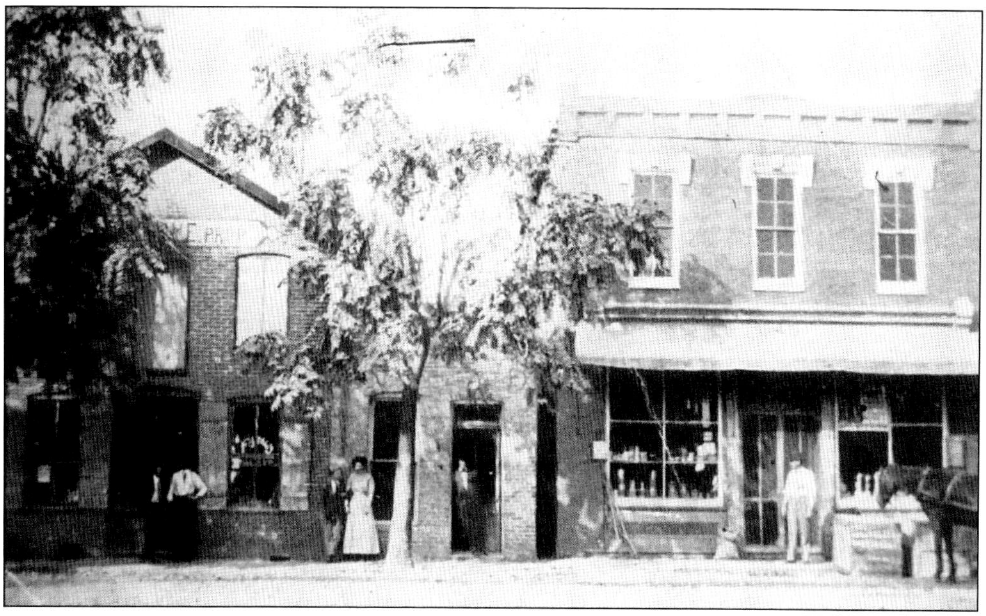

A SONORA STREET SCENE, 1908. In this old postcard view of Main Street in Sonora are, from left to right, the R.B. "Lit" Hodge building, containing the Tom Brunk Store, the office of Dr. J.F. Glasscock, and the Mason Brothers Store (operated by Levi and Wilbur Mason), where the post office was kept for many years. At its peak, Sonora was the largest town between Elizabethtown and Glasgow.

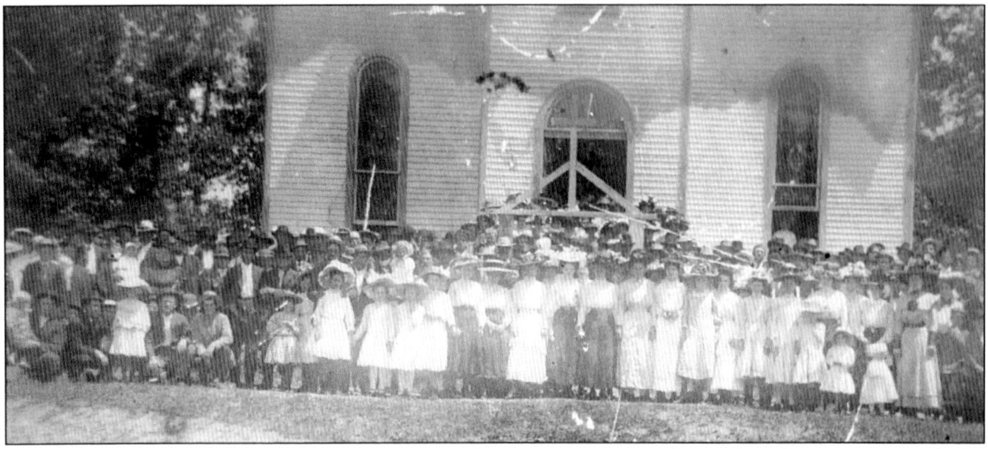

THE ST. JOHN CATHOLIC CHURCH, 1900. The congregation of St. John the Baptist Catholic Church, near Rineyville, gathers in front of their newly constructed church. It was the fourth building to house the congregation, which was founded in 1812 by pioneer priest Rev. Charles Nerinckx. This "Rhudes Creek Congregation" first met in a simple log building, identified as St. Ignatius. In 1835, the name was changed to St. John the Baptist. The church was brick-veneered in the 1960s, and continues to serve the congregation today.

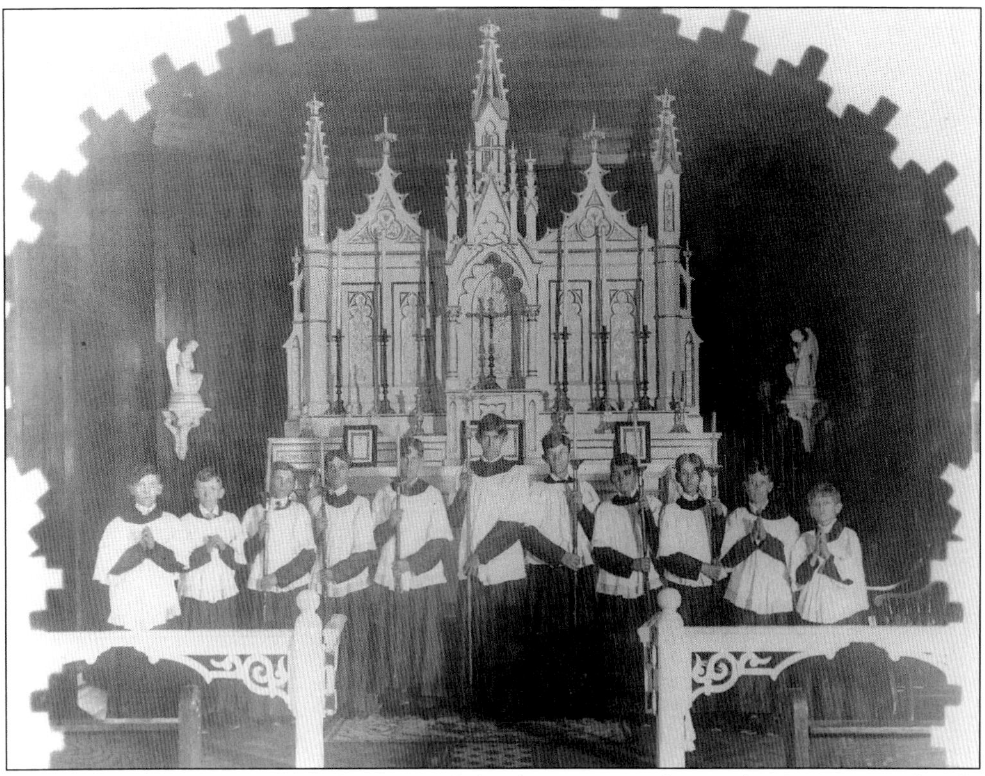

ST. JOHN ALTAR BOYS, 1908. This group of altar boys pose inside St. John the Baptist Church, near Rineyville, in 1908. Rev. J.J. Abell was pastor at the time. Pictured, from left to right, are Frank Vessels, George Stewart, Ernest Woosley, Ray Thomas, Milburn Fields, Les Wilmoth, Ozzie Vessels, Charles Thomas, C. Zee Riney, Willie Williams, and Leo Thomas. The three Thomas boys were brothers as were the two Vessels boys.

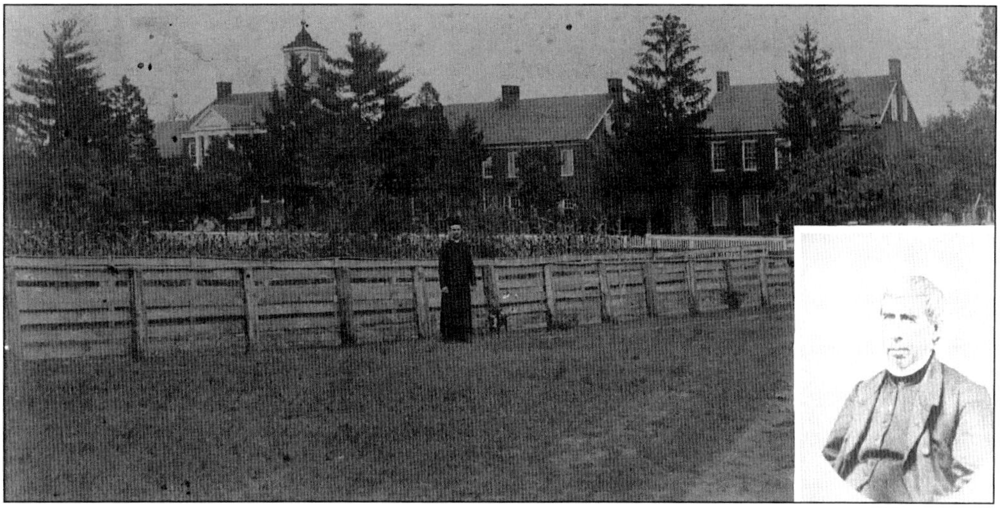

Bethlehem Academy, 1880s. In 1830, the Sisters of Loretto established an all-girls school on a 580-acre farm between Cecilia and Rineyville. Arriving on December 24, the Sisters christened the school "Bethlehem Academy," in honor of Christ's birth. The center portion of the building was originally built as a residence in 1818 by George Helm, father of Governor John L. Helm. The first school here was operated out of a small loom house, located behind the main residence. Rev. Augustine Degauquire (inset), resident pastor from 1839 to 1870, had the left and right wings added to the building in the 1840s. A successful boarding school was operated here for 129 years before closing in 1959.

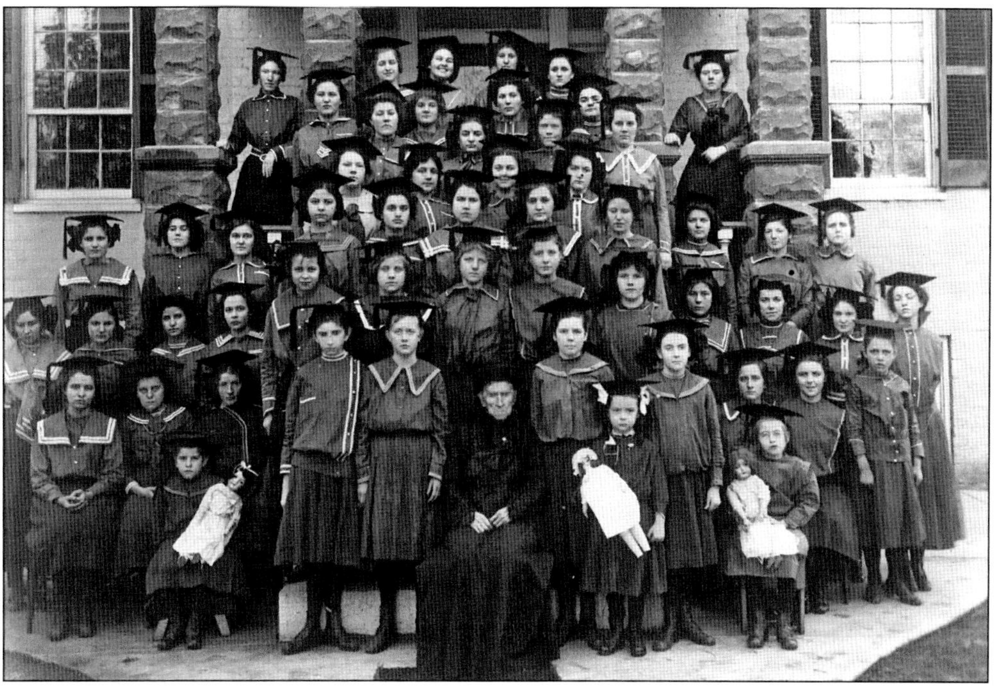

The Bethlehem Student Body, 1914. The students of Bethlehem Academy pose on the front steps of the school on January 22, 1914. The lady seated in front is Honor Frances Wise, who was 98 years old, the school's oldest living alumnus. This photo provides a good indication of the strict dress code maintained at the school.

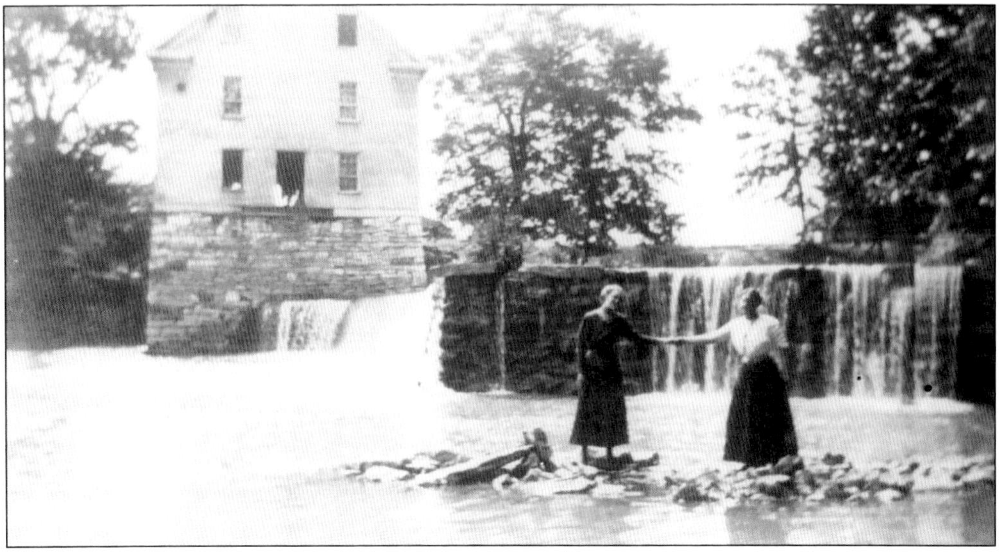

Star Mills, 1915. Located on the Nolin River, this water-powered mill was constructed around 1870. Its popularity soon drew others to the area, and soon a general store, blacksmith shop, cooper's shop, and several residences were built here. The post office was established here on April 26, 1893, but was discontinued two years later. Another post office was opened in 1901, under the name of "Warner," in the store of Parker W. Robertson. It lasted until 1904. The three-story mill was swept away in the swift waters of the 1937 flood. The old stone dam remains today as a relic of a much simpler time.

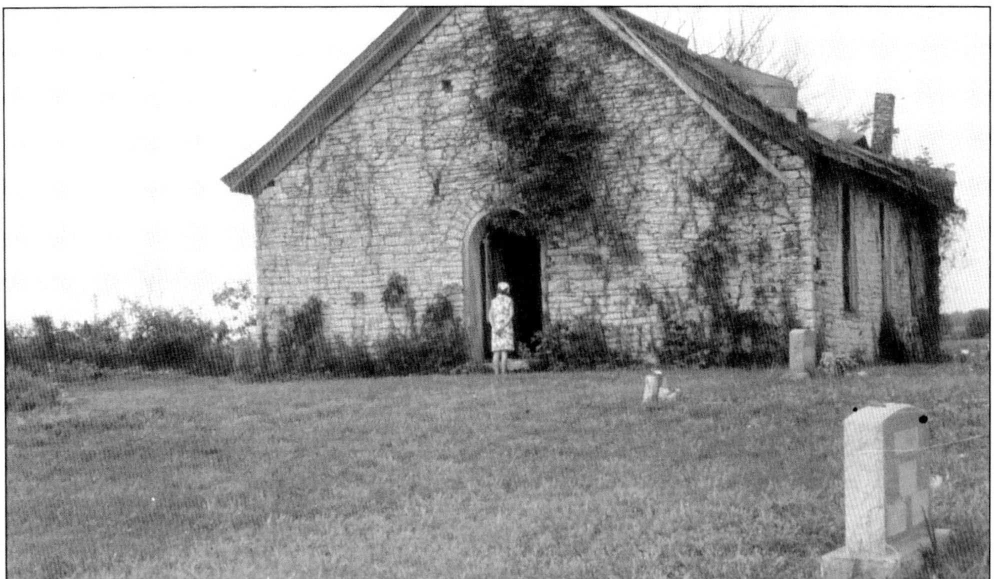

The Old Stone Church, 1920s. This primitive church was built near Star Mills (*c.* 1824) of stones provided by the Morrison family, who were prominent in the area. First known as "Union Church," it was shared by the Baptist, Methodist, Presbyterian, and Christian denominations for many years. Many attended from as far away as White Mills. The building was abandoned and remained vacant for many years before being dismantled. A small cemetery still remains on the old church site.

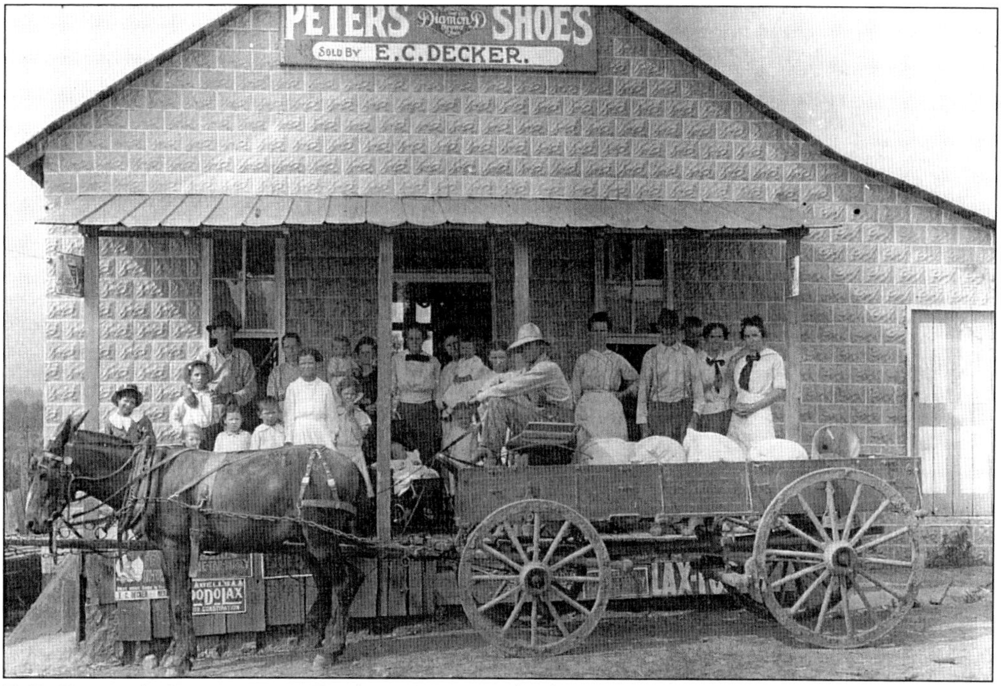

E.C. Decker's Store, 1900. Decker's Store was built near the railroad in "New Stephensburg" during the late 1800s. A store was conducted in the building by several different owners, and the post office was kept in it for many years, before it was torn down in the 1940s.

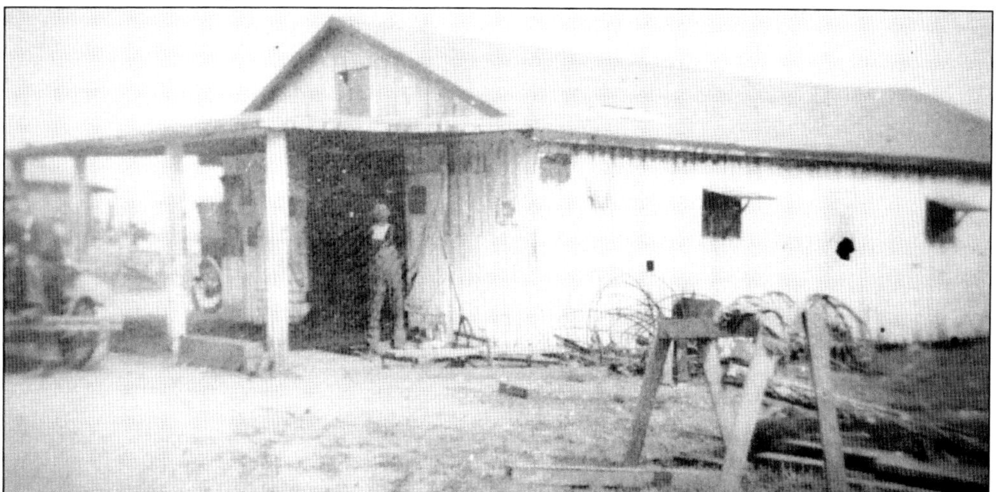

Young's Blacksmith Shop, 1917. The original town of Stephensburg was established on the old stagecoach pike that leads from Elizabethtown to Leitchfield. Hardin County's third post office was established here in the old brick home of Stephen Southern, the first postmaster, on December 23, 1829. Several stores, a blacksmith shop, three churches, two hotels, a saddle shop, and several saloons were built here, before the E&P Railroad was constructed near the town in 1870. Stagecoaches soon gave way to the much-faster train service, resulting in a drastic population decline. In this photo, taken in 1929, Joe Owsley Young stands on the porch of his blacksmith shop along Kentucky Highway 62 in Old Stephensburg. Young moved the building here from the town of Harcourt when that town started to decline.

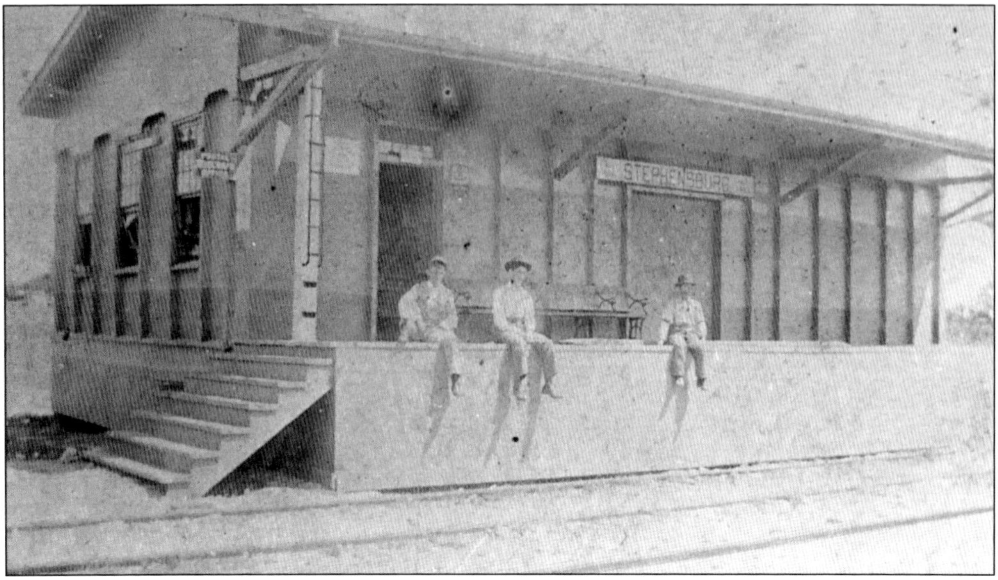

The Stephensburg Depot, 1900. The depot was built in "New Stephensburg," shortly after the E&P Railroad (later the Illinois Central) was constructed, in 1870. It held its place of prominence in the center of town for almost 60 years. The town received many visitors in the early part of this century who came to fish and camp at the large lake near town. The railroad abandoned the depot in the 1930s, and it was then torn down. When the Leitchfield road was built in the 1920s, the population gradually shifted back to Old Stephensburg.

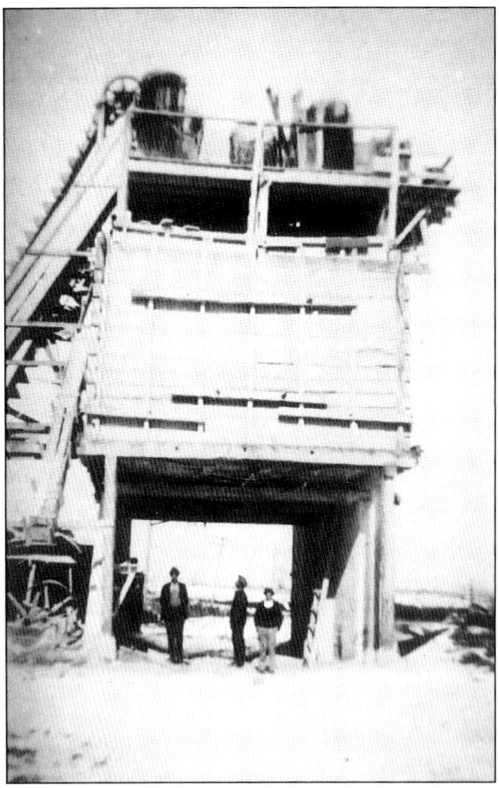

The Lil Mae Stone Company, 1920. A large limestone rock quarry, known as the Lil Mae Rock Quarry, was opened near Stephensburg in the late teens. Many town residents were employed at the quarry, which provided much of the crushed limestone used to build and improve area roads for many years. In this photo, several men stand under the "old crusher." The quarry closed many years ago, but the large caverns cut into the rock are still there.

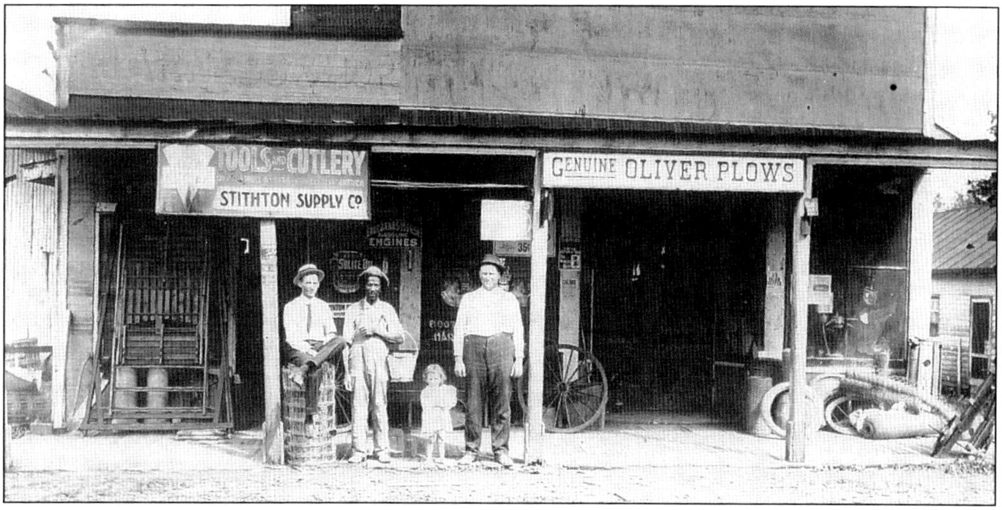

The Stithton Supply Company, 1908. Located on North Main Street, the Stithton Supply Company was purchased by A.C. "Conn" Corbett in 1908, and operated in conjunction with W.P. Ray and Bradford Wise. Pictured here are Conn Corbett (standing at right) and Jim Corbett (child). The other two men are unidentified. Edd Miller's blacksmith shop was located next door. Mr. Corbett moved the business to New Haven in 1918, when the government took over Stithton.

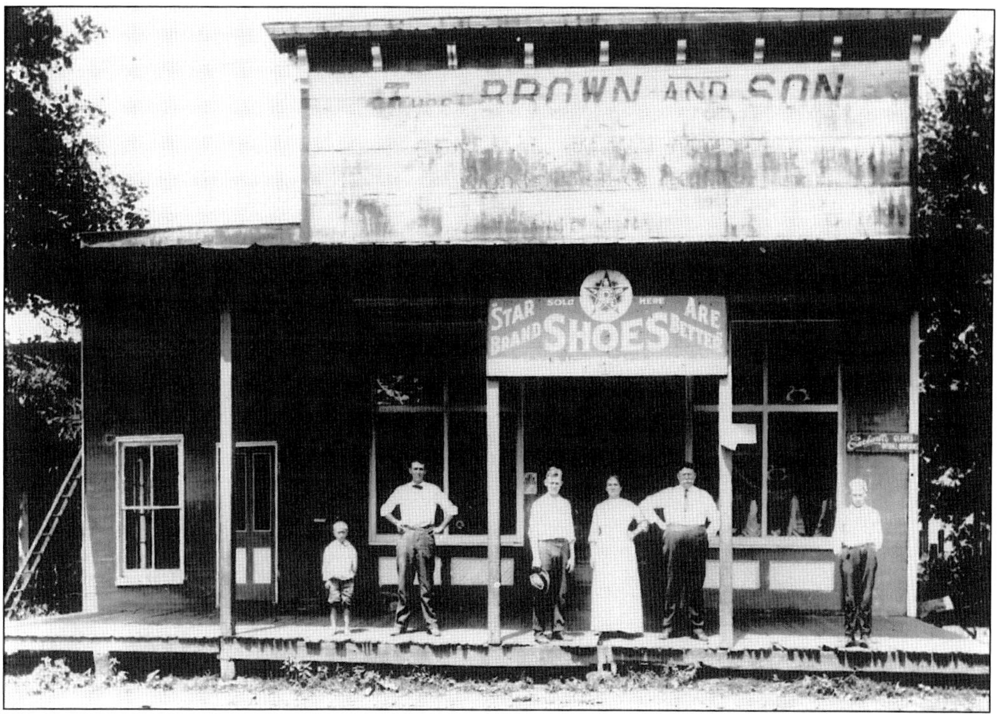

The Tom Brown and Son Store, 1910. Tom Brown and his son Will operated this store in Stithton for many years, selling groceries and dry goods. Mr. Brown, a well-respected member of the community, was on the board of directors of the Peoples Bank of Stithton. Here, Tom Brown and his wife, Sally, stand side-by-side under the "Star Brand Shoes" sign on the porch of the store around 1910.

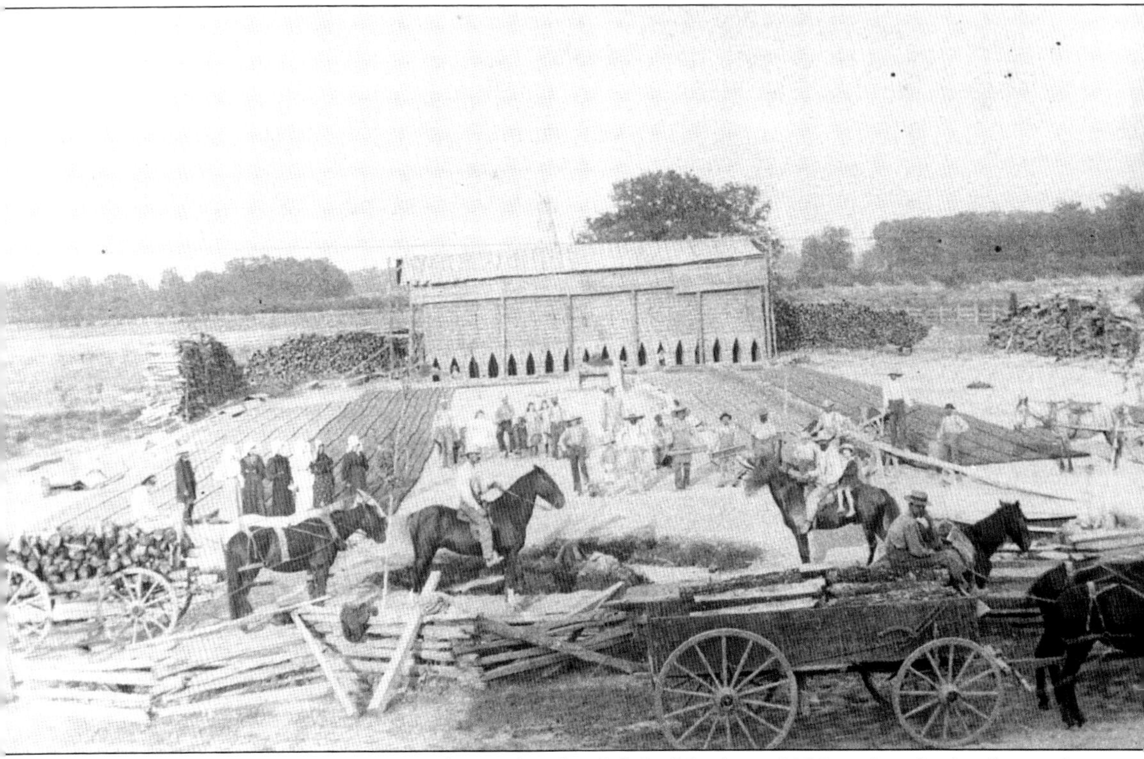

The Old Brick Kiln, 1898. This is the "brick kiln," built in 1898 to fire the bricks used in the construction of the St. Patrick Catholic Church, in Stithton. Constructed in the church lot, the kiln was tended around the clock by volunteer families, who took 24-hour shifts. A.C. "Conn" Corbett and Robert Corbett were in charge of operations. As can be seen here, men and women worked side-by-side to accomplish the task. It is the only known photo of this type of kiln.

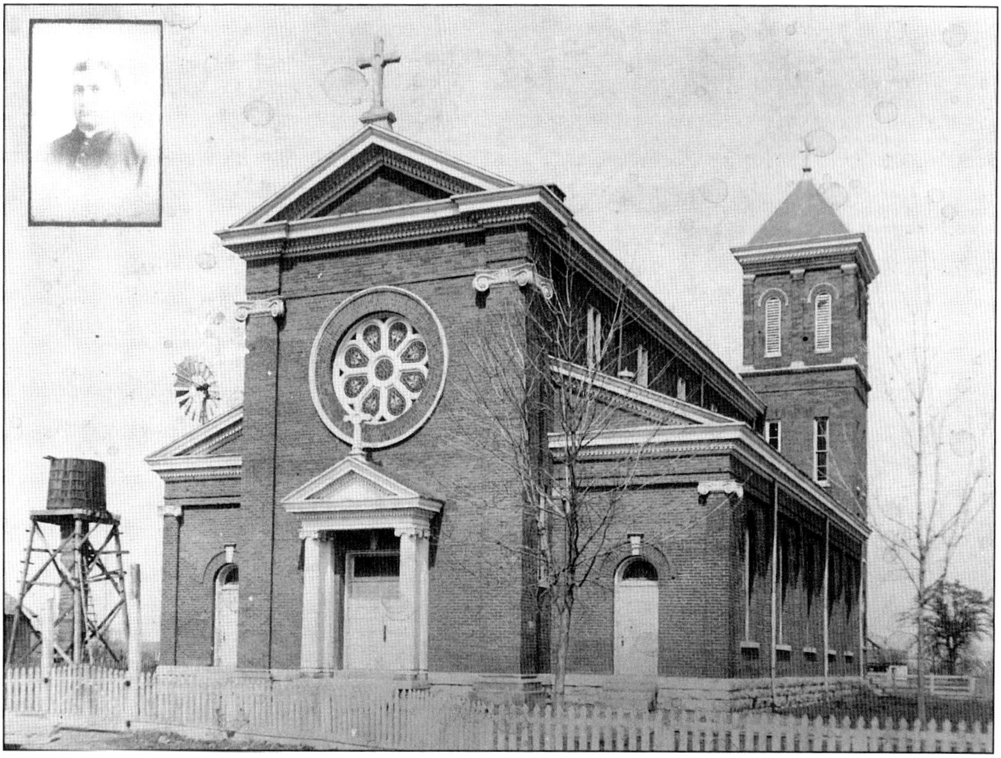

THE ST. PATRICK CATHOLIC CHURCH, 1906. This church is the only remaining structure that was once part of the town of Stithton. It was built under the meticulous direction of the parish's first resident pastor, Rev. James L. Whelan (inset), at a cost of $12,000. Bricks for the building were burned on the site by members of the congregation. The cornerstone was blessed on August 4, 1899, and the church was opened for services in 1900. It was considered the most handsome country church in the state at that time. In 1918, the federal government converted the church into a motion picture hall and used it as such until 1938. It was renovated and reopened as main Post Chapel on May 30, 1939.

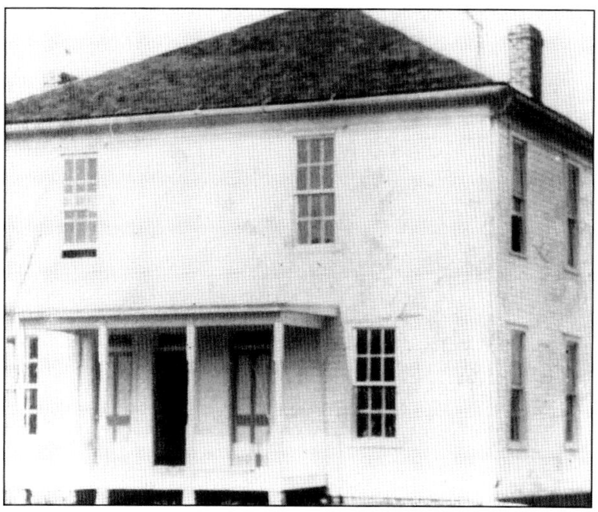

THE ST. PATRICK SCHOOL, 1913. Shortly after Rev. R.C Ruff became the third resident pastor of St. Patrick Church in 1912, the Catholics of Stithton focused their efforts on the establishment of a parochial school. The building was completed and dedicated on August 26, 1913, and taught by the Ursuline Sisters of Mount St. Joseph in Daviess County, Kentucky. The school enjoyed a successful five-year existence before the federal government took over the area and established Camp Henry Knox in 1918.

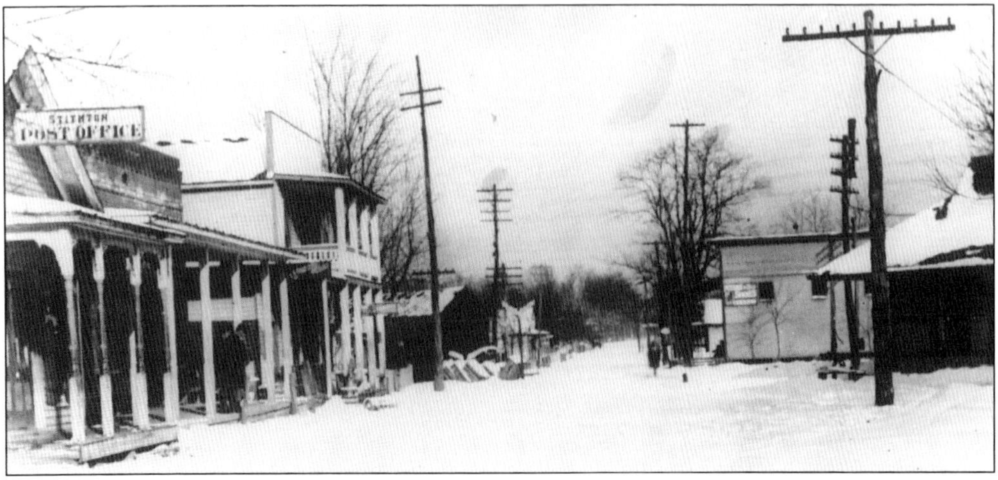

A STITHTON STREET SCENE, 1910. The town of Stithton was located in the heart of what is now the main post area of Fort Knox. The entire town, and thousands of surrounding acres, were seized by the federal government in 1918. The town was leveled, except for St. Patrick's Catholic Church, which was kept as the post chapel. This winter street scene looks down Main Street in Stithton and shows, from left to right, the post office, H. Brady's Store, the hotel, the I.C. Railroad crossing, Sam Mossbarger's Store, and the Illinois Central Railroad depot.

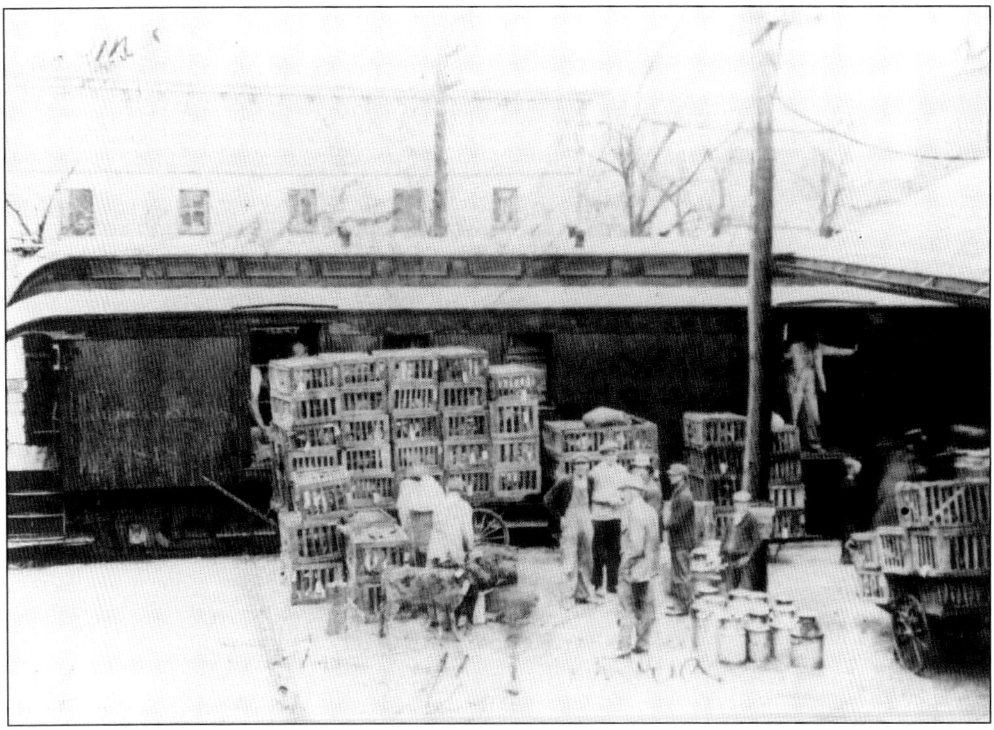

A STITHTON DEPOT SCENE, 1905. The E&P Railroad made its way through the rural farming community of Stithton in 1873. In this photo, a freight car is being loaded with crates of chickens, probably to be sold in Louisville. Milk cans and the depot are at right. Sam Mossbarger and Son's Store is behind the boxcar, and Stithton Bank is at the upper right.

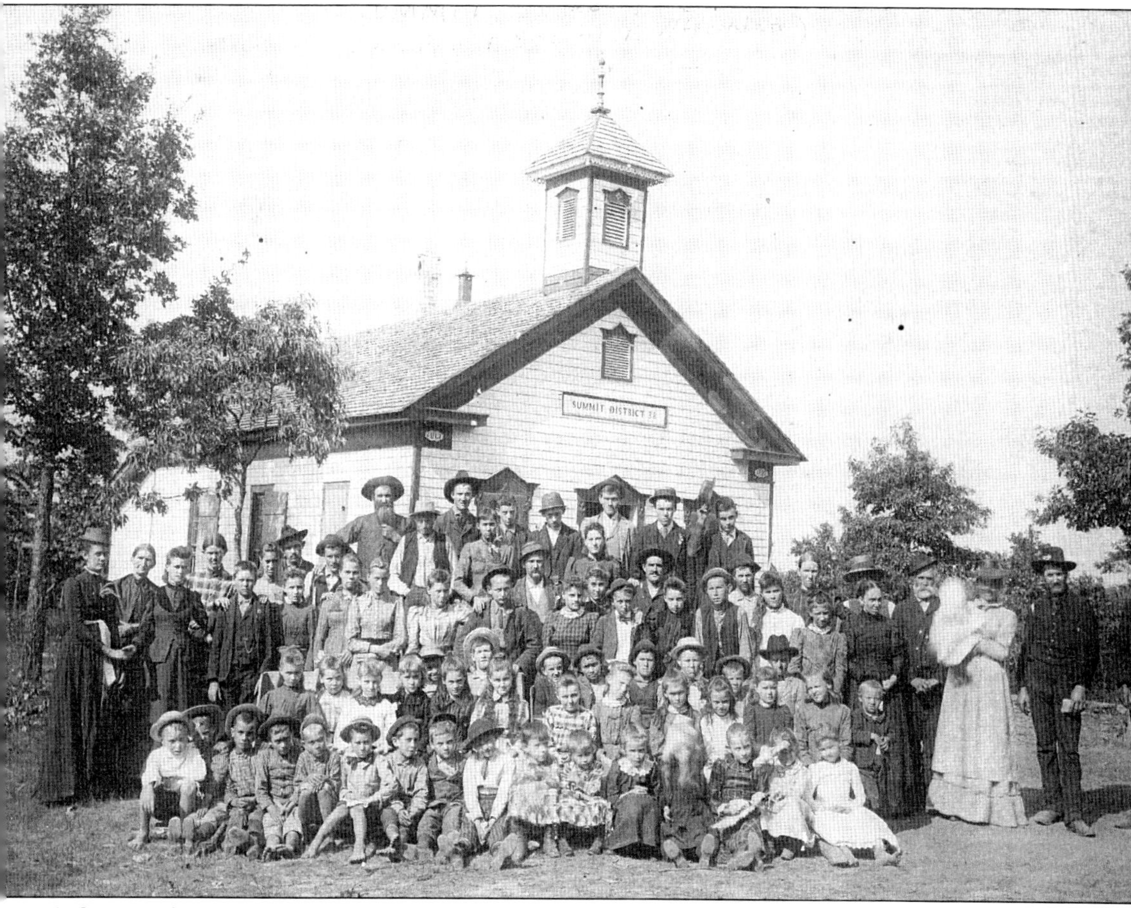

A SUMMIT SCHOOL DEDICATION, JULY 7, 1892. A group of students and other locals pose in front of Summit School on Dedication Day in 1892. The three older gentlemen, on the right, are Civil War veterans, dressed in uniform. W.A. Dever, who stands second from the right, built the school. It was considered the best one-room school in the county and was designed with many decorative features. It held its place on a small country road near Summit until 1978, when it was moved to Freeman Lake Park in Elizabethtown.

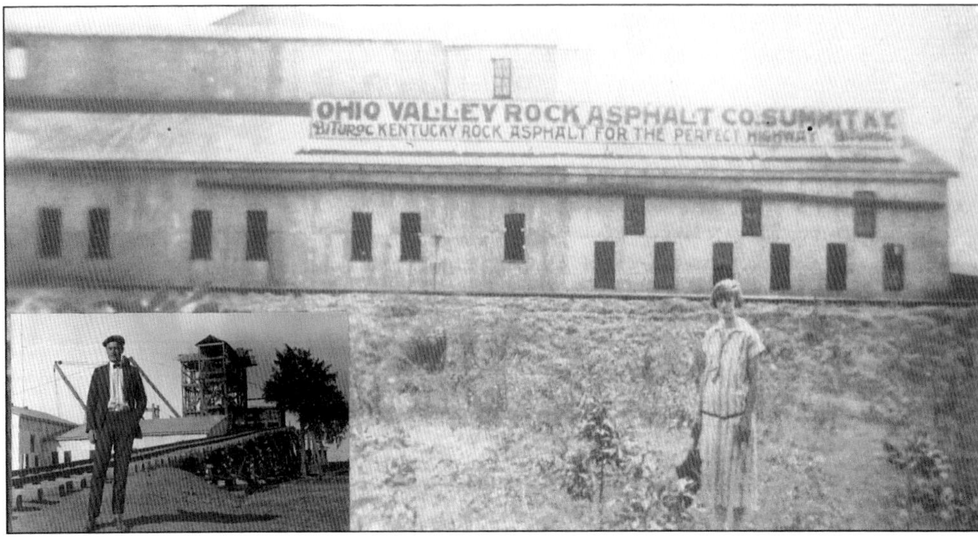

THE OHIO VALLEY ROCK ASPHALT COMPANY, 1920S. Around 1920, a Rock Asphalt mining and processing plant was established near Summit, along the Illinois Central tracks. Many area roads were paved with asphalt from this plant, and great quantities were shipped to other areas. The company, which put Summit on the map and provided jobs for many local men, closed due to bankruptcy in 1946. Russell Richardson (inset) stands near the plant around 1928.

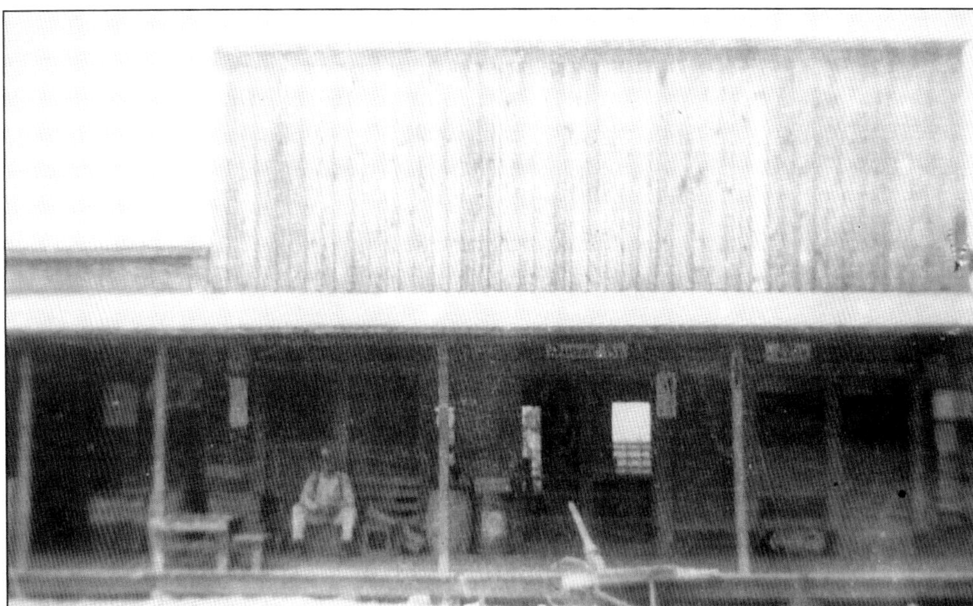

THE TAUL TABB GENERAL STORE, 1922. The town of Summit received its name when the E&P Railroad was being built through the area in 1870. Since it was the highest point on the line, it was called "Summit." The post office was established here on October 16, 1874, in a store owned by Jesse St. Clare, the first postmaster. During its prime, Summit had two stores (run by David F. South and James "Taul" Tabb), a hotel, two restaurants, a photo gallery, and a silent movie house. Mr. Tabb was in business when this photo was taken in 1922. The store is still in operation.

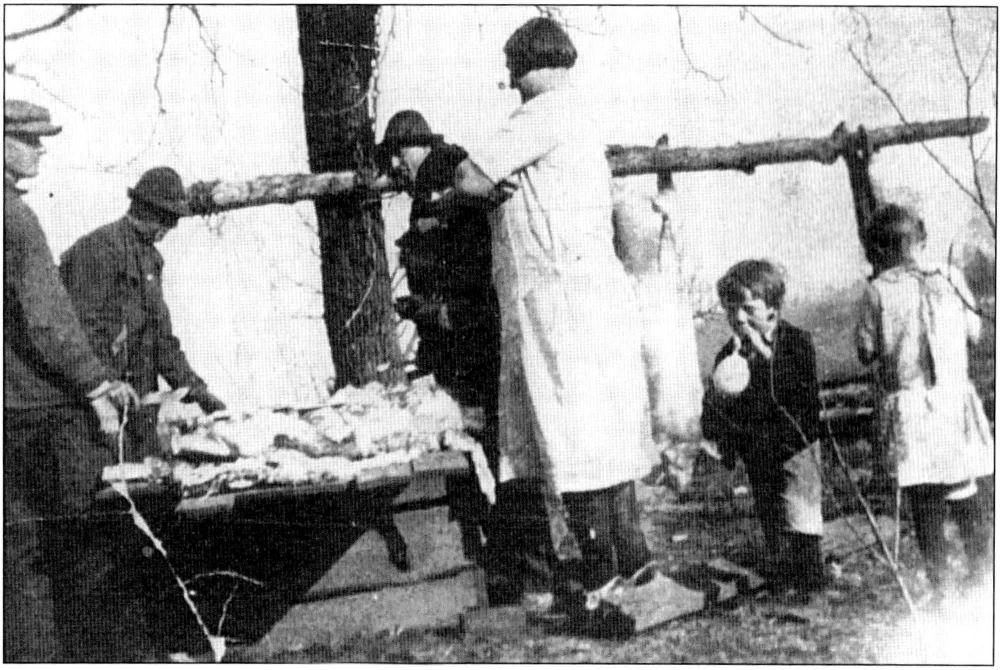

Hog Killing Day, 1924. From left to right, Clifford Bush, Linzie Bush, Walter Bush, Archie Bush, David Humes, Maeola Humes, Pete Bush, and Wilma Bush participate in the hog butchering process near the Talley-Oak Hill Store in the Talley neighborhood of the Maxine community in LaRue County. Slabs of meat and buckets of lard were the end result of the day's work. The children, Pete and Wilma Bush, are blowing hog bladders into makeshift balloons, a common form of entertainment for farm children in those days.

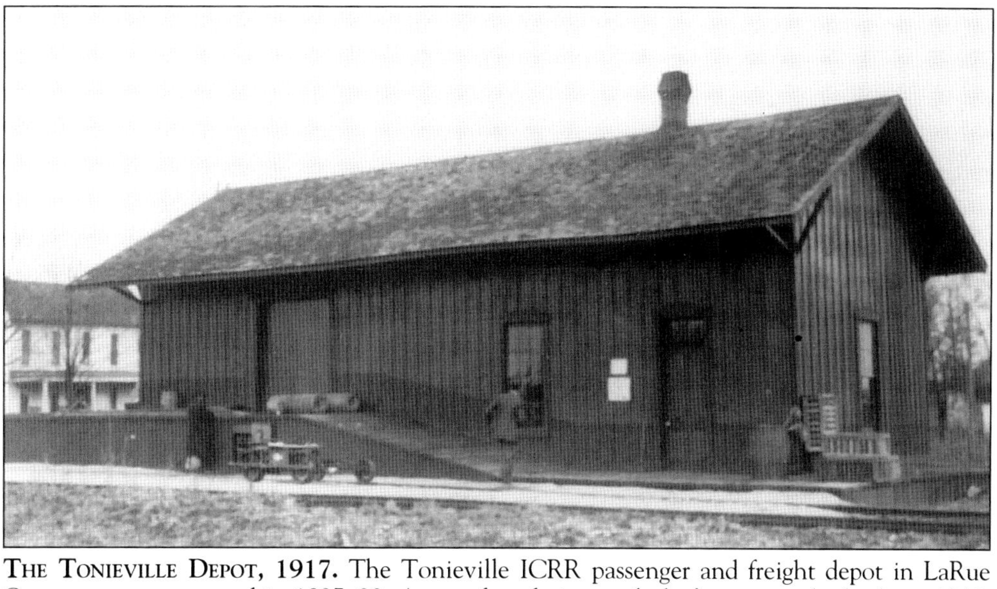

The Tonieville Depot, 1917. The Tonieville ICRR passenger and freight depot in LaRue County was constructed in 1897–98. A new foundation and platforms were built about 1912. This photograph also shows the Ben Crawford residence at left. Large crowds gathered around the depot and cheered for Presidents Theodore Roosevelt (1909), William Howard Taft (1911), and Woodrow Wilson (1916) when their trains passed through on the way to Hodgenville.

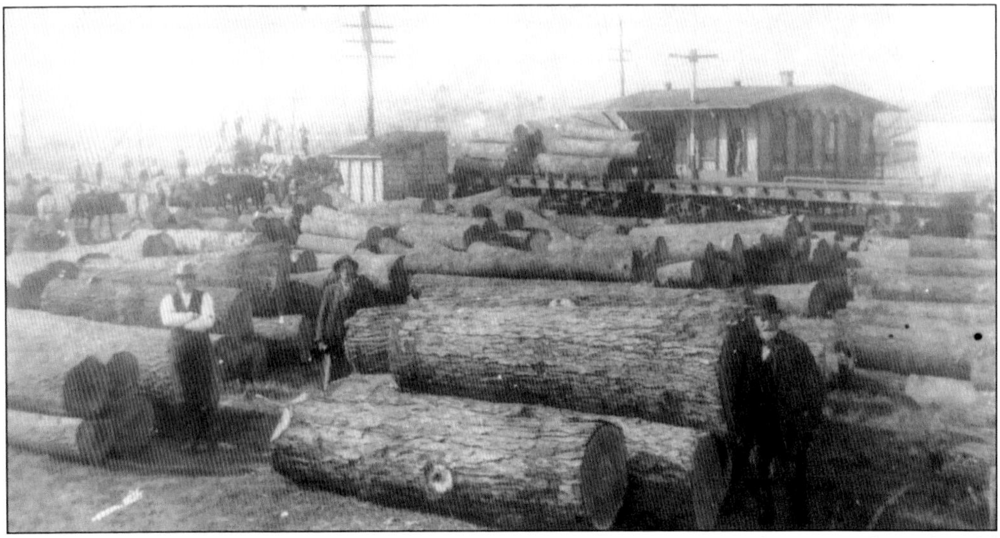

The Tunnel Hill Depot, 1898. The Tunnel Hill community acquired its name from the old L&N Railroad tunnel that was cut through a nearby hill in the 1850s. The depot, shown here, was built in 1864. The small village also included a hotel, general store, and blacksmith shop. Logs are being loaded on flatcars for shipment. The general store can be seen to the right of the depot. Standing in the doorway of the depot is Felix McMillen, the local telegraph operator and agent. The depot was extensively remodeled in 1912 and has since been removed.

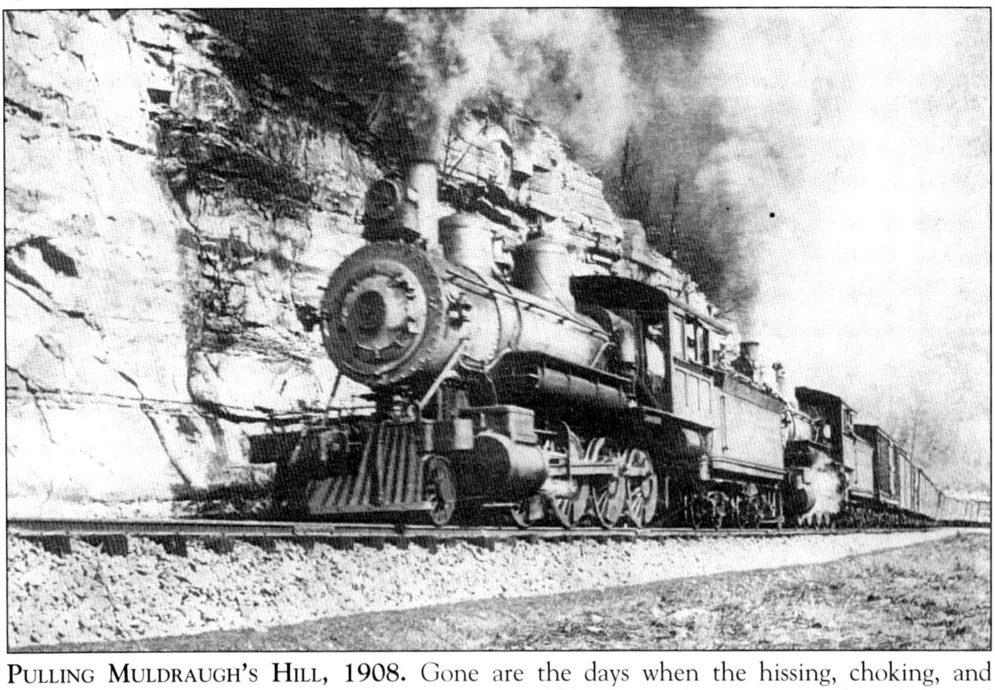

Pulling Muldraugh's Hill, 1908. Gone are the days when the hissing, choking, and screeching sounds of the old steam locomotives would bring people scurrying to their doors and porches to see who was getting on and off the train. A common sight for more than a century in Hardin County, the mighty steam engines eventually bowed to diesel-powered engines. Here, two of those engines help pull a long freight train up the steep ascent of Muldraugh's Hill, near Tunnel Hill, on the L&N Railroad.

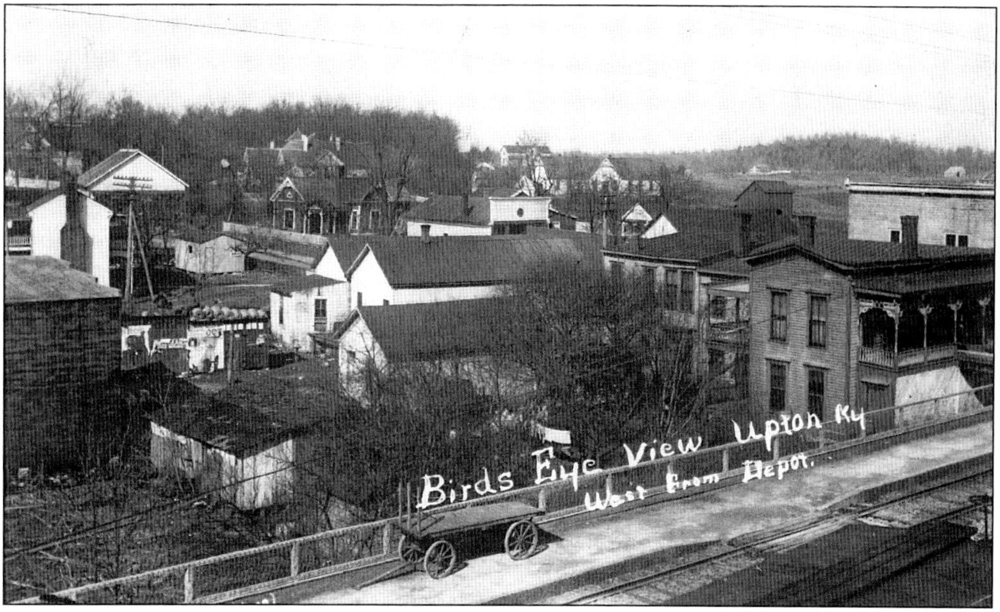

A Bird's-eye View of Upton, 1910. This postcard view of Upton shows almost the entire west-side business district in 1910. The white building, seen above the roofs in the center of the photo, is the H.Y. Davis Banking Company. The long white building on the hill in the background is the Upton Institute (college). The large building to the far right is the G.M. Dixon and Son store. The building beside the railroad is the hotel.

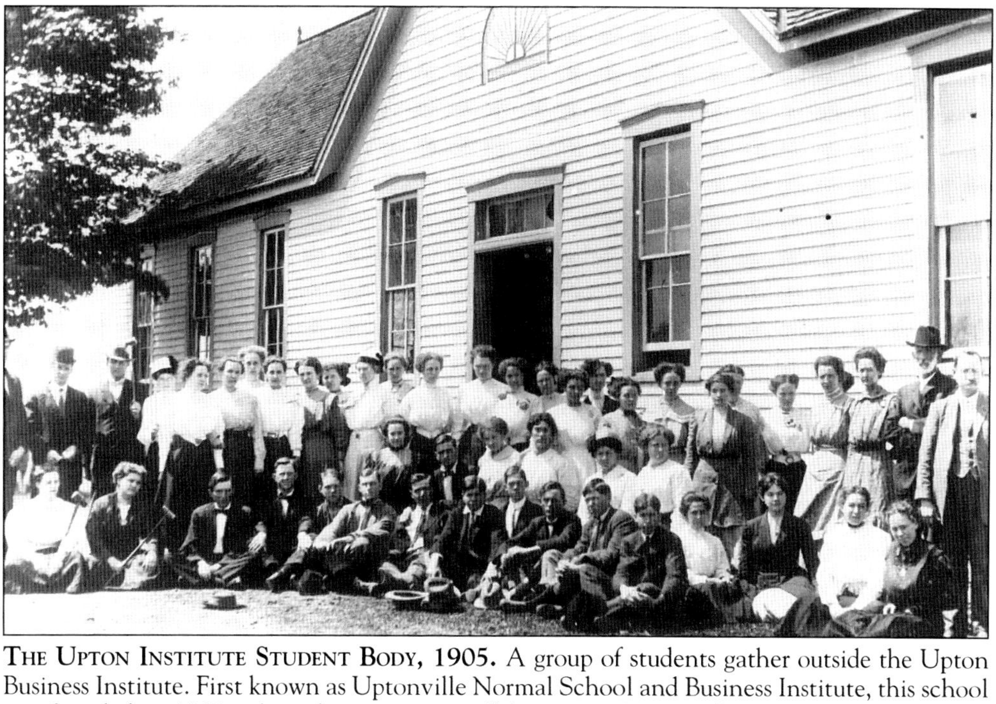

The Upton Institute Student Body, 1905. A group of students gather outside the Upton Business Institute. First known as Uptonville Normal School and Business Institute, this school was founded in 1889, when the town was still known as Uptonville. Serving as a school of higher learning for local students planning careers in business and teaching, its popularity lent much prestige to the small community.

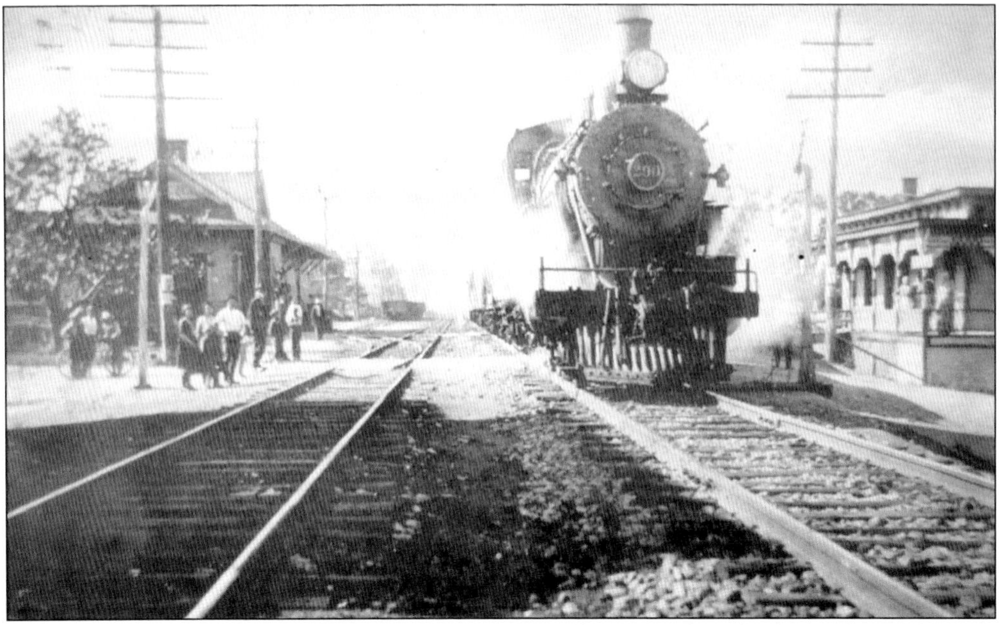

AN UPTON RAILROAD SCENE, 1908. Upton, partially situated in both Hardin and Larue Counties, was given birth by the advent of the railroad. This view, from a postcard dated 1908, shows an old L&N steam engine as it stops to pick up passengers at the train station (left). The hotel can be seen at right. Upton is Hardin County's southernmost township.

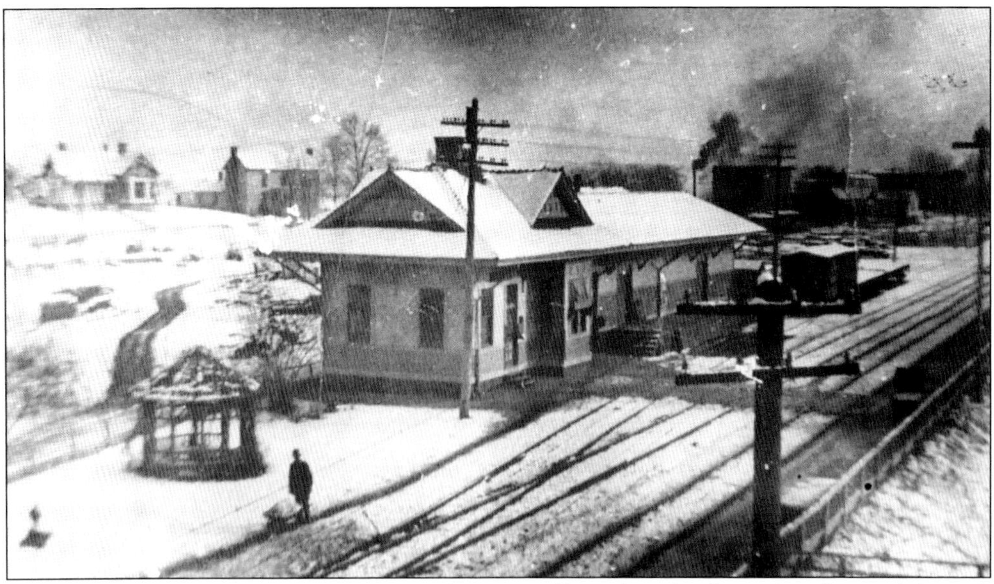

THE UPTON DEPOT, 1910. In the 1850s, the Louisville and Nashville Railroad passed through property owned by George Upton. Upton went to great lengths to assure that a town would materialize on his property by offering a free lot to anyone who would build a home on it. He also donated a lot for the public school and built a depot, which he later sold to the railroad. When the post office was established on April 8, 1856, it was named Uptonville in his honor. The town's name changed to Upton in 1892.

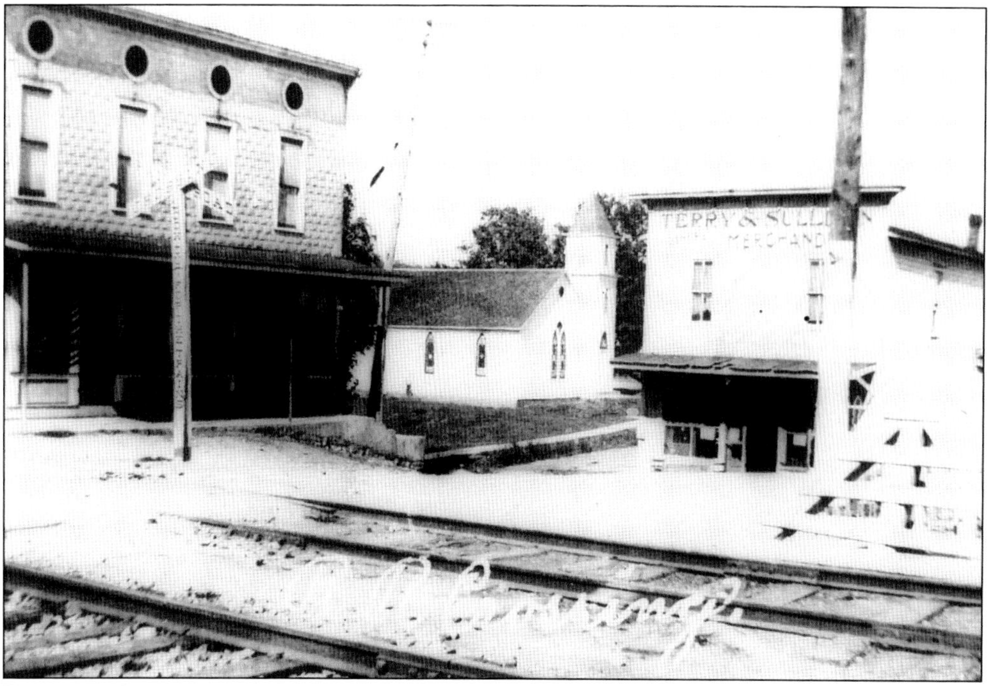

THE EAST SIDE OF UPTON, 1920S. Here are some of the businesses located on the east side of the railroad tracks in Upton around 1920. They are, from left to right, the Evans and Foster Store (operated by Tom Evans and Will Foster), the Methodist church, and Terry & Sullivan's Store. The drug store was located in the Evans and Foster building for many years.

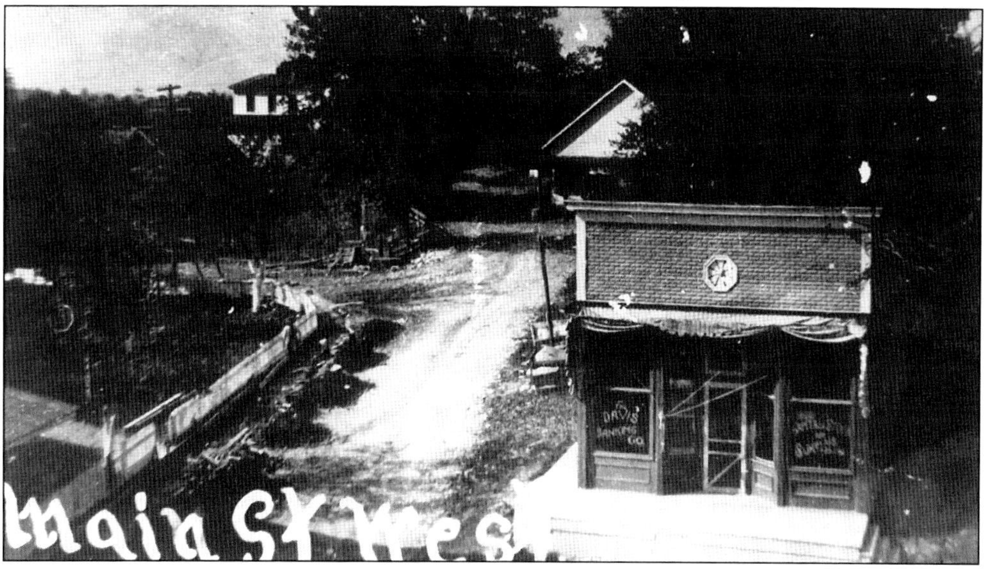

THE DAVIS BANKING COMPANY, 1920S. Upton received its first bank in 1905, with the establishment of the Davis Banking Company. The bank was founded by H.Y. Davis and other members of the Davis family of Cave City Kentucky. H.Y. Davis served as first president, and H.Y. Davis Jr. was cashier. The bank's name was changed to Bank of Upton in June 1949. In May 1957, the bank was purchased by First Hardin National Bank of Elizabethtown, and operated as a branch bank.

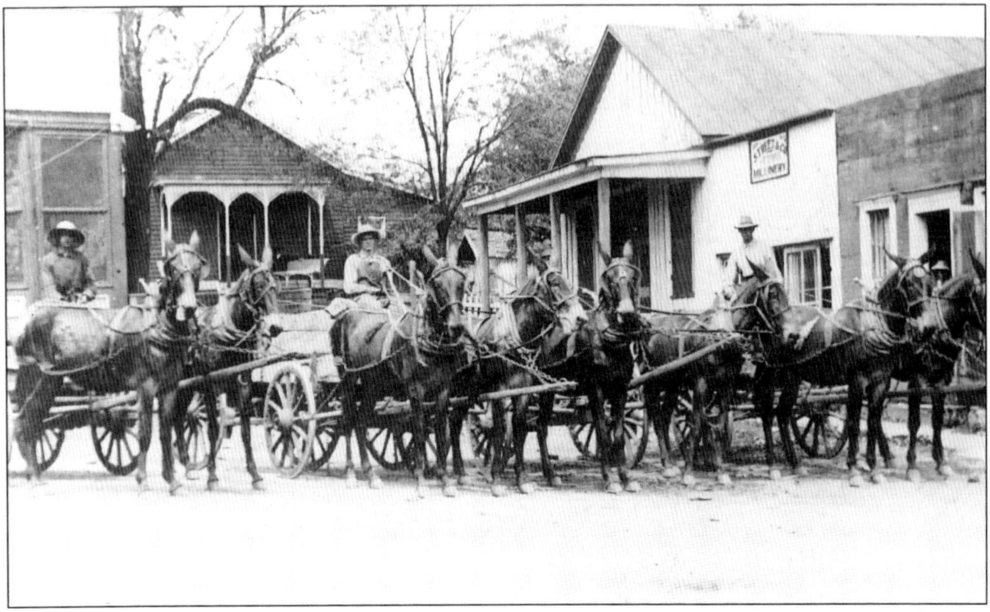

Teaming Up at Upton, 1917. Most rural farmers took great pride in their mule and horse "teams," and gave them pet names. Many responded only to the commands of their masters' voices, and were a source of pride and prestige to those who owned them. Here, several farmers show off their teams in the heart of Upton. Shown, from left to right, are Upton Bank, the Upton Telephone Exchange, and Riders Store.

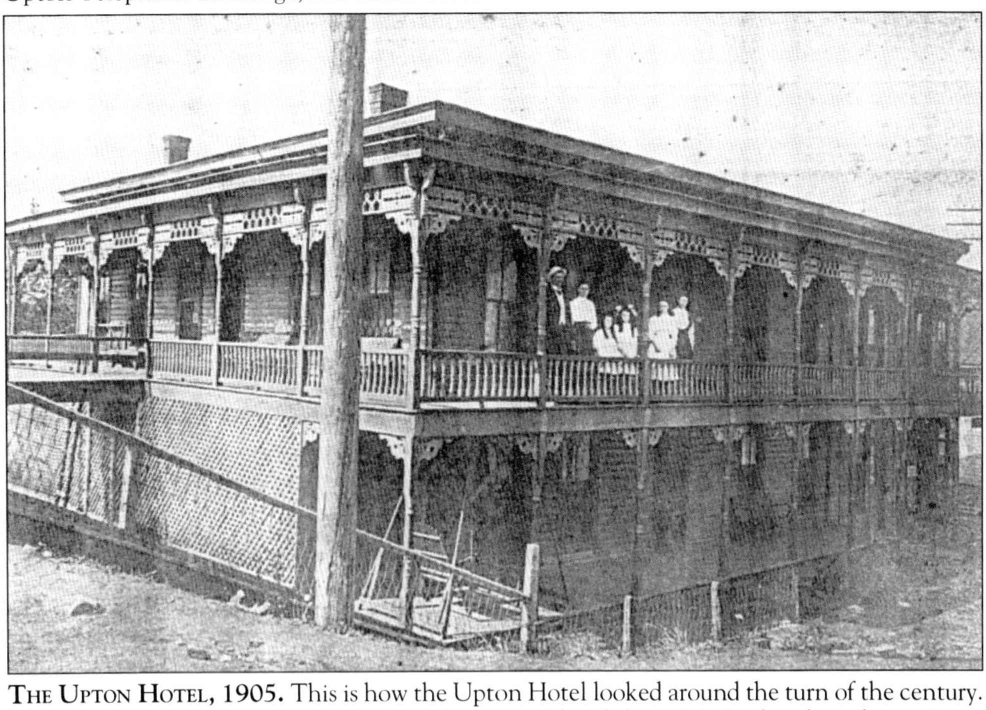

The Upton Hotel, 1905. This is how the Upton Hotel looked around the turn of the century. The two-story structure was situated on the west side of the L&N Railroad tracks on Main Street, directly across from the depot. It was first operated by G.W. Upton, and held a place of prominence in the community for many years.

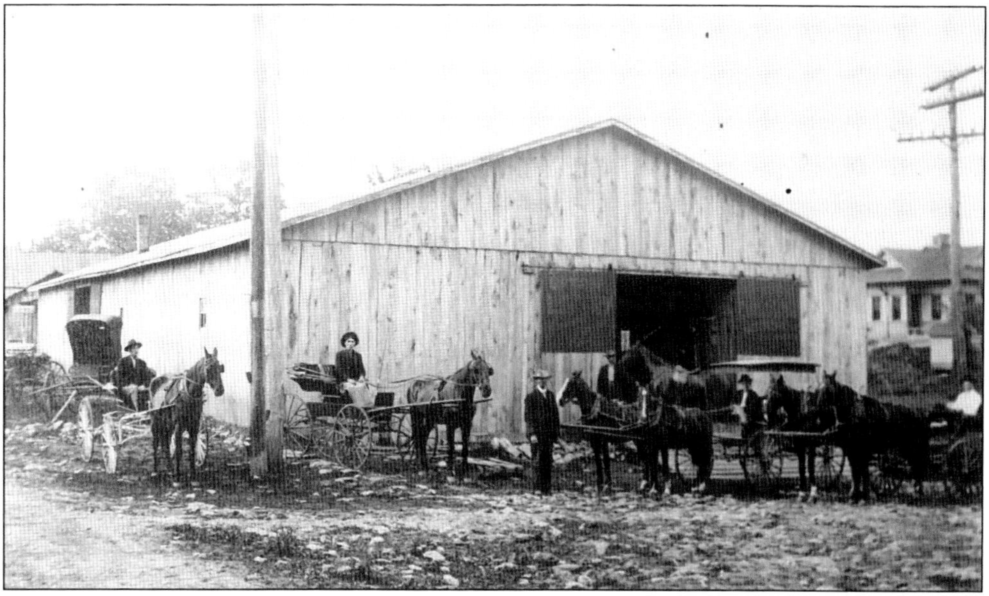

The Upton Livery Stable, 1910. A group of wagons and buggies line up in front of F. Wash Skaggs livery stable in Upton. The stable was located near the L&N depot, which can be seen at the right. Many horses were kept on hand to rent to visitors who arrived by train and needed transportation to their local destinations. The advent of the automobile eliminated the need for livery stables in the 1920s.

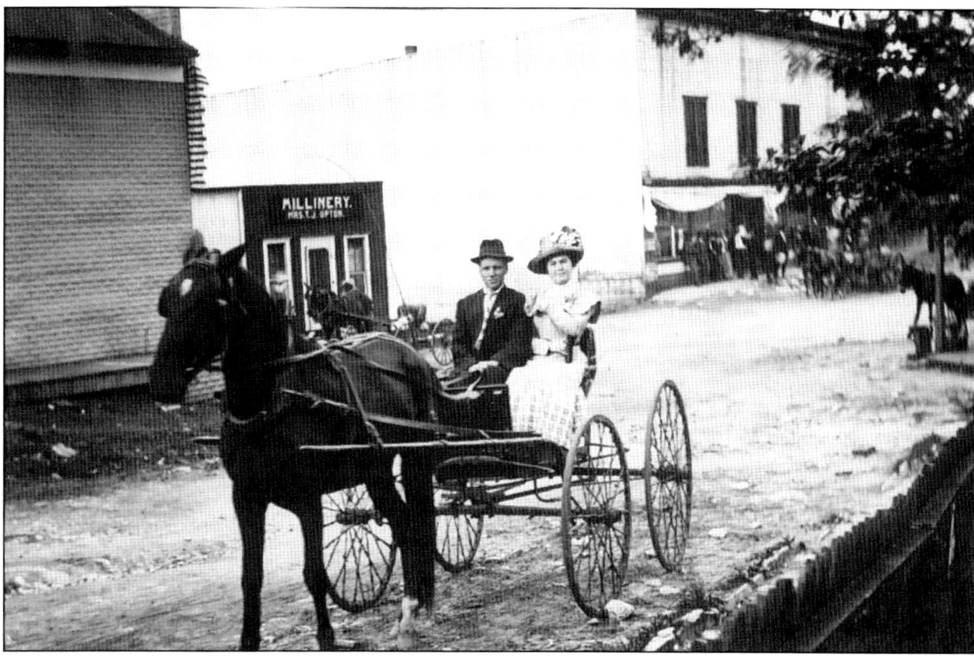

Traveling First Class in Upton, c. 1910. Augustus Burke and Mary Caswell appear to have just purchased a stylish hat for Ms. Caswell from Mrs. T.J. Upton's Millinery, a hat store in Upton. The G.M. Dixon and Son general merchandise store (top right) was operated by the Dixon family for more than 50 years. The front corner of the Upton Banking Company is at left.

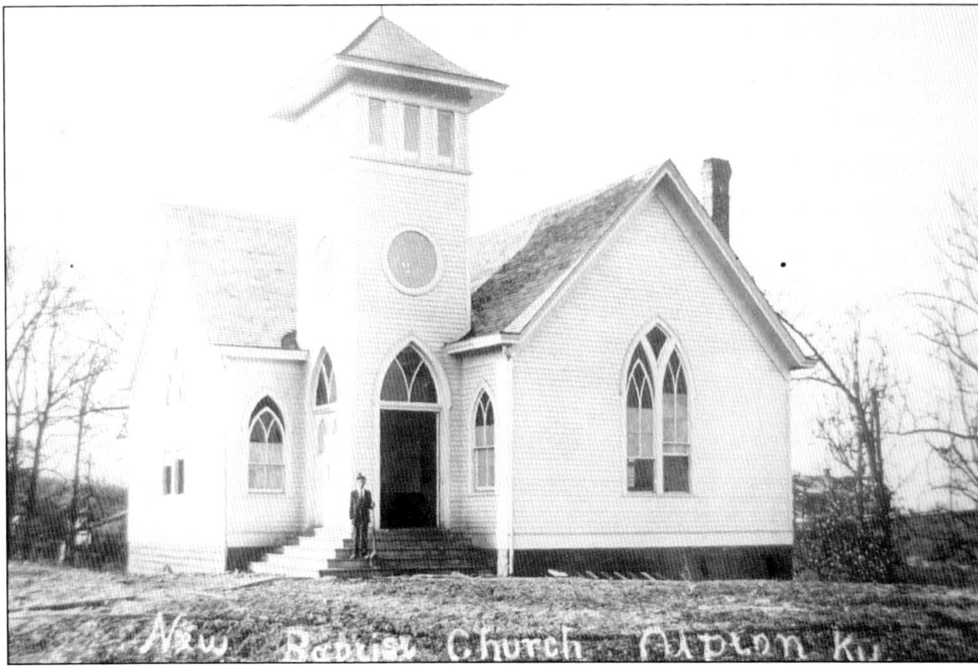

THE UPTON BAPTIST CHURCH, 1908. THE Upton Baptist Church was organized July 20, 1872, with 33 charter members. The first building met the congregation's needs until the structure shown here was dedicated on October 24, 1908. The man on the steps is Rev. T. Riley Davis, who was pastor of the church from 1908 to 1911. The building measured 40 feet by 40 feet and was built at a cost of $2,000.

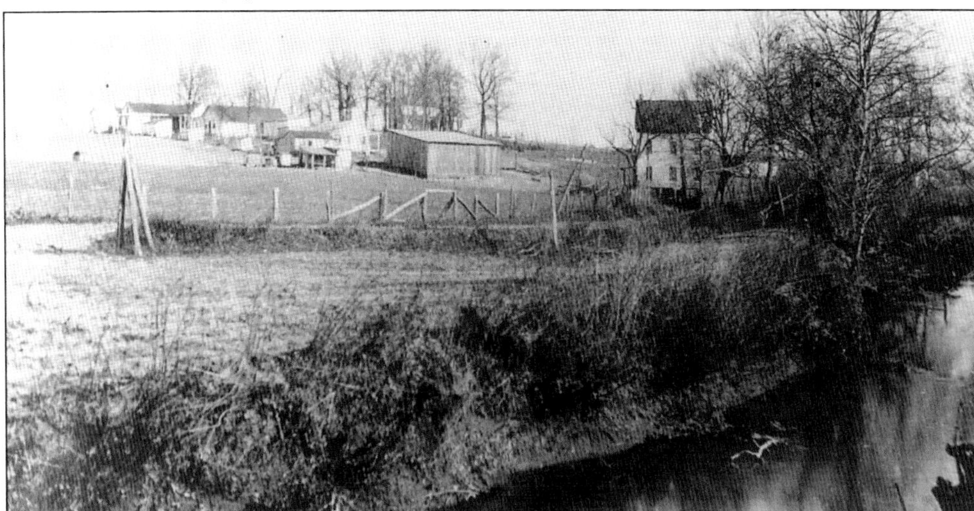

VERTREES MILL, 1920. The Vertrees community had its beginnings along the old stagecoach road leading from Elizabethtown to Hardinsburg. About 1830 this road was intersected by the Salt River Road, and a small village formed nearby. The community was named for Joseph Vertrees, who built the first cabin in the area in 1810. A mill (shown here at far right), built on Rough Creek, was operated by members of the Vertrees family for many years. On the hill behind the mill was a store operated by Milt and Ida Cralle. The post office here was established on July 6, 1881, with George W. Taber as postmaster.

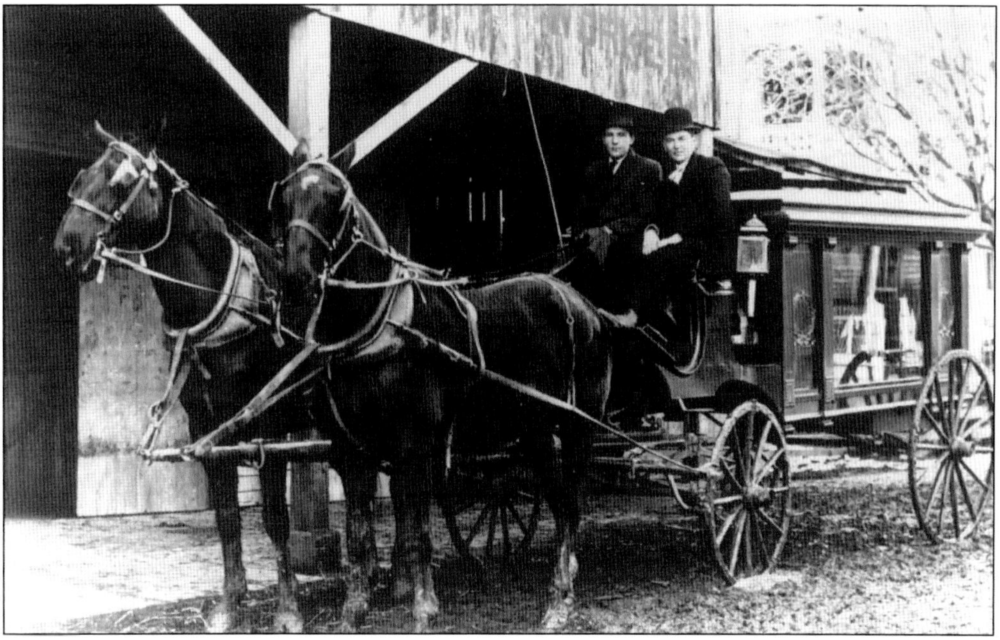

AN EARLY HORSE-DRAWN HEARSE, 1900. The "Cadillac" of its time, this early horse-drawn hearse was typical of those used by early funeral directors. Usually surrounded on all sides by glass, these simple-but-elegant vehicles carried the deceased from their homes to local cemeteries. At that time, most bodies were kept at home as the family kept vigil with the body in a ceremony known as a "wake." This hearse was owned and driven by Lum Craycroft and Will Selby of Vine Grove.

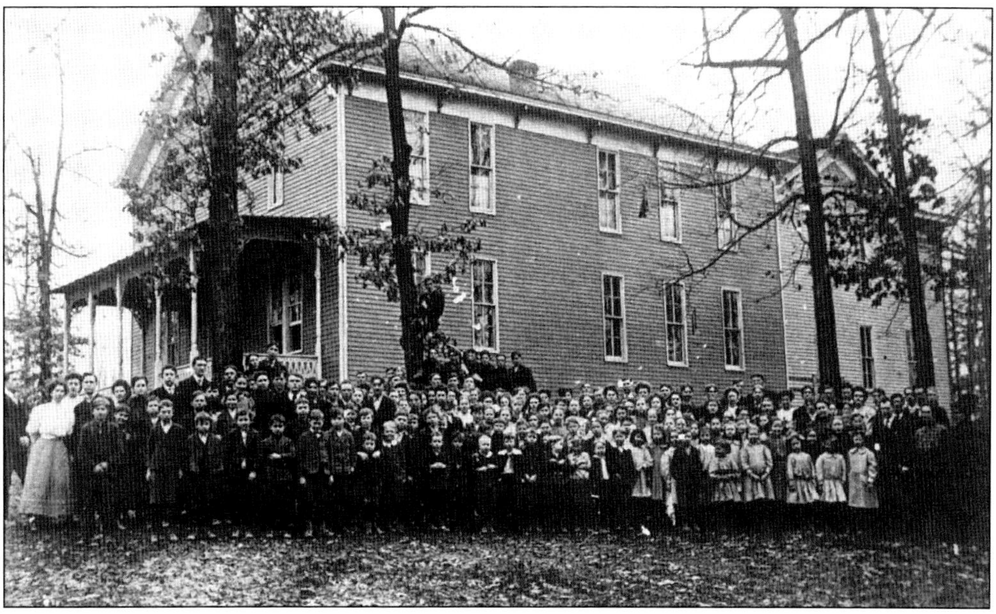

THE VINE GROVE SCHOOL AND STUDENT BODY, 1905. The first school at Vine Grove was opened in 1876 by Rev. P.F. Hagan and Professor Haynes. It was replaced in 1892 with the large frame structure shown here, known as Vine Grove College. In 1911, an addition was made to the building, and a high school added. The building was destroyed by fire in 1924.

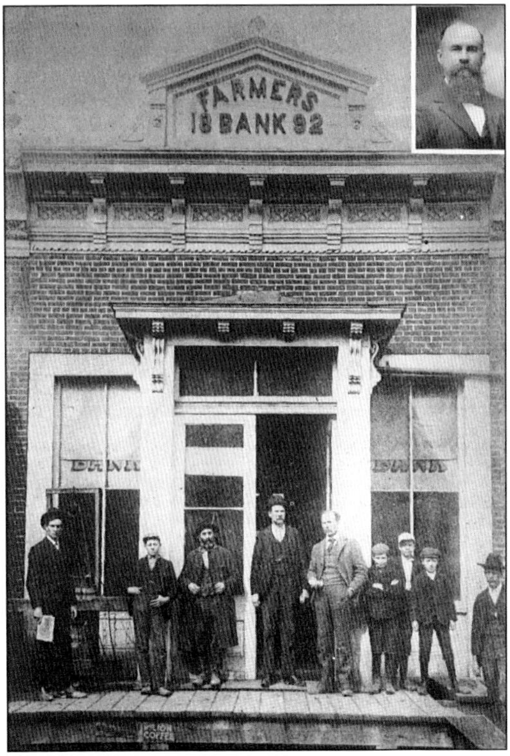

The Farmers Bank of Vine Grove, 1900. This was the first building to house the Farmers Bank of Vine Grove. Construction began in 1892, but the bank did not open for business until May 15, 1893. John O. Hibbs (inset) was the bank's first president, and G.E. McMurtry was cashier. A second story was added to the building in 1903. Over the years other physical changes have been made, but the main branch of the bank has been at the present location since its founding.

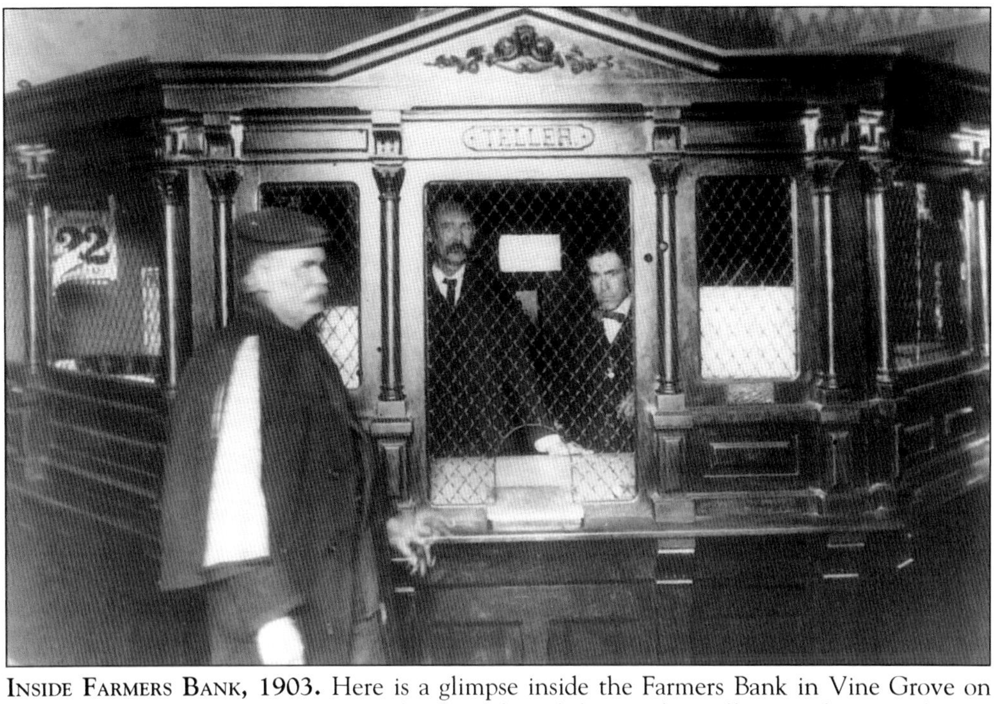

Inside Farmers Bank, 1903. Here is a glimpse inside the Farmers Bank in Vine Grove on January 22, 1903. At the teller window are, from left to right, Bill Macy (customer), Edd McMurtry (cashier), and Lon Hibbs (bookkeeper). Farmers Bank is Hardin County's oldest locally owned bank still in business.

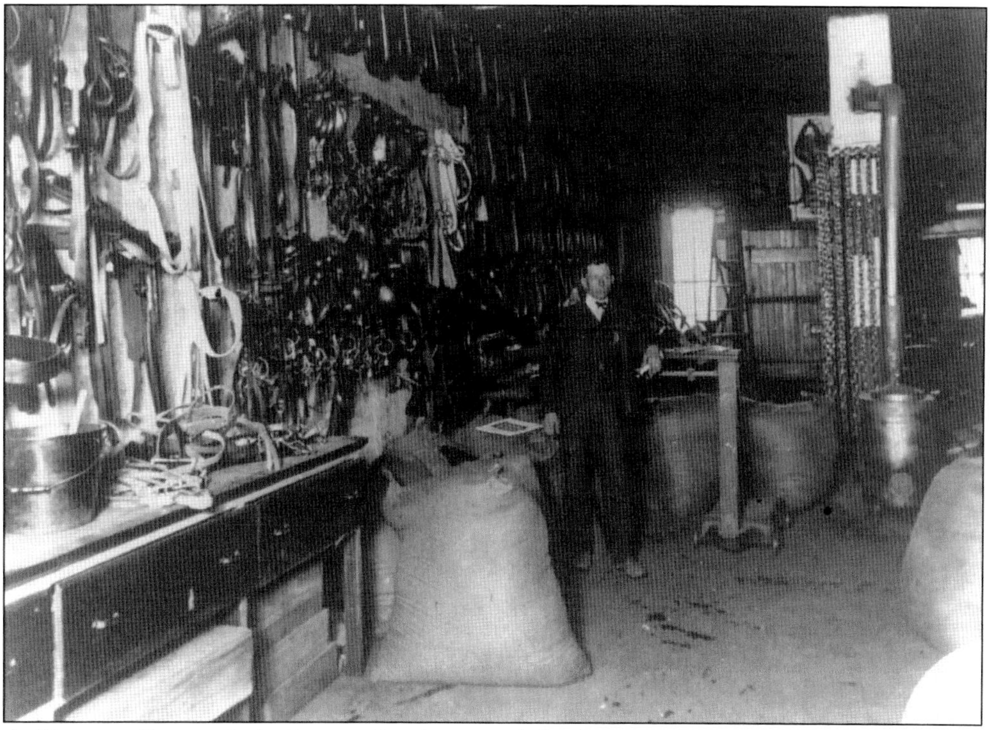

A Harness Shop, 1908. George Grief operated this harness shop in Vine Grove. At that time in history, the harness shop was as important to our ancestors as our present-day auto repair shops are to us. Since the horse provided every family with a means of transportation and power for farm machinery, a proper-fitting harness was a necessity. People living in smaller communities could purchase their harnesses at their local general store.

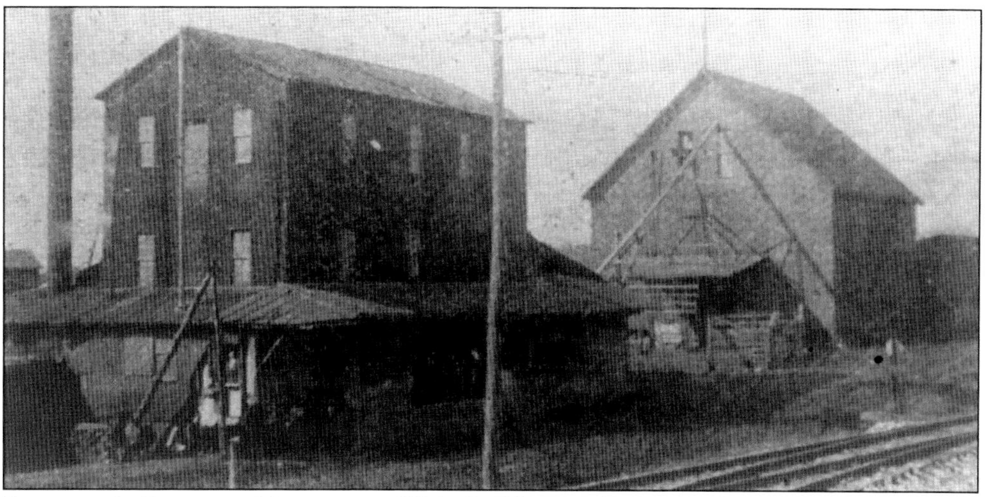

Burkhart's Flouring Mill, 1900. W.A. Burkhart and Sons operated this large flour and grain mill, located adjacent to the railroad tracks in Vine Grove, for many years. It was a popular landmark in the town for over 50 years. Local farmers would bring their wheat and corn crops to the mill to be processed into flour for their own needs, and corn was ground for livestock feed. Most milling was done on a percentage basis, and the miller would keep a portion of the finished product in exchange for his services.

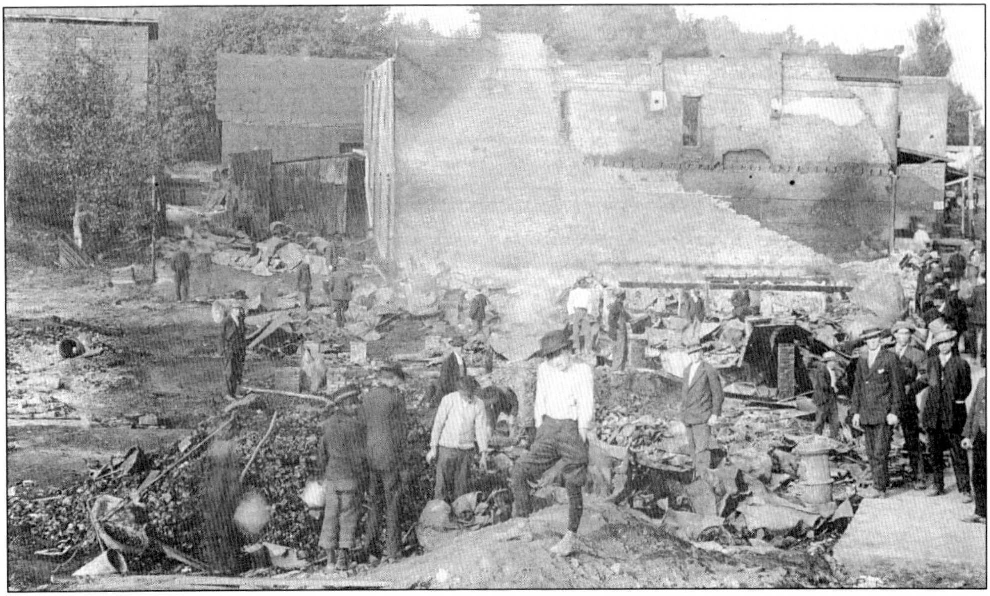

ONE OF THE VINE GROVE FIRES, 1908. Downtown Vine Grove suffered two disastrous fires only three years apart. In 1905, the north side of Main Street was leveled with the exception of the Farmers Bank building and the Burkhart residence. In 1908, the south side of Main Street was nearly wiped out. Since most towns were arranged with buildings connected to one another, they were extremely vulnerable to fast-spreading flames. At that time, little could be done to stop the spreading fire, and "bucket brigades," formed by local residents, had little effect. In this photo, taken in the aftermath of the 1908 fire, residents and sight-seers sift through the rubble.

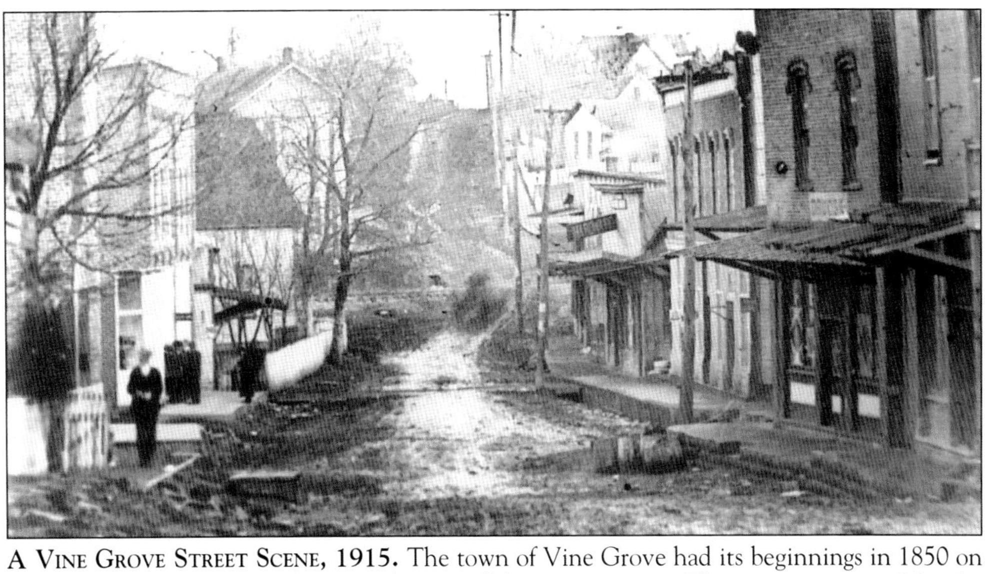

A VINE GROVE STREET SCENE, 1915. The town of Vine Grove had its beginnings in 1850 on the banks of Otter Creek, about a mile west of the present town. The town was named for the dense growth of wild grape vines that grew among the large oak trees in that vicinity. In 1873, the E&P Railroad passed nearby, and the locals moved their homes and businesses closer to the railroad. The new Vine Grove grew quickly, and soon became Hardin County's second largest town. This photo was taken around 1915, before paved streets were constructed.

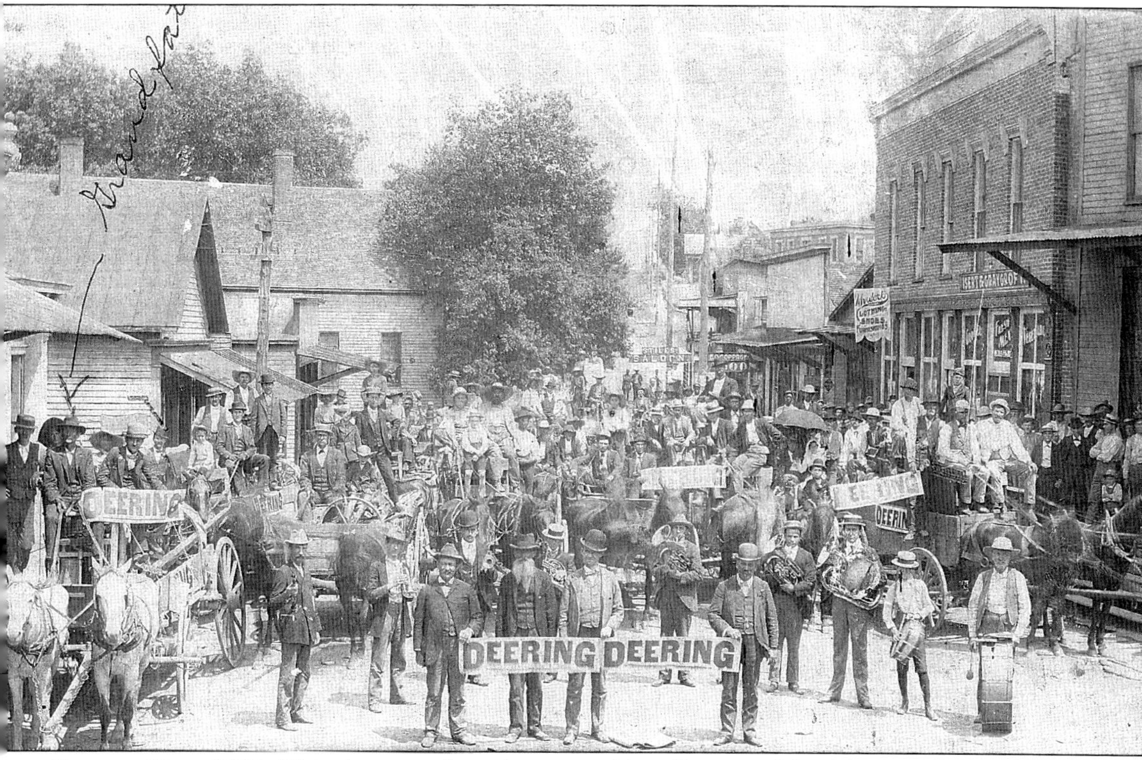

DEERING DAY, 1900. This photo, made in downtown Vine Grove on May 26, 1900, depicts the magnitude of social importance that the displaying of new farm machinery had on a community around the turn of the century. Deering was a highly respected manufacturer of horse-drawn farming equipment. Each year, local agents for the manufacturer sponsored an exhibition of the newest farm machinery. The event drew large crowds, complete with carnival atmosphere and politicians. J.H. Carman and Son was an agent for Vine Grove.

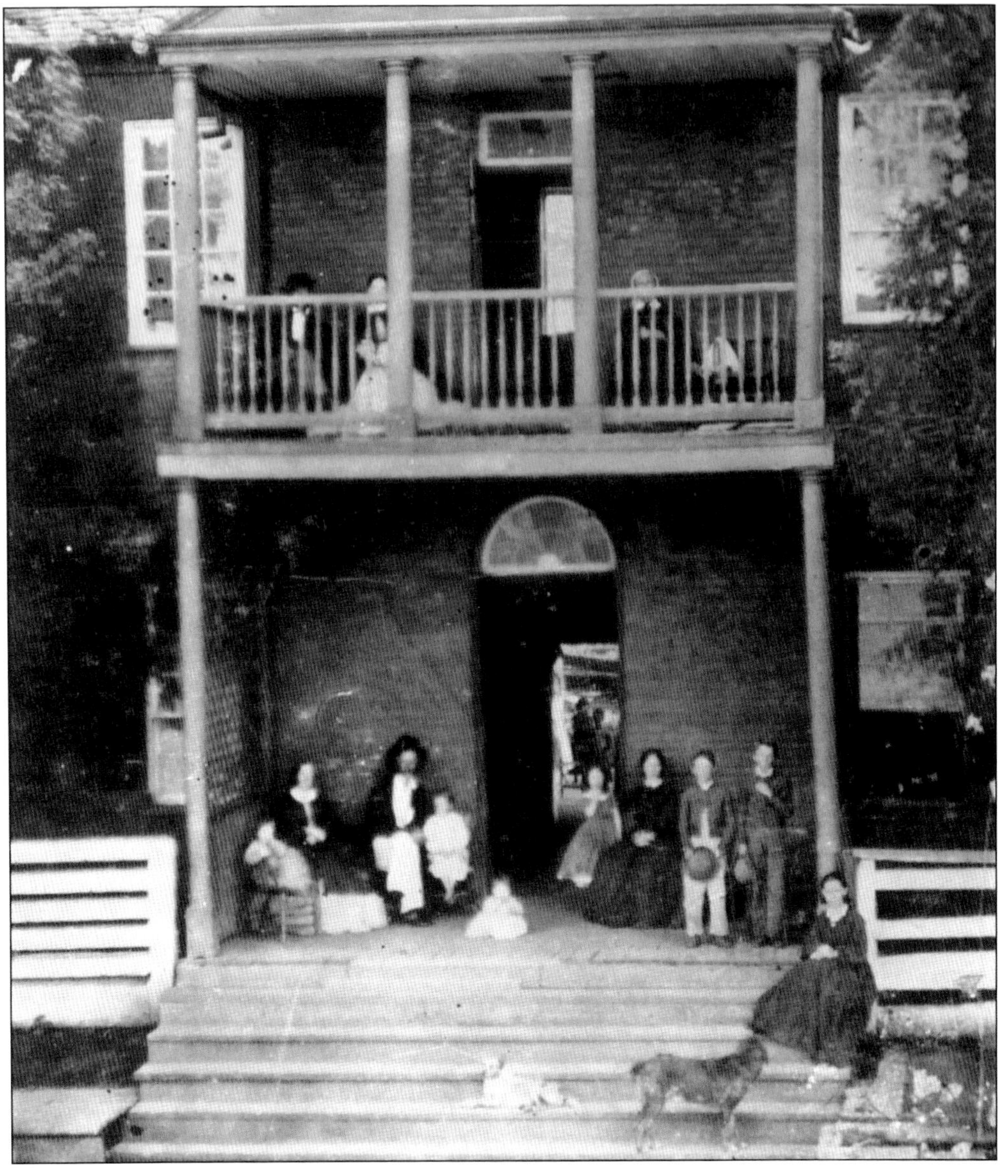

The James Young Home. James Young , a member of a group of Virginians who came to the area in 1776 and were known as "Shane, Sweeny, and Company," along with Samuel Pearman, laid off the streets and lots of the town of West Point on a 150-acre tract of land. It was officially declared a town by order of the Hardin County Court in July 1798. Young built the first cabin in West Point and was a very prominent and influential businessman. He operated ferries across the Ohio and Salt Rivers and owned several large warehouses on the banks of the Ohio. In 1792, he built and operated a large inn near the mouth of Salt River. In 1805, he built a large, two-story brick home across the street from his inn. Young is also credited as being the father of the Louisville and Nashville Turnpike, which began construction in 1829 and opened the area for over-land travel. Samuel Beale Thomas, who was operating a stagecoach line on the pike, married Young's daughter Zorado in 1833. Upon the death of Young's wife in 1839, he gave the house to Zorado. Young died on July 11, 1849, and the Thomases kept the house until 1853. The home remains today as a tribute to one of Hardin County's earliest settlers.

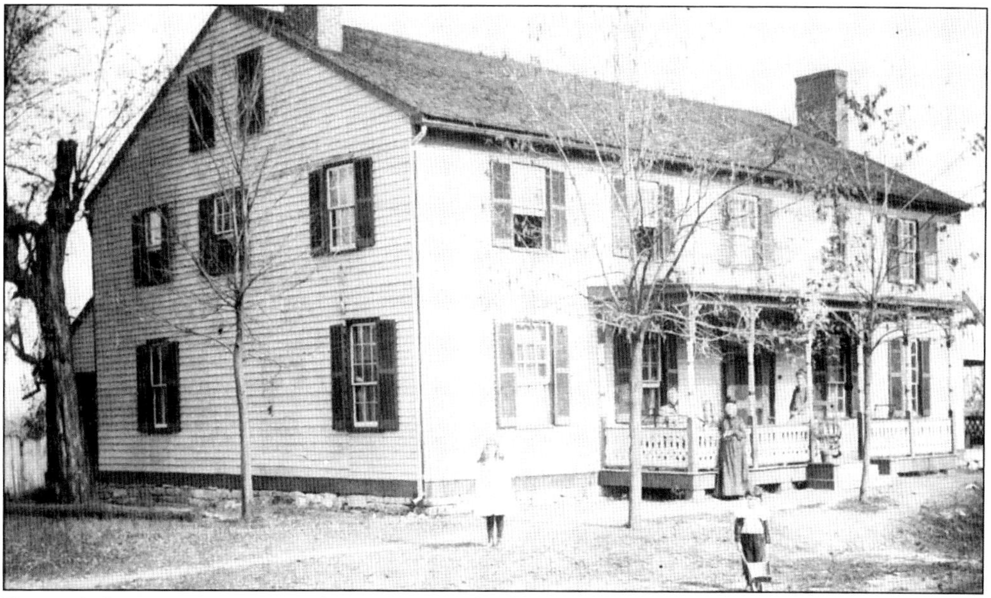

YOUNG'S INN, 1900. In 1792, James Young, the founder of West Point, built this two-story log inn on the banks above the Salt River at West Point. The inn became a popular, over-night rest stop for those traveling the Ohio and Salt Rivers. When the Louisville and Nashville Turnpike was built in 1929, it passed directly in front of the inn and supplied additional customers who traveled by stagecoach. Among the famous personalities to visit Young's Inn over the years were John James Audubon, Henry Clay, Clara Barton, James Buchannon, Jenny Lind, P.T. Barnum, Andrew Jackson, and Wendell Wilkie. The building was briefly used as headquarters for Union General William Tecumseh Sherman during the Civil War. The inn was later converted to a private residence, and remains today as an irreplaceable link to the early history of West Point.

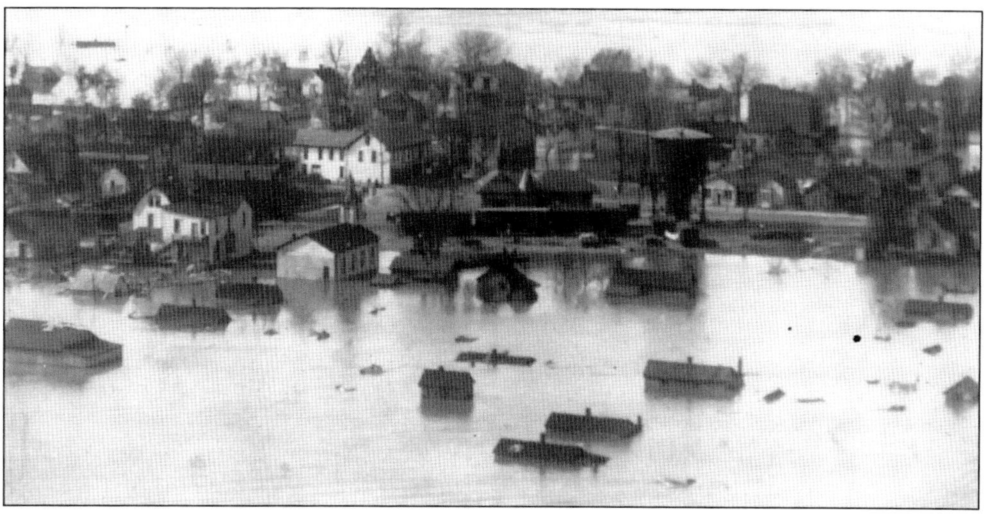

A FLOOD AT WEST POINT, 1913. Through the years, the mighty Ohio River has spilled over into the West Point community many times. The image here depicts the town of West Point during the 1913 flood. The photo was taken from a hill near town. Frequent flooding has prevented the town from growing much over the years, but many are willing to "pay the price" to live in this historic community.

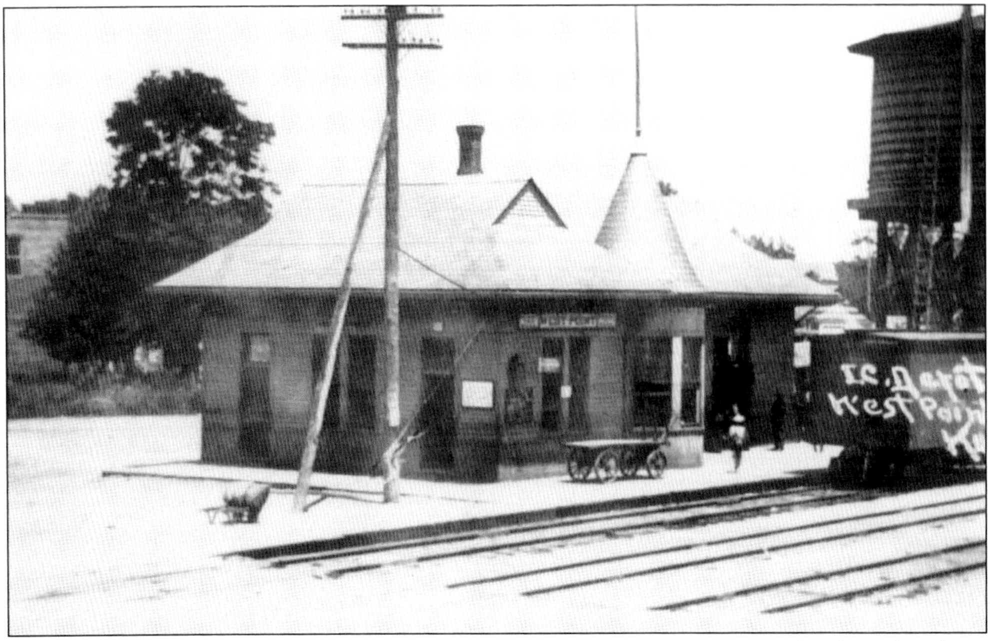

THE ILLINOIS CENTRAL RAILROAD DEPOT, 1908. The Elizabethtown and Paducah Railroad was constructed through West Point in 1873. The line was later operated as the Chesapeake, Ohio, and Southwestern Railroad. On August 1, 1896, it became the property of the Illinois Central Railroad, which operated it for over 60 years. The depot, shown here, was built by Illinois Central around the turn of the century to replace the first structure, built in 1874. Its unusual design made it one of the most attractive depots in the county.

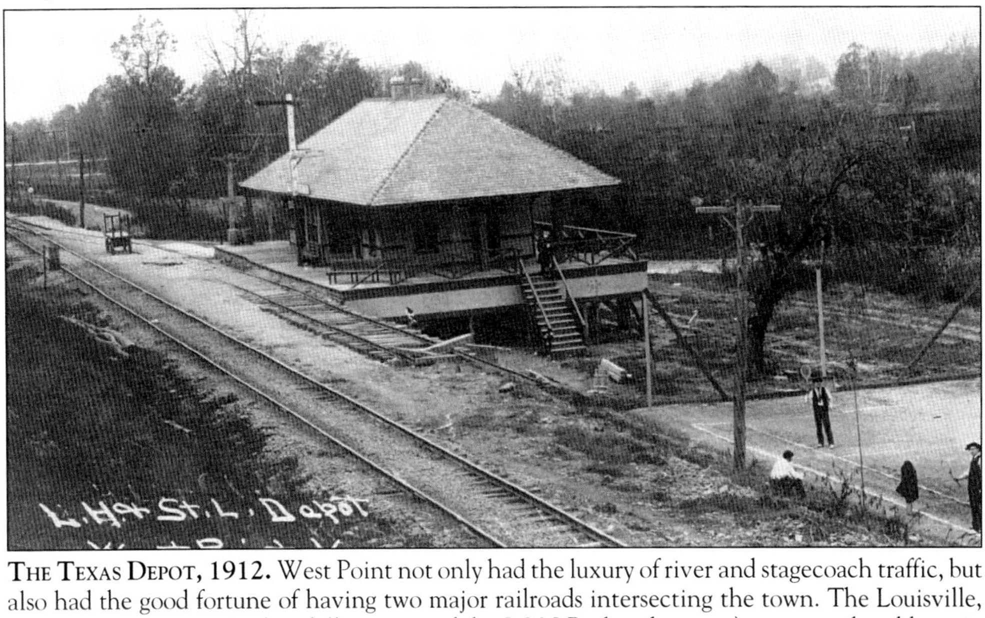

THE TEXAS DEPOT, 1912. West Point not only had the luxury of river and stagecoach traffic, but also had the good fortune of having two major railroads intersecting the town. The Louisville, St. Louis, and Texas Railroad (later part of the L&N Railroad system) was completed here in 1889. The depot, shown here, was completed on the "Texas Line" in 1905. Steps descending from the depot led to the "Chautauqua grounds," which contained a tennis court that proved very popular with the locals.

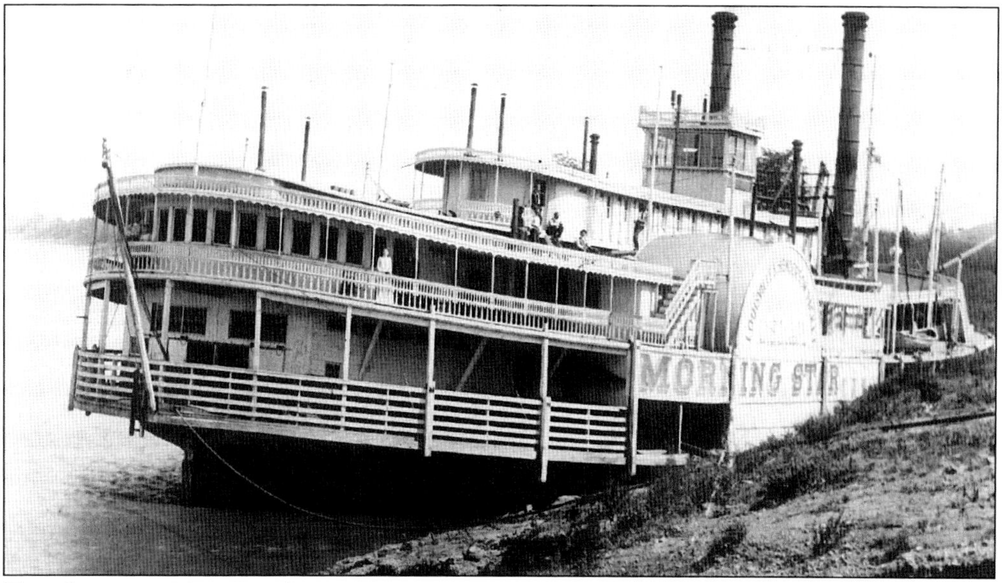

The Steamer *Morning Star*, 1900. West Point rapidly became a strategic commercial shipping port and one of the most famous river towns in the state. With few navigable roads in the early years, the vast majority of travel and shipping took place on the river. Flatboats were soon replaced with steam-powered craft, which dominated the rivers for almost a century. The mighty steamboats could be fitted to most any enterprise including stores, sawmills, theaters (showboats), and even churches. West Point witnessed the rise and fall of the great steamboat era of the 1800s, with their tall stacks belching thick black smoke and musical whistles playing familiar tunes. Shown here is one of those great steamboats, the *Morning Star*, which frequented the wharf at West Point.

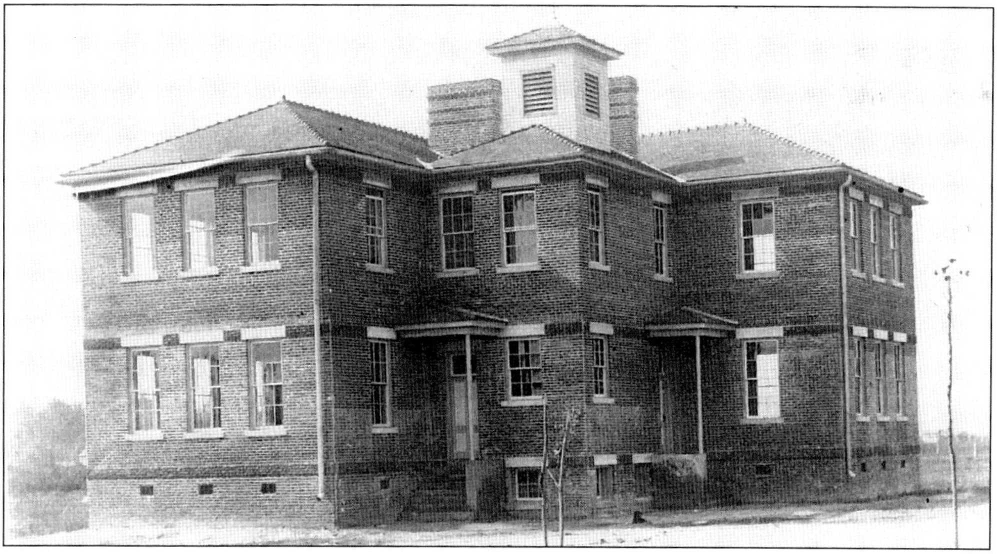

The West Point School. The first school building in West Point was undoubtedly a log structure. Over the years, different schools were built to accommodate the growing number of children in the town. This large school was built in West Point in 1909 as a graded/high school and served the area for many years. It was the pride of the community, and was considered one of the finest schools in the county.

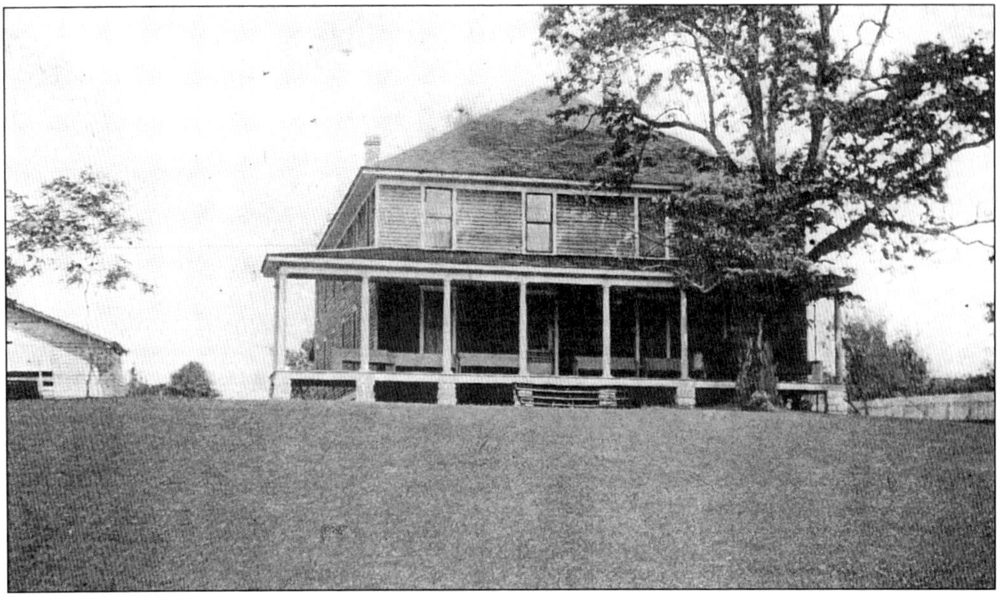

The Hatfield Hotel, 1908. Built in 1907 to accommodate the growing numbers of summer visitors to White Mills, this two-story building was constructed by Doug Hatfield and contained 22 guest rooms and a dining room that seated one hundred people. The building was constructed entirely of creosoted lumber. Mr. Hatfield's sisters, Lena and Betty, assisted him in operating the hotel until 1938, when it closed due to a decline in tourists.

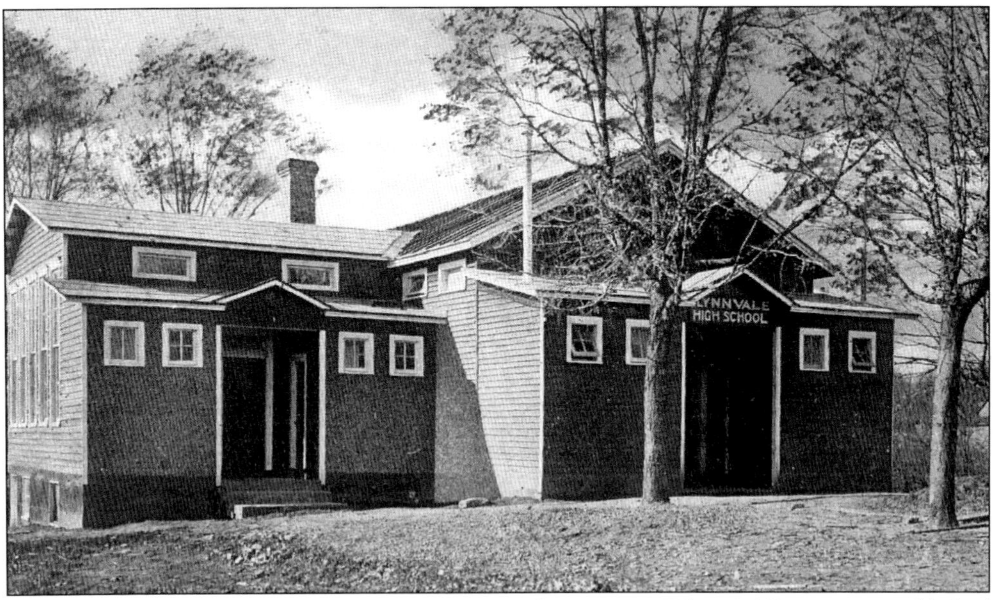

Lynnvale High School, 1921. In 1893, a group of prominent White Mills citizens established the Lynnvale Academy. Upon completion of a one-story frame building, Professor W.E. Maddera became the first teacher. Subjects taught at the school included Latin, geometry, philosophy, and other advanced subjects. In 1921, the school's name was changed to Lynnvale High School, and it continued as such until 1933, when the present brick school was built.

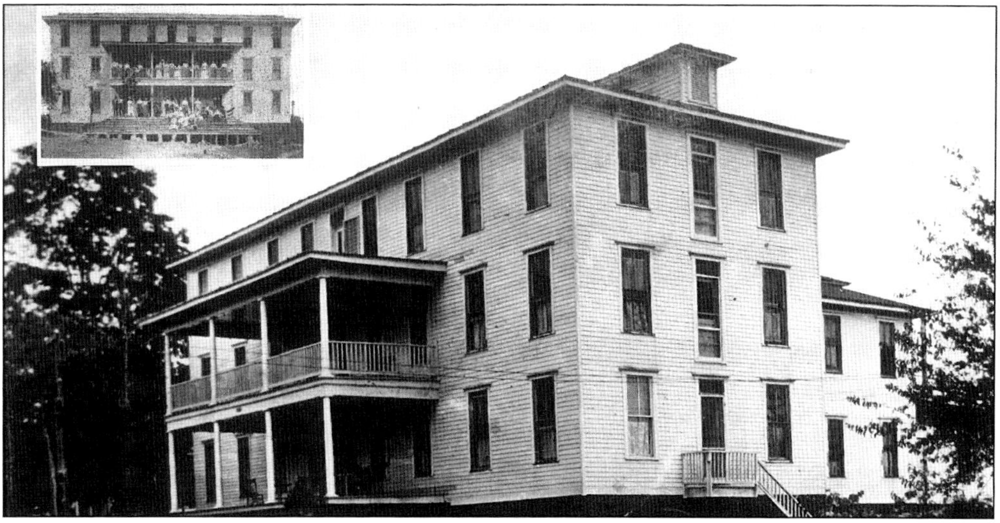

THE RICHARDSON HOTEL, 1908. The White Mills Hotel was built in 1907 through the partnership of three siblings: Dr. Hayward A. Richardson (the town dentist), Marshall T. Richardson, and Lucretia Richardson Barnes. Electricity for the hotel was produced at the nearby mill owned by their father, Joe D. Richardson. It was the first building in the area to have electric lights. The three-story hotel contained 50 guest rooms, indoor baths, and a dining room which seated three hundred people. Guests were transported from the railroad depot at Eastview in a fringed surrey. Hotel rates were $3.50 per day, with meals included. Activities included fishing, boating, swimming, hiking, and evening dancing. In 1949, the property was sold to the Christian Camp Assembly, and the third floor of the hotel was removed. It continues to be the civic center of the White Mills community.

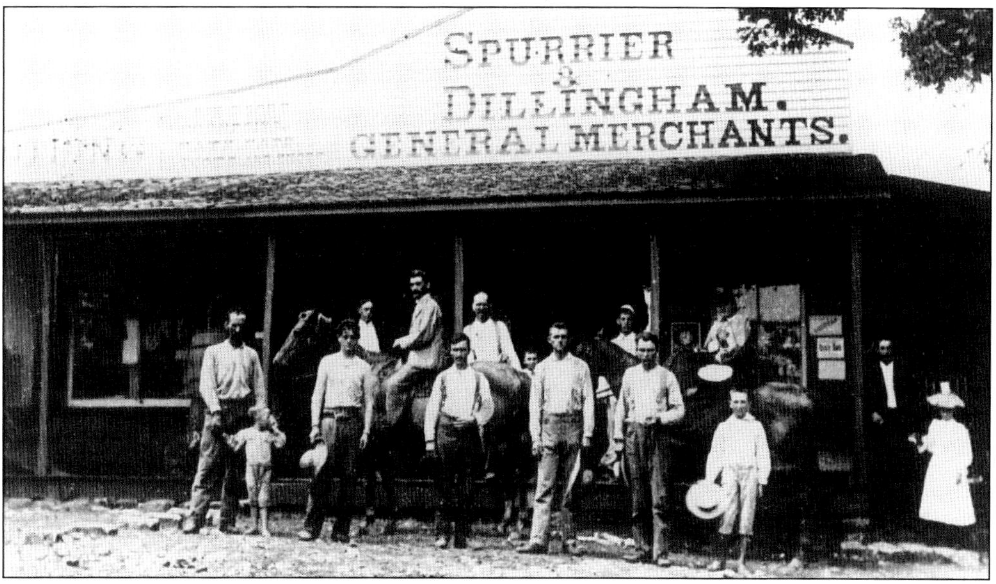

THE SPURRIER AND DILLINGHAM STORE, 1896. The first store in White Mills was built by Philip Bunger in the late 1850s, shortly after the second mill was built by Dan Wortham. About 1915, as the White Mills community grew, this small village supported four stores. The largest of these was operated by the Spurrier and Dillingham families. It sold everything from farm implements to clothing. The original building survives today, but was closed as a store in 1987.

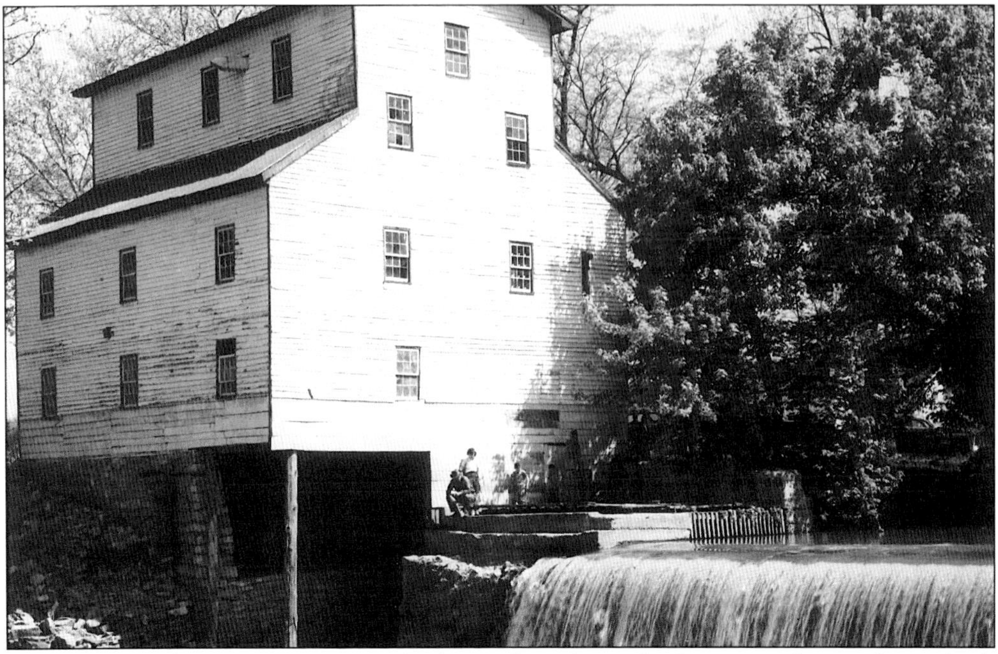

The Wortham/Richardson Mill. The first mill on the Nolin River in White Mills was built about 1830 and was washed away c. 1853. The next mill was constructed by Dan Wortham in 1855. It was later purchased by Joe D. Richardson, who constructed a large stone dam across the river, making it one foot higher than the original dam. In 1889, his son, Marshall Richardson, constructed a building on the bluff above the river to house a wool-carding machine, which was powered by electricity from the mill. When the hotel was built nearby in 1907, it, too, used electricity from the mill. The demand for the mill gradually declined over the years, as milling became more of a nostalgia than a necessity. Both the mill and hotel were sold to the Christian Church Assembly in 1949. The building was vacant for several years before being torn down in 1965. It was the last mill on the Nolin River to fade into history.

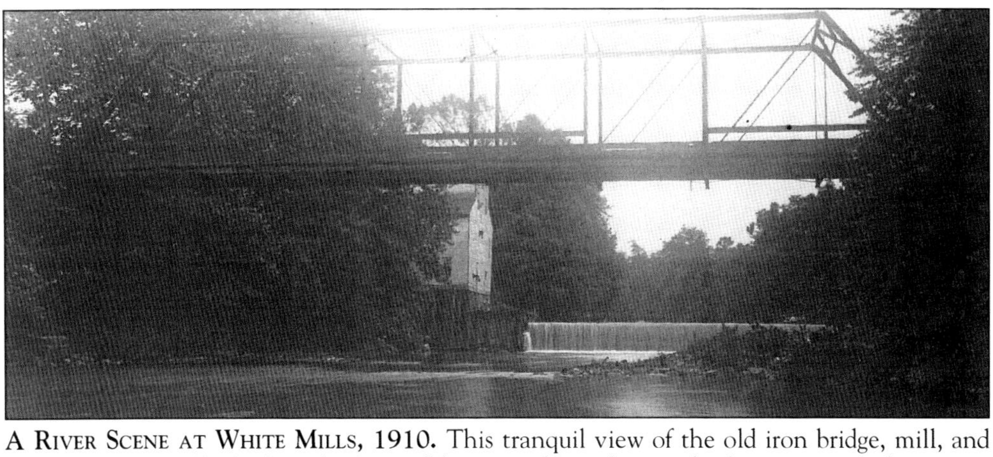

A River Scene at White Mills, 1910. This tranquil view of the old iron bridge, mill, and dam at White Mills displays the beautiful surroundings that made the area a popular tourist attraction for almost 50 years. The old bridge, built in 1889, was a vital link for the people on both sides of the Nolin River. It has survived numerous floods, the worst of these being the "Great Flood of 1937," which raged 9 feet above the floor of the bridge. It is still in use today, with the distinction of being the only one-lane iron bridge remaining in Hardin County.

Two

Lincoln's Legacy in Hardin and LaRue Counties

No county or area of Kentucky can claim a closer connection to, or relationship with, Abraham Lincoln than can the counties of Hardin and LaRue. Lincoln's parents, Thomas and Nancy Lincoln, resided at three different places in Hardin County during their early married life together. At each of these three residences, one of their three children was born—Sarah in Elizabethtown in 1807, Abraham at the Sinking Spring farm near Hodgenville in 1809, and Thomas Jr. at the Knob Creek farm, about 7 miles east of Hodgenville, sometime between 1811 and 1816.

The Hardin/LaRue-Lincoln connection was perpetuated and preserved during the early part of this century by the construction, dedication, and acceptance by the federal government of the stately Memorial Building at the birthplace farm, the accompanying three successive Presidential visits, and the dedication of the Weinman statue of Lincoln in the square in Hodgenville, together with celebrations and other related occurrences. This chapter portrays and discusses these and other Lincoln-related events, places, and people as they were photographed from 1880 to 1930.

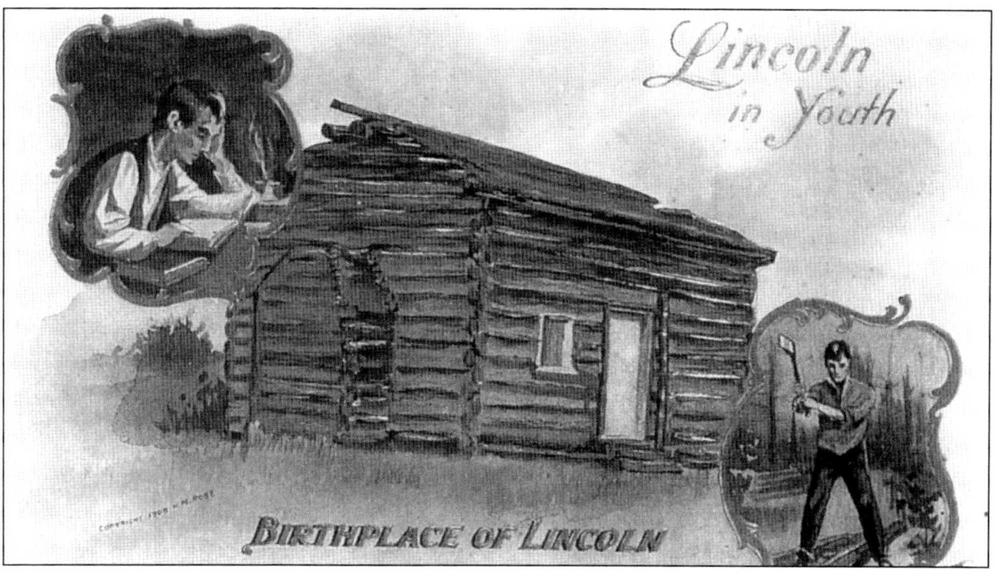

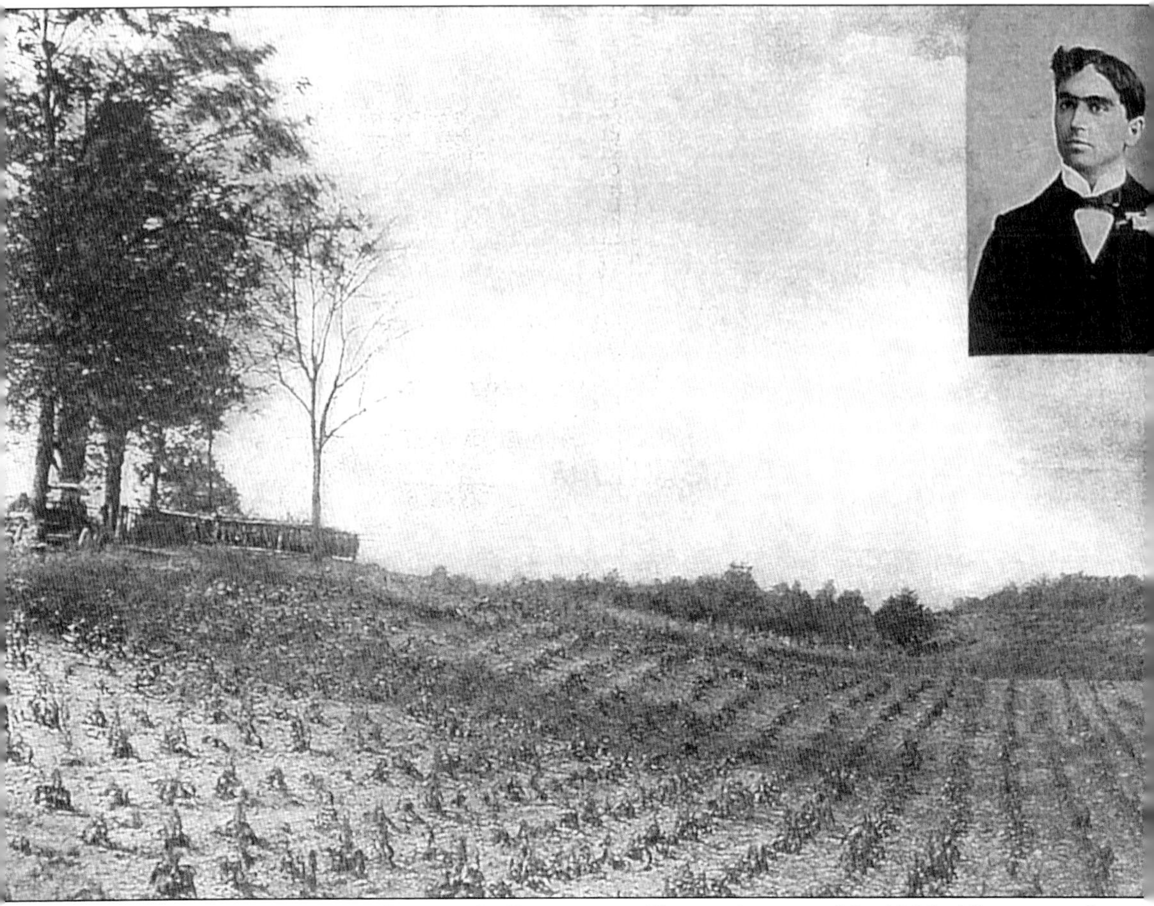

The Sale of Abraham Lincoln's Birthplace Farm, August 28, 1905. The original log cabin in which Lincoln was born occupied the knoll on the right in this 1905 picture. Pursuant to a judgment and order of sale entered in the May 1905 term of LaRue Circuit Court, prominent Hodgenville attorney L.B. Handley (inset) was appointed special commissioner to sell the Abraham Lincoln birthplace farm at public auction. Richard Lloyd Jones, on behalf of Robert J. Collier of *Collier's* magazine, was the high bidder at $3,600. Collier's sole objective, as stated in the February 10, 1906 issue of *Collier's* magazine, was "to protect this shrine from further vandalism and . . . to turn it over to the people of the United States, to be held forever by them as a garden spot in the nation's history . . ." To this end, Collier and his magazine caused to be organized and incorporated, under the laws of Kentucky, the Lincoln Farm Association, whose expressed purpose was to develop the Lincoln birthplace farm into a national park. He conveyed the land to the association in 1907. The first work of the association, whose board of trustees was comprised of 28 well-known patriotic citizens, was to restore the log cabin to its original location and to enhance the Sinking Spring and surrounding areas. The second goal was to collect money to pay for the construction of a suitable building in which to preserve the cabin, prior to deeding the farm to the government. Thomas B. Kirkpatrick, postmaster of Hodgenville, made the first contribution to the Lincoln Farm Association by mailing a check in the amount of $5 to *Collier's* magazine. Thousands of contributions followed by public spirit-minded people throughout the United States. Many were made by children, and most of the people contributed amounts of 25¢ to $25, as initially requested by the association. All contributors received engraved membership certificates in recognition of their gifts. In 1905, at the time of the (*continued on page 113*)

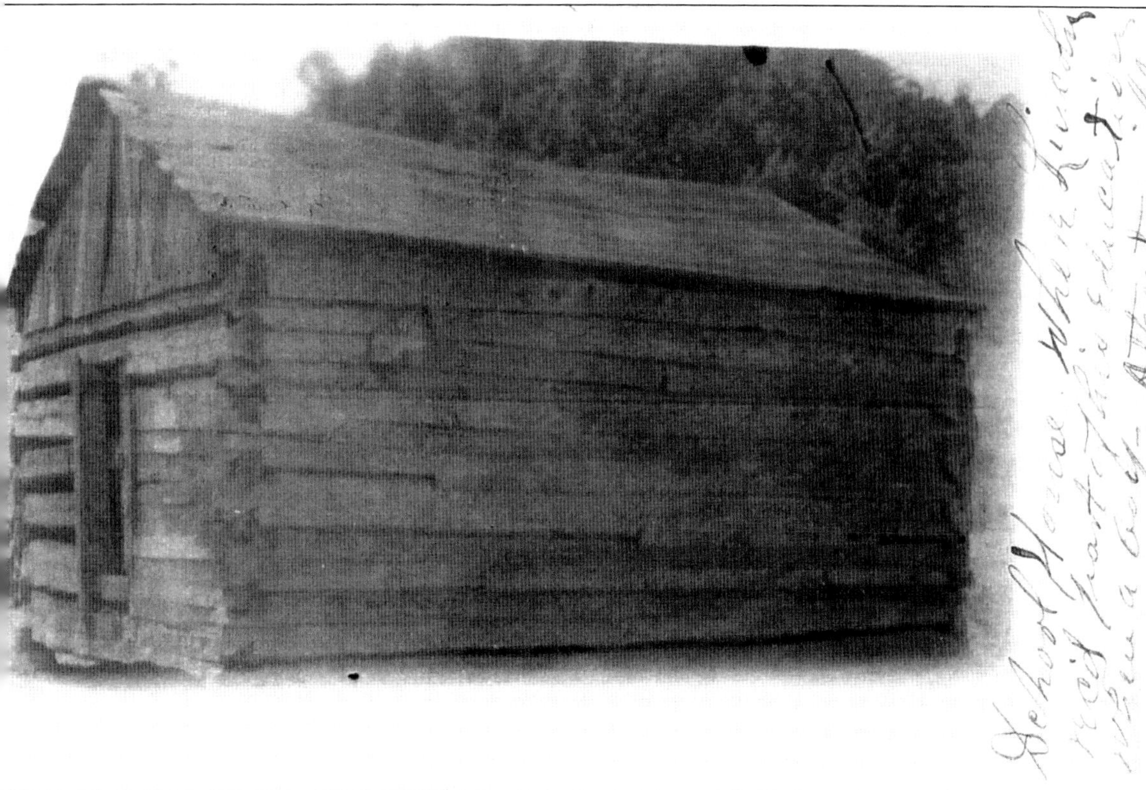

LINCOLN'S FIRST SCHOOL, 1910. In 1815, while the Lincoln family resided on the Knob Creek farm, Abraham and his sister Sarah attended two ABC schools. The first was located in this small log house, about 2 miles from Athertonville. The knowledgeable and widely respected Zachariah Riney was their teacher at this schoolhouse, also known as a "blab" school. Taken shortly before it was dismantled, this is the only known real-photo postcard of the schoolhouse. On May 15, 1910, the sender wrote, "School House where Lincoln rec'd part of his education when a boy—Athertonville, Ky."

(*continued from page 112*) commissioner's sale, the 143 carefully numbered logs comprising the cabin in which Lincoln was believed to have been born had been shipped by Methodist preacher James W. Bigham, on behalf of the farm and cabin's owner, A.W. Dennett, to Nashville and exhibited at the Tennessee Centennial Exposition. After a lengthy exhibition itinerary, the cabin was purchased by David Crear of New York City, who stored the logs in the basement of the old Poffenhausen mansion at College Point in Long Island. In February 1906, Norman Hapgood, a member of the board of trustees of the Lincoln Farm Association, purchased the logs from Crear for $1,000. On June 6, 1906, under military escort, they were sent by flatcar from Pennsylvania Station in New York City to Louisville, where the reconstructed cabin became the feature of the Kentucky Homecoming Week festivities. The cabin remained in Louisville until it was taken to the birthplace farm for the laying of the cornerstone of the Memorial Building on February 12, 1909. After the ceremony, the cabin was returned to Louisville, where it was stored in a fire-proof storage building. When the Memorial Building was completed in 1911, the cabin was reconstructed within its walls, where it has since remained.

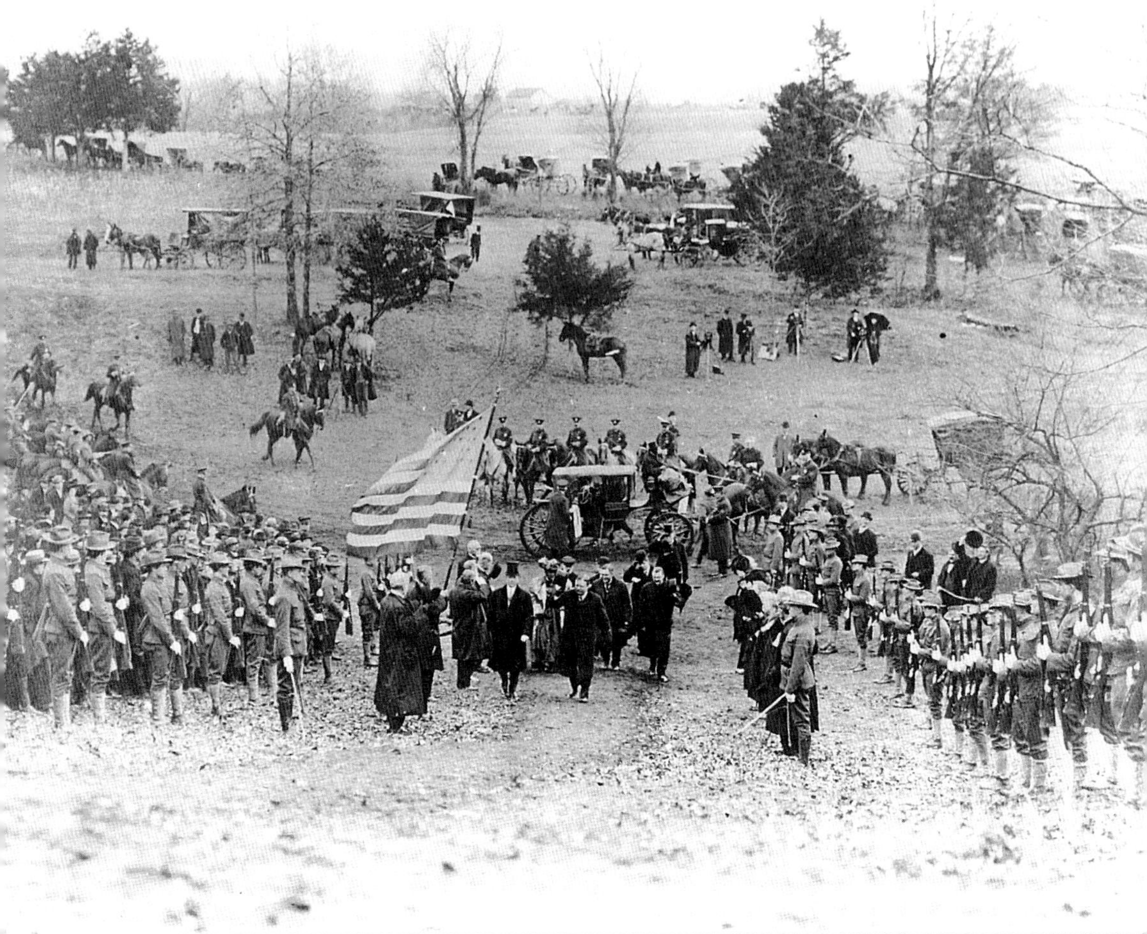

PRESIDENT THEODORE ROOSEVELT ARRIVING AT LINCOLN'S BIRTHPLACE, FEBRUARY 12, 1909. President Roosevelt and his entourage ascend the hill leading to the recently reconstructed, one-room log cabin near Hodgenville in which Abraham Lincoln was believed to have been born. The occasion marked the first visit by a presiding President to the place of nativity of Kentucky's most famous and revered native son, and occurred on the 100th anniversary of Lincoln's birth. While the cornerstone was suspended in the grasp of a derrick, President Roosevelt concluded his address by characterizing Lincoln as "The mightiest of the mighty men who mastered the mighty days." The program continued with orations by Kentucky Governor Augustus Wilson, Lincoln Farm Association President/Governor Joseph Folk, Federal Army General James Grant Wilson, and Confederate Army General Luke E. Wright.

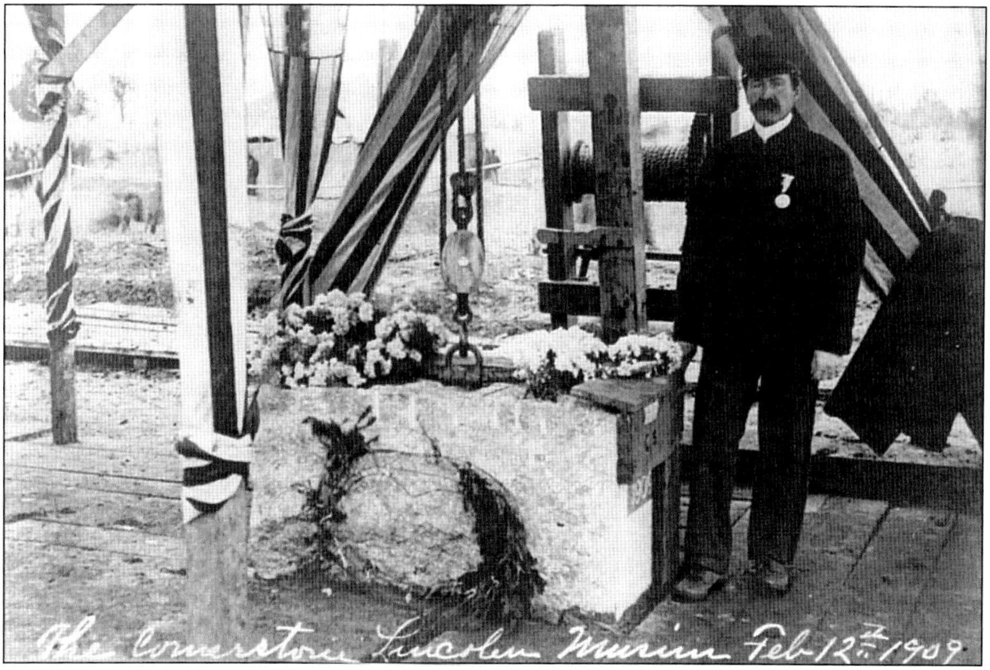

LAYING THE CORNERSTONE OF THE MEMORIAL BUILDING, FEBRUARY 12, 1909. At the conclusion of the formal addresses, the speakers left the platform and joined the officers of the Lincoln Farm Association at the cornerstone. Governor Folk handed a copy of the United States Constitution to President Roosevelt, who deposited it into a metal box located in the center of the cornerstone. Then occurred one of the most impressive moments of this great occasion, as Governor Folk handed a copy of the Emancipation Proclamation to Isaiah T. Montgomery of Mississippi, a former slave of Confederate President Jefferson Davis. Taking it in his hand, Montgomery turned to the crowd and said, in part: "At this, the birthplace of the immortal Lincoln, I speak as one of the four million slaves that received the priceless boon of liberty through a stroke of his pen, and as a representative of ten millions of negro citizens of our beloved country." As he then proceeded to place the document into the box, he continued, "I deposit this proclamation . . . First, on behalf of ten millions of grateful people who will ever remember the noble man who espoused their helpless cause without hope of fee or reward and . . . Second, on behalf of a free and united people still impressed with the presence of grave and unsolved difficulties, yet all alike cherishing the life and example of this great man, looking upward full of hope, with an abiding faith in the great Author of our national destiny." Following a tremendous round of applause, other documents were then placed in the metal box by many of the dignitaries who were present for the occasion. After the stone was ready for placement, President Roosevelt applied the first mortar with a silver trowel. The cornerstone, a block of Connecticut granite weighing 3,000 pounds, is located at the front right corner of the Memorial Building and is inscribed, "February Twelfth 1909." The unidentified man standing next to the cornerstone is wearing a Lincoln Centennial medallion on his coat.

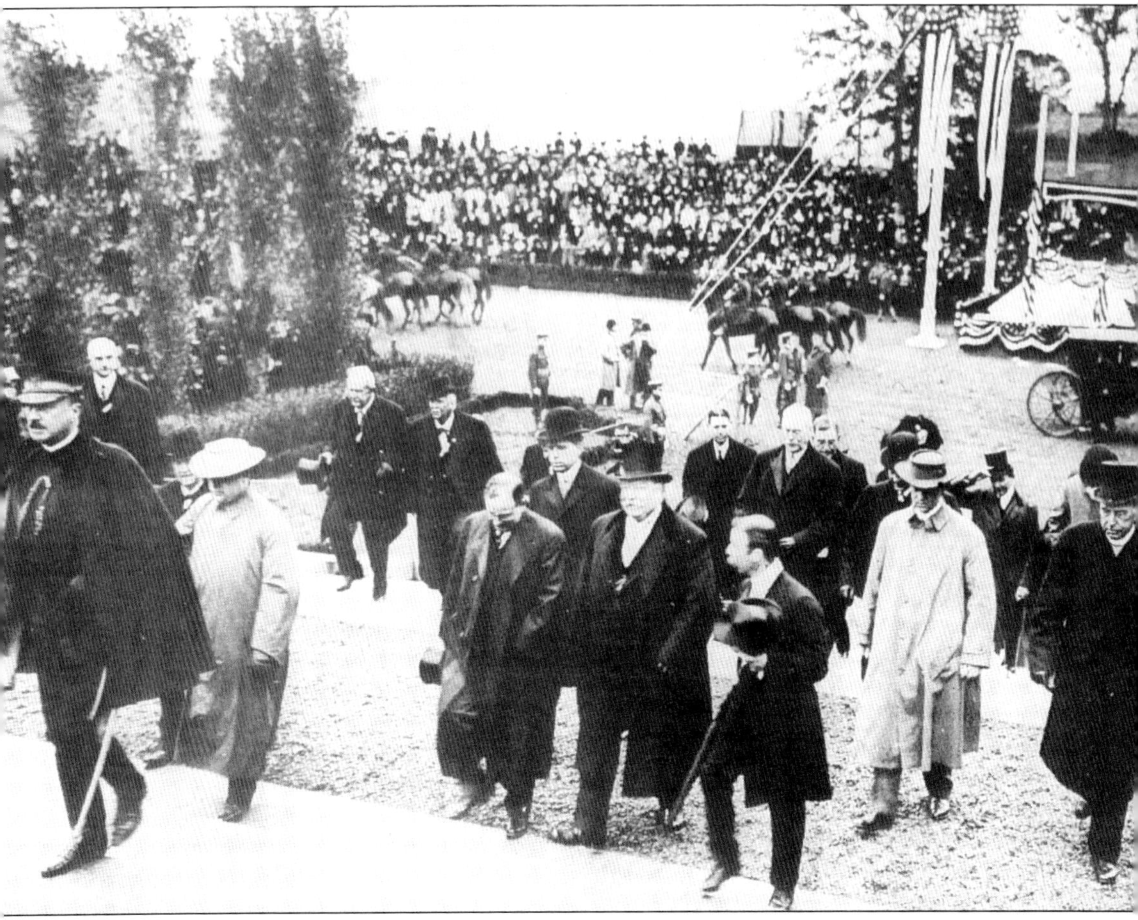

President William Howard Taft Approaching the Memorial Building at Lincoln's Birthplace, November 9, 1911. President Taft and his entourage ascend the 56 granite steps leading to the newly constructed Memorial Building at Lincoln's birthplace. On this day, November 9, 1911, over three thousand people witnessed former Missouri Governor Joseph M. Folk, on behalf of the Lincoln Farm Association, turn the Lincoln birthplace farm, Memorial Building, and cabin over to the Commonwealth of Kentucky. Kentucky Governor Augustus Willson accepted the trust and stated that Kentucky would add to the $50,000 trust fund established by the association for the farm's maintenance. Other speakers on this occasion were Idaho Senator William A. Borah, General John C. Black, and Henry Watterson. Clarence H. Mackay, treasurer of the association, spoke of the Memorial Building, "It is the gift of both the affluent and the lowly. . . It is a simple, direct tribute of a grateful people to the memory of a great American." Noted New York architect John Russell Pope designed the structure, which was constructed of Stony Creek Connecticut pink granite and Tennessee marble by Norcross Brothers, a contracting company from Worchester, Massachusetts.

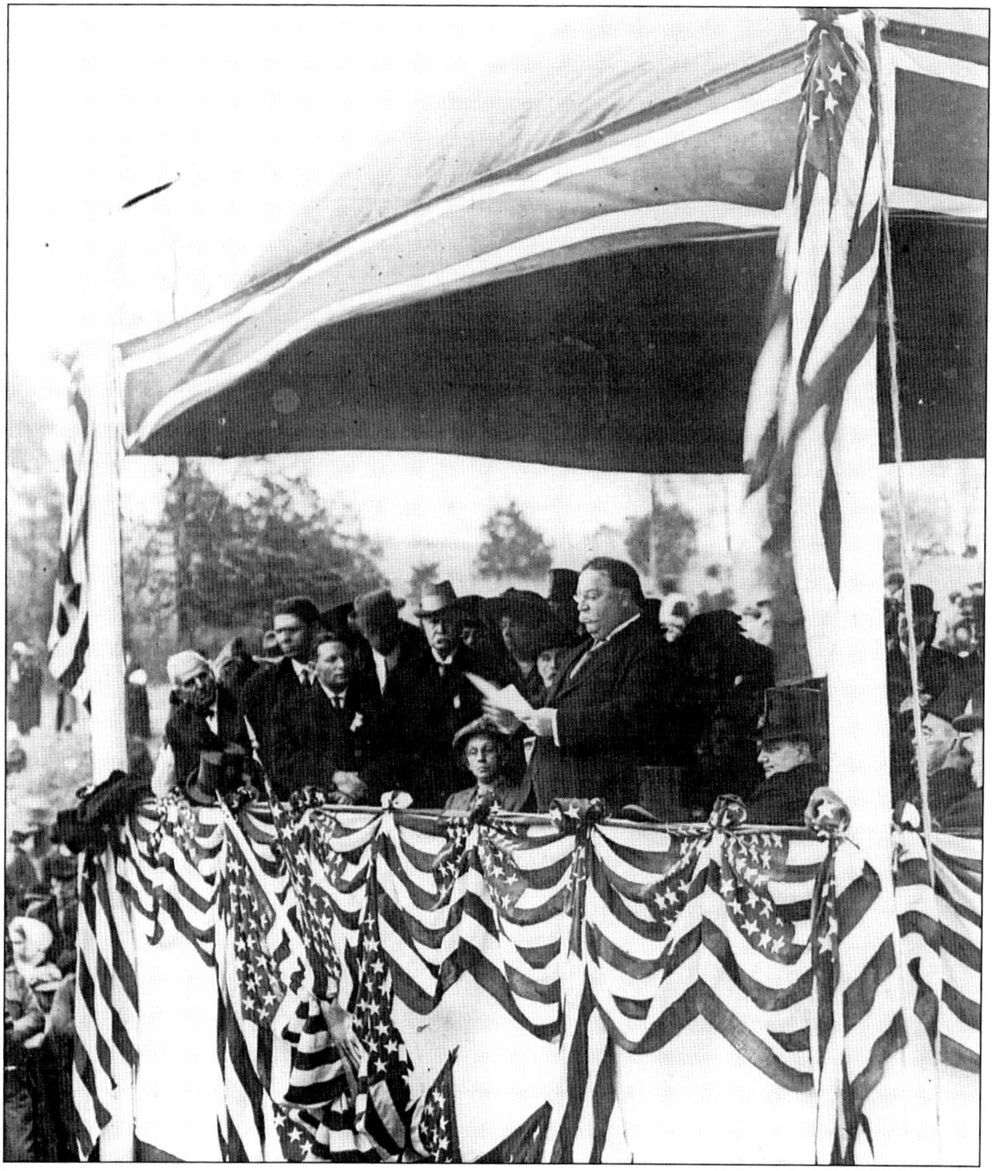

PRESIDENT WILLIAM HOWARD TAFT DELIVERING HIS ADDRESS AT LINCOLN'S BIRTHPLACE, NOVEMBER 9, 1911. The following are selected excerpts from President Taft's address at the dedicatory services: "The explanation of Lincoln and his wonderful character from his origin and environment is almost as difficult as the explanation of Shakespeare; but the passion of the world grows for more intimate knowledge of his personality and a deeper inquiry into the circumstances of his wonderful life. Nothing of his characteristics is too incidental for those who study over again his great speeches and messages and trace again the amazing story from the lowly home in Kentucky whence he sprang to the height of his glory in his martyrdom. It is eminently appropriate that the farm where Lincoln was born should come into public possession and should have erected on it a suitable memorial . . . The great reason [for the memorial] is the constant reminder it furnishes of the unexplained and unexplainable growth and development, from the humblest and homeliest soil of Lincoln's genius, intellect, heart and character. . ."

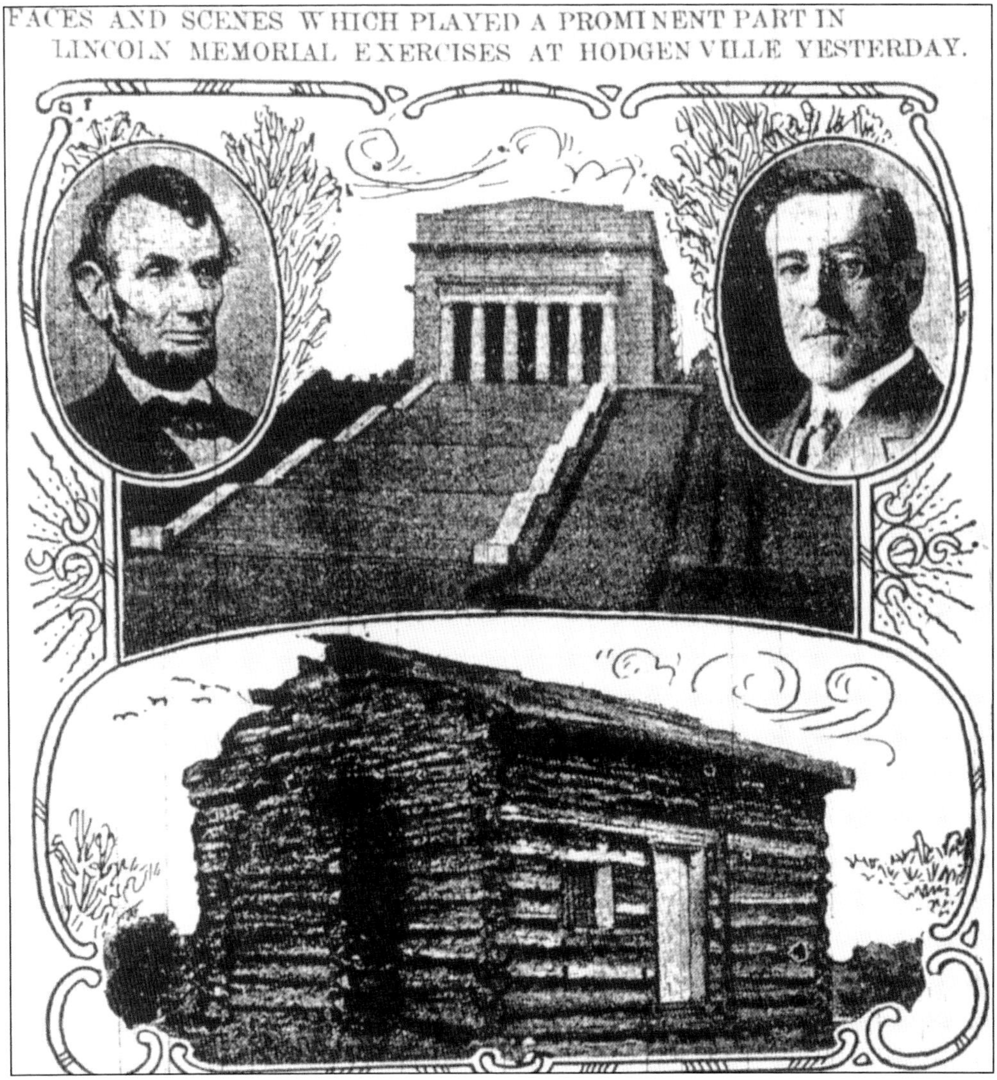

President Woodrow Wilson at Lincoln's Birthplace, September 4, 1916. Woodrow Wilson became the third successive President to visit Hodgenville and Abraham Lincoln's birthplace when he came by special train from Louisville on Labor Day, September 4, 1916. He spent about five minutes at the Lincoln statue, then proceeded by automobile to the recently constructed Memorial Building, where he examined the enclosed cabin. Wilson's address, in which he accepted the Lincoln Memorial on behalf of the government, was brief but couched in the language of a brilliant educator and former university president. He stated, in part, "This little hut was the cradle of one of the great sons of men, a man of singular, delightful, vital genius who presently emerged upon the great stage of the nation's history . . . A natural ruler of men." Confederate veteran General John B. Castleman opened the program by delivering a brief address and then introducing Kentucky Governor Joseph W. Folk. His short but well-received speech was followed by the lengthy oration of Senator John Sharp Williams. Robert J. Collier then formally presented the deed to the birthplace farm and the endowment fund of $50,000 to Secretary of War Newton D. Baker, who received it by authority of the president. (This montage, published in the September 5, 1916 issue of the *Lexington Herald*, is reprinted with permission of the *Lexington Herald-Leader*.)

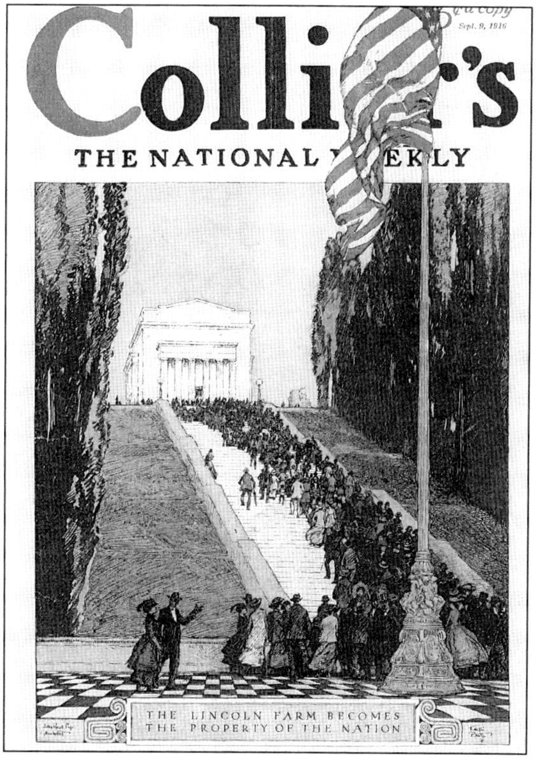

COLLIER'S MAGAZINE REPORTING THE LINCOLN FARM BECOMING THE PROPERTY OF THE NATION, SEPTEMBER 9, 1916. The cover of *Collier's* Weekly Magazine, dated September 9, 1916, is shown here. The addresses of Robert J. Collier and President Woodrow Wilson, delivered at the Memorial Building on September 4, 1916, are contained in this issue.

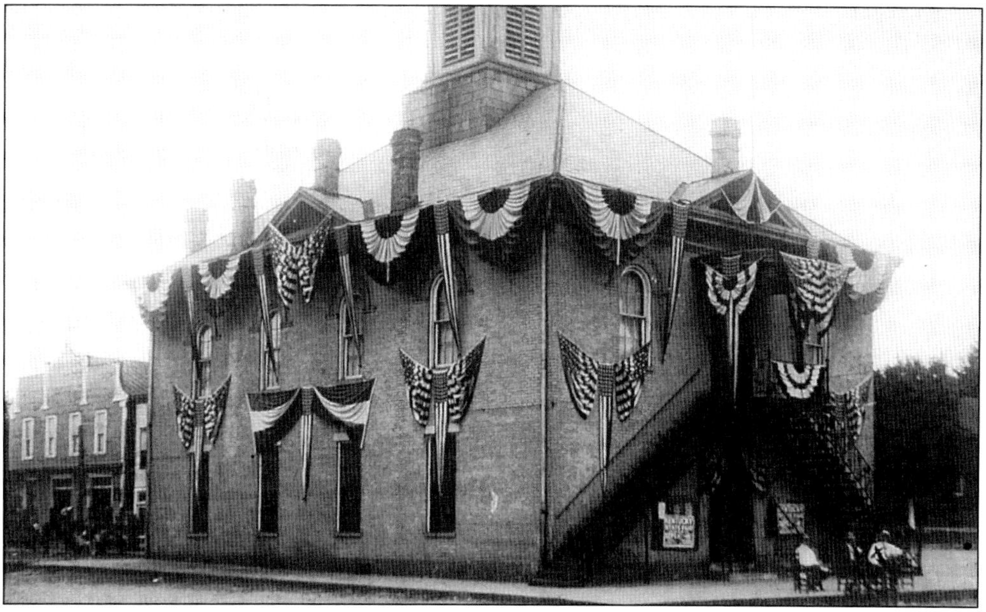

THE LARUE COUNTY COURTHOUSE, 1916. The courthouse was beautifully decorated for the visit of President Woodrow Wilson on September 4, 1916. This one-of-a-kind, real-photo postcard was mailed to H.R. Creal in Birmingham, Alabama, on September 8, 1916. The following message appears on the back side: "You would hardly distinguish Papa in this picture so I marked him with an X." This two-story, brick building was constructed 1865–67, renovated in 1892, and dismantled in 1967.

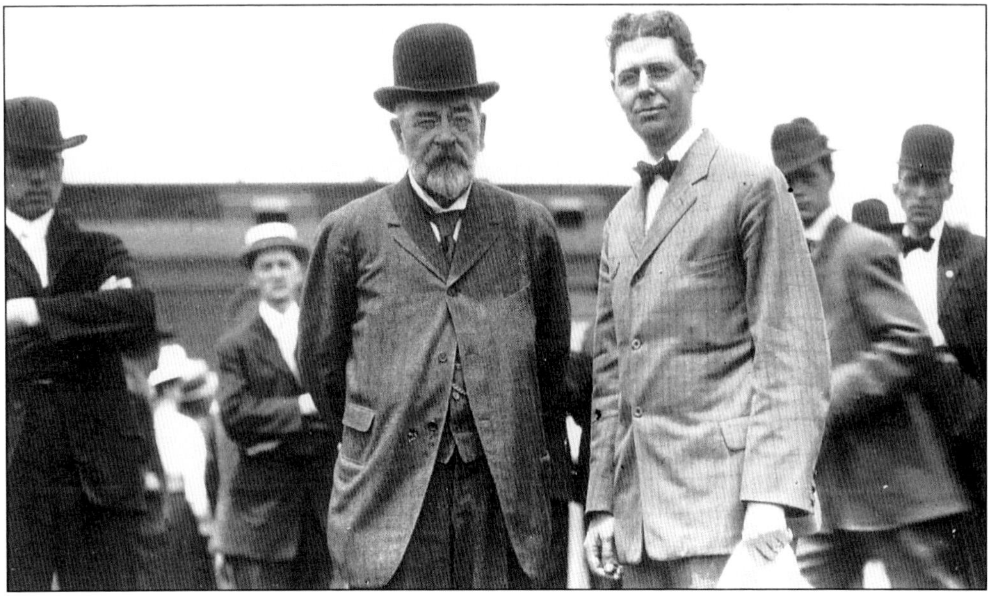

ROBERT TODD LINCOLN AND RICHARD LLOYD JONES, MAY 31, 1909. Robert Todd Lincoln (left), the 65-year-old son of Abraham Lincoln, meets with Richard Lloyd Jones, secretary of the Lincoln Farm Association, with whom originated the movement to preserve Lincoln's birthplace, at the Hodgenville Depot. Lincoln later remarked, at the unveiling of the statue, that the bronze sculpture was a "noble likeness" of his father. In November 1909, Lincoln mailed a check in the amount of $1,000 to the Ladies Lincoln League in Hodgenville to help pay for necessary improvements and the future preservation of the plot of ground around the base of the Lincoln Statue.

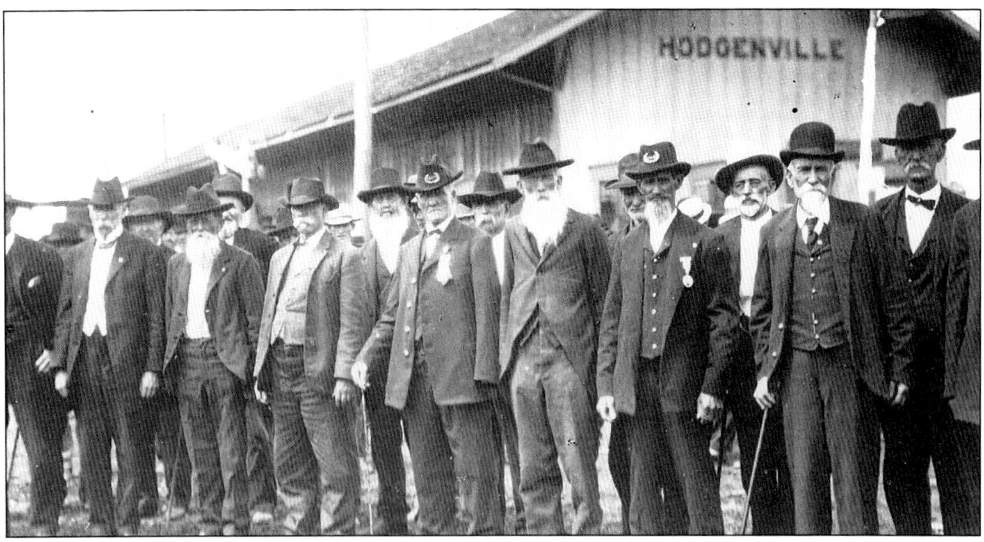

CIVIL WAR VETERANS, MAY 31, 1909. These men have assembled at the Hodgenville Depot to greet Robert Todd Lincoln upon his arrival on the morning of May 31, 1909. They formed an honor guard for the son of the former president, whose sculpted likeness would soon be unveiled at the Hodgenville Town Square. Although he had planned to visit the cabin and birthplace site later that day, Lincoln became ill during the unveiling ceremony and retired to his train car.

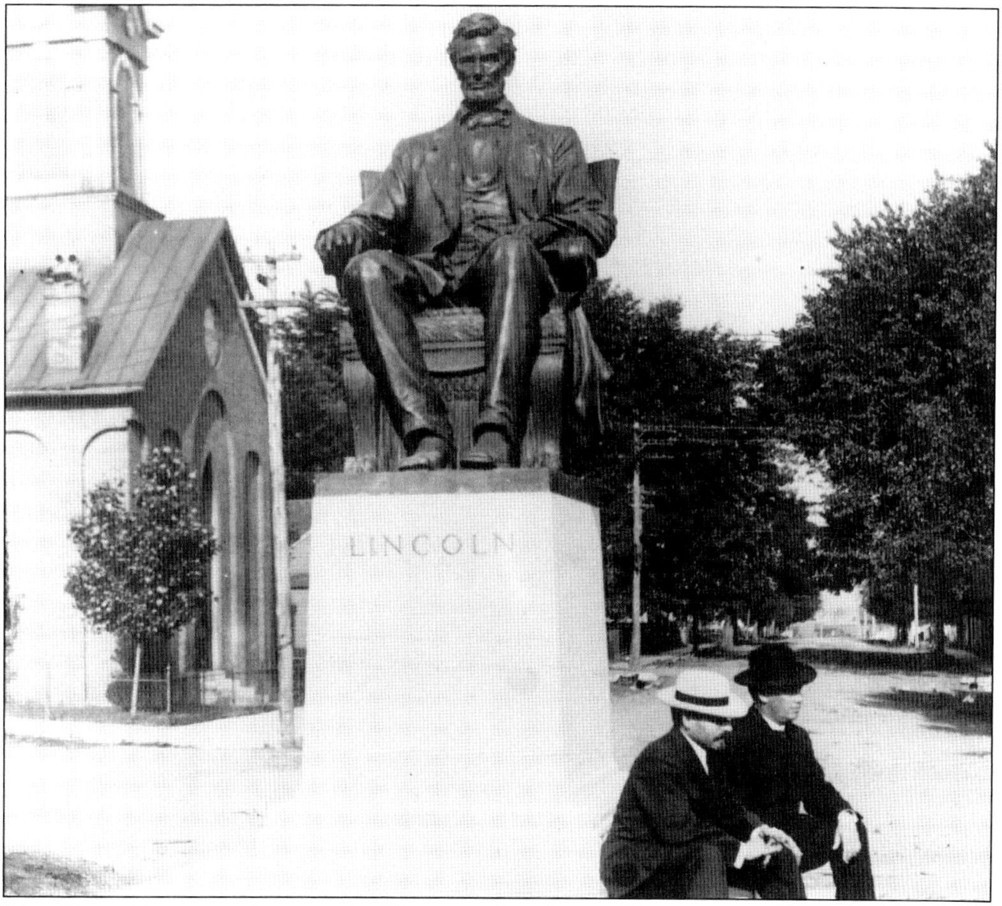

NEW YORK SCULPTOR ADOLPH A. WEINMAN (LEFT) AND HODGENVILLE ATTORNEY CHARLES WILLIAMS AT THE LINCOLN MONUMENT, MAY 31, 1909. The unveiling of the Lincoln statue, sculpted by Adolph A. Weinman, culminated the grandest day in Hodgenville's history. The following list of exercises is contained in the souvenir program of the Lincoln Monument unveiling: Invocation by Rabbi Enlow; address "The Kentucky Pioneer" by Judge Ed C. O'Rear; address by Colonel Henry Watterson; address by Hon. Edward J. McDermott; "The Blue and the Gray" by Miss Florence Hansbrough Howard; unveiling of Lincoln statue by Mrs. Ben Hardin Helm; "America" by Band and Audience; Acceptance of Statue on Behalf of Lincoln Tablet Commission by Judge George Du Relle; Acceptance of Statue for the State of Kentucky by Gov. Augustus E. Willson; Acceptance of Statue for the People of LaRue County by Hon. D. H. Smith. The acceptance speech on behalf of the LaRue County people was given instead by the Honorable Charles Williams. The eloquent Hodgenville attorney stated, in part, "We have met, and by our presence, speech and the unveiling of this likeness again pay tribute to the memory of LaRue County's boy, Kentucky's son and the Nation's hero. In the purity of his boyhood days [the citizenship of LaRue County] gave him that simplicity of life that was ever mingled with his heroic character. Though another state may have developed him, he carried from his boyhood home . . . the elements of character that enabled him to win his deathless fame. We gave him to the nation. After many, many years she returns to us not his body or his ashes, but this bronze figure she gives unto us as a pledge of appreciation. . . We accept it that it may stand before coming generations who will pause beside its figure in its mute eloquence, pleading with them and inspiring in them a hope that we may ever have . . . a Government of the people, by the people and for the people."

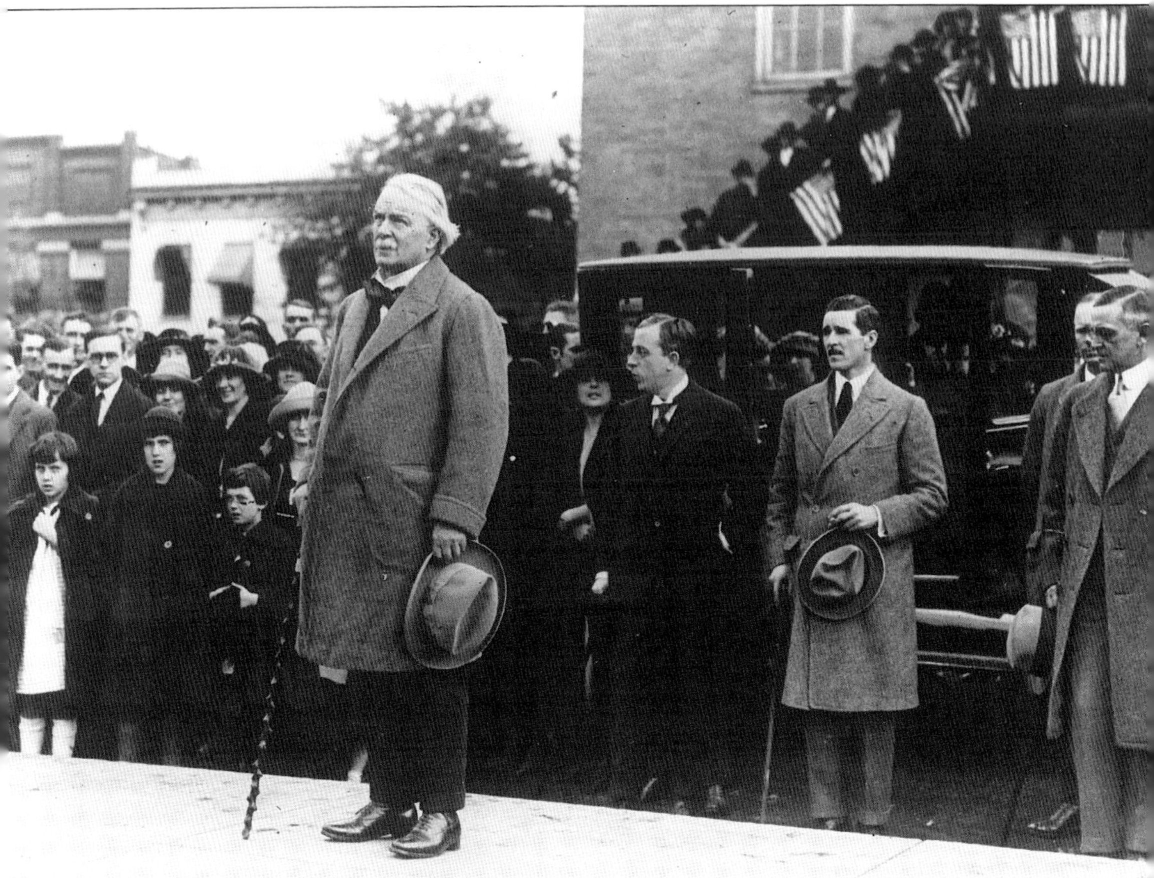

DAVID LLOYD GEORGE AT THE LINCOLN STATUE, OCTOBER 21, 1923. The former English Prime Minister stands before the statue of Abraham Lincoln in Hodgenville on October 21, 1923. The *New York World* reported that he was met at Hodgenville by several hundred Kentuckians who still live in a sparsely settled region, and who habitually refer to the great president as "Abe." The distinguished visitor stopped in front of the old courthouse to inspect the monument of Lincoln, and was received by citizens and schoolchildren, the latter singing "God Save the King" and "America" as he stood before them. In a tribute, Lloyd George once stated, "I doubt whether any statesman who ever lived sank so deeply into the hearts of the people of many lands as Abraham Lincoln did . . . In his life he was a great American. He is an American no longer. He is one of those giant figures, of whom there are very few in history, who lose their nationality in death. They are no longer Greek or Hebrew or English or American—they belong to mankind." (Photograph courtesy of the Lincoln Museum, Fort Wayne, Indiana, #1944.)

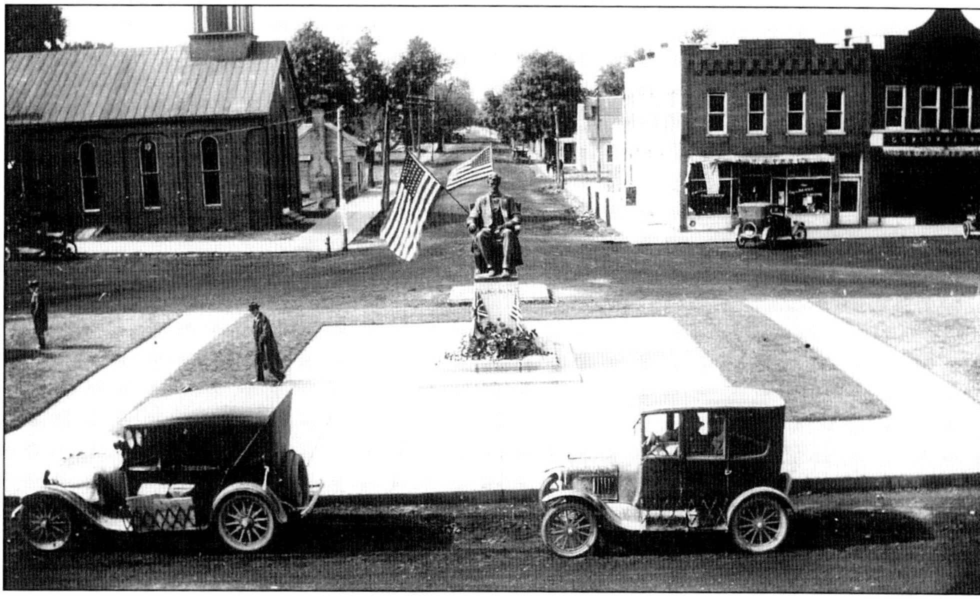

Town Square and the Lincoln Statue, October 21, 1923. The Hodgenville Town Square and Lincoln statue are depicted as they appeared on the day of David Lloyd George's visit. After later viewing the Lincoln cabin and drinking from the famous spring, Lloyd George asked a child, "Where are you from, little girl?" "I'm from Buffalo," she said. "Why, you've come a long way, haven't you?" "Yes sir, 2 miles," she replied. The famous British statesman did not know that LaRue County has its own Buffalo.

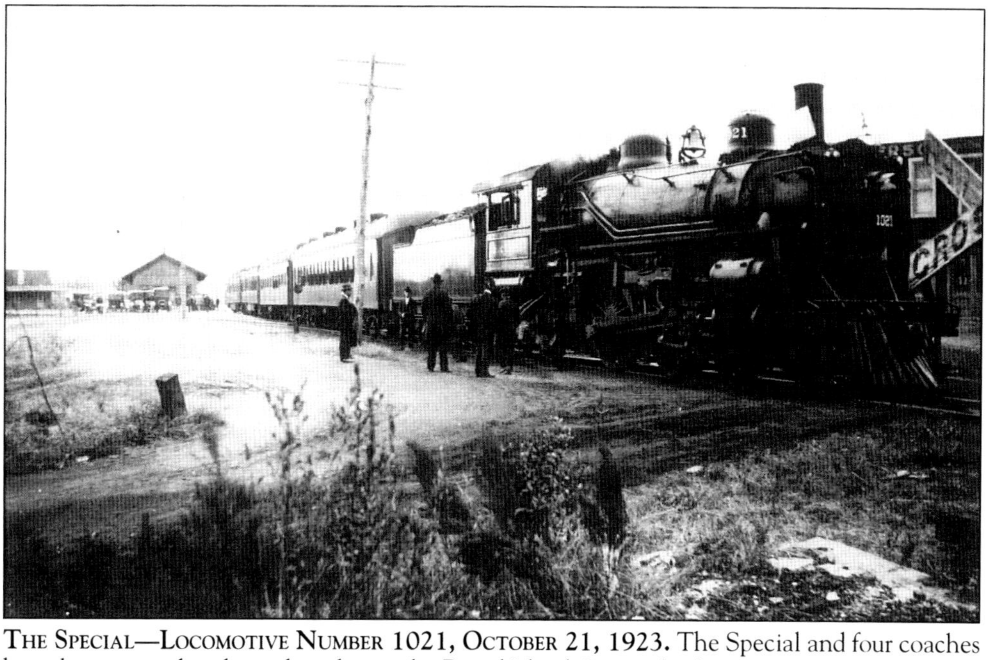

The Special—Locomotive Number 1021, October 21, 1923. The Special and four coaches have been turned and stand ready to take David Lloyd George back to Louisville. Six railroad officials engage in conversation alongside the train. A portion of the D.E. Patterson Hardware Store can be seen behind the locomotive and railroad crossing sign. In the distance are the Hodgenville depot, a few parked cars, and a stockyard building.

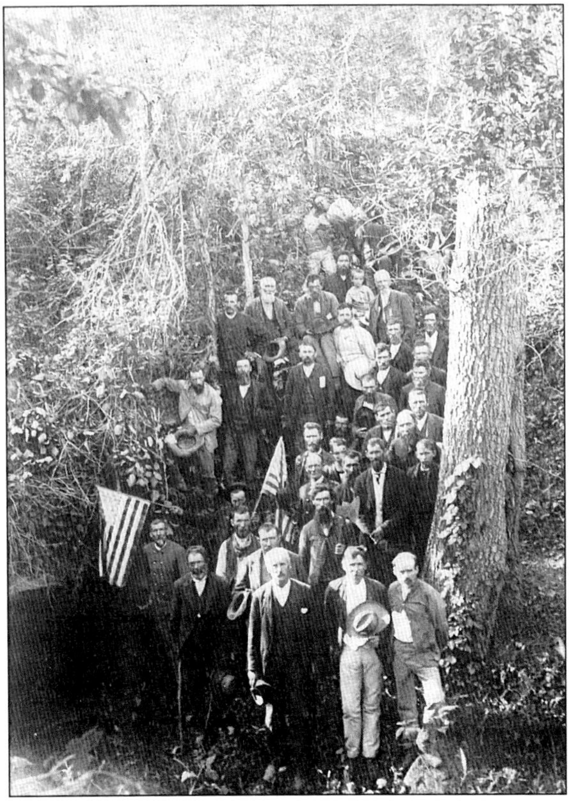

SINKING SPRING AT LINCOLN'S BIRTHPLACE, JULY 4, 1888. These men, many of whom are Civil War veterans, have gathered at the spring on the Lincoln farm near Hodgenville to celebrate the Fourth of July in 1888. It was in the 1880s that many people first considered holiday pilgrimages to the historic spring to participate in brief patriotic ceremonies in honor of the renowned President. In March 1898, Kentucky Governor William O. Bradley commissioned James Speed Jr., son of one of Lincoln's closest friends, to travel to the Lincoln farm to obtain a jug of spring water. His daughter, Hallie Speed, knelt by the famous spring and filled the jug with sparkling water which was donated by A.W. Dennett, the owner of the birthplace farm. On March 24, 1898, the governor's young daughter, Christine Bradley, christened the new battleship *Kentucky* by breaking the jug against its hull and launching the great ship on its maiden voyage.

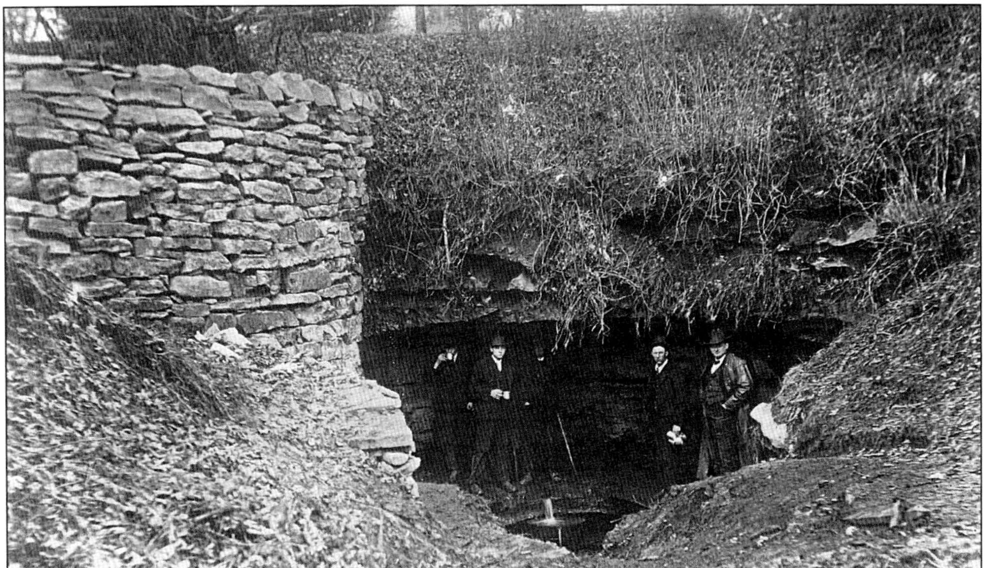

SINKING SPRING AT LINCOLN'S BIRTHPLACE, c. 1909. This real-photo postcard shows five men at the famous spring near Lincoln's birthplace. A rain barrel, or wash tub, had been placed in the well so that water could be contained and then scooped out in metal cups for drinking purposes. Abraham Lincoln drank his first water from the "Sinking Spring," which also served as the source of water supply for the Lincoln family.

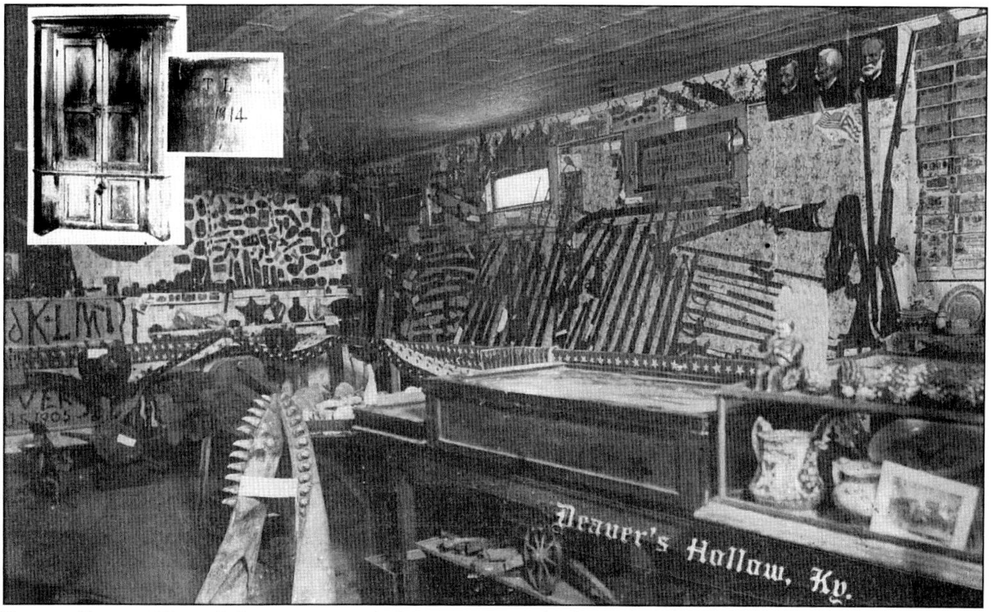

INSIDE BLACK HOOF MUSEUM, 1905. Here is a rare look inside W.A. Dever's famous museum, which reveals many of the items in his personal collection. At left can be seen a portion of the many Native-American artifacts that Dever found on the farm. To the right is his priceless gun, knife, and sword collection, most of which dated to the Civil War. Also at right is a collection of rare paper currency. Among other items on display are early American pottery, clocks, and primitive furniture. One furniture item is a corner cupboard (inset) made in 1814 by Thomas Lincoln, the father of President Abraham Lincoln. The cupboard was later sold to the J.B. Speed Museum in Louisville, Kentucky, where it remains on display.

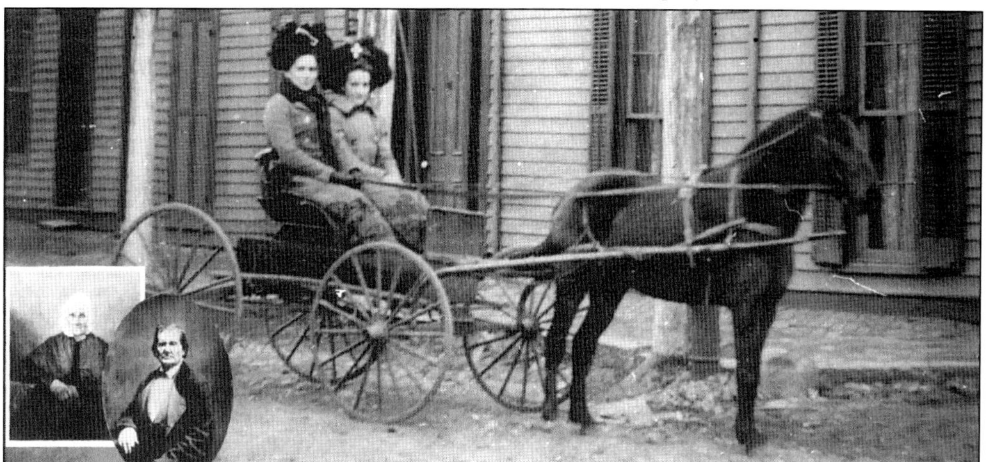

THE PATTON HOUSE, C. 1910. This house, once located on North Main Street in Elizabethtown, is known for being the house where Thomas Lincoln (father of President Abraham Lincoln) married his second wife, Sarah Bush Johnston (photos inset), on December 2, 1819. At that time, the house belonged to a prominent Elizabethtown lawyer by the name of Benjamin Chapeze, one of Sarah's neighbors. Initially constructed in 1798 by Aaron Rawlings on original town lot number 25, it was built with logs cut from trees located on the property. After passing through numerous owners, the house was torn down in 1921.

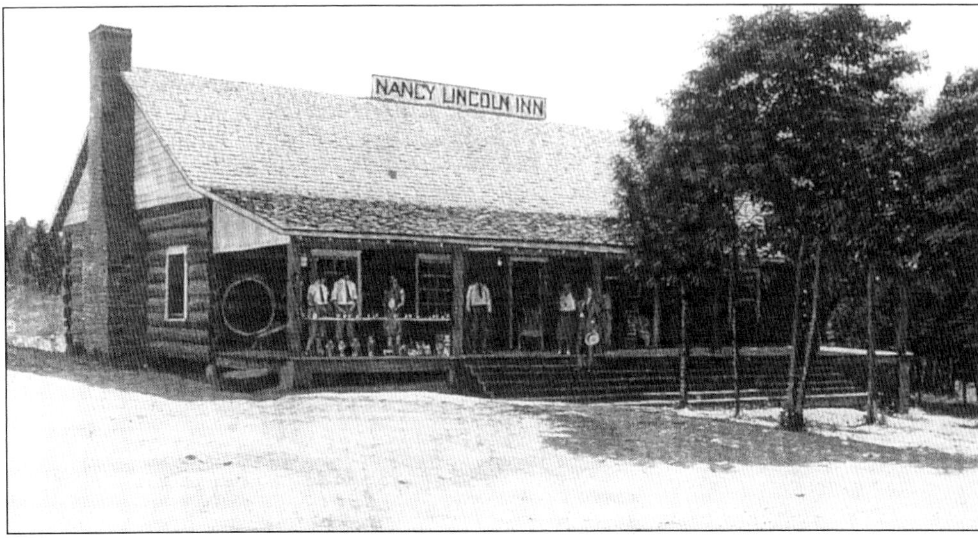

The Nancy Lincoln Inn, c. 1930. A souvenir shop and museum located near Abraham Lincoln's birthplace, the Nancy Lincoln Inn was constructed in 1928 by James Richard "Jim" Howell, a LaRue Countian born in 1879. The inn, named for Abraham Lincoln's mother, was built of many grand chestnut logs. Meals were served in the early years, and the four cabins still located adjacent to the inn were rented to tourists who wished to spend the night near the site where Lincoln was born.

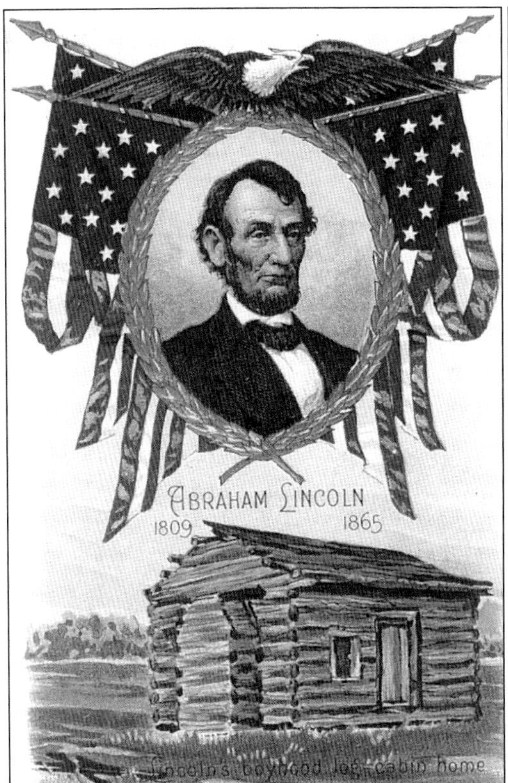

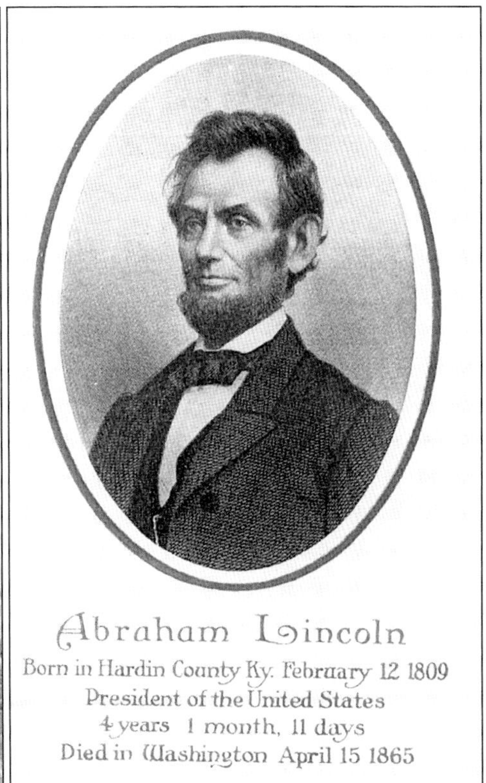

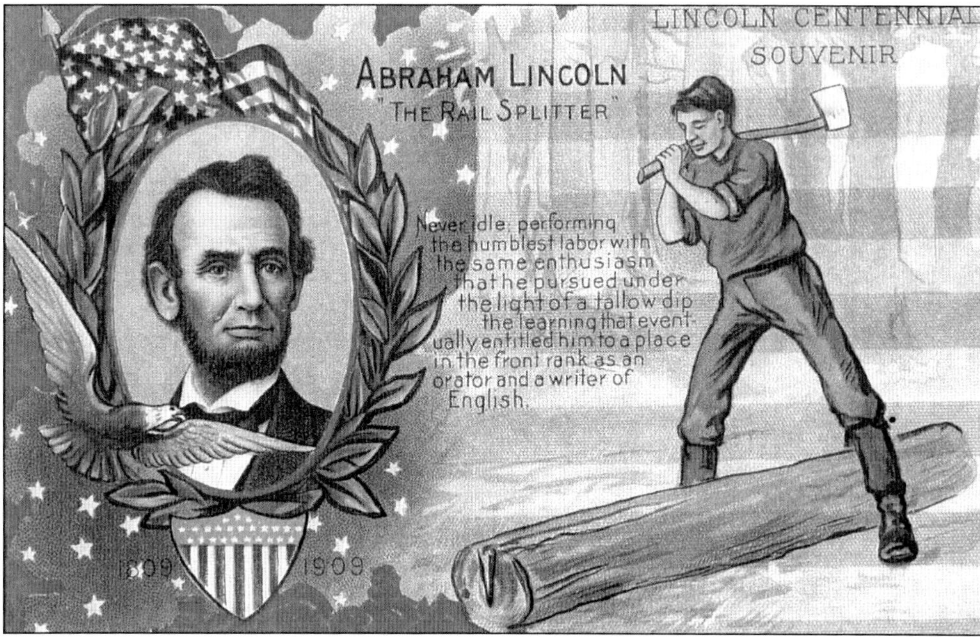

THE CENTENNIAL OF LINCOLN'S BIRTH, 1909. The year 1909 marked the centennial of the birth of Abraham Lincoln, the man most people then believed, and today still believe, was America's greatest president. Making the Lincoln centennial especially personal and relevant was the fact that a large percentage of the population had been alive at the time of his presidency and assassination. Less than a half-century had passed since Lincoln was first elected in 1860. Of the original 1.5 million Union veterans of the Civil War, several hundred thousand were still alive, many of them members of the GAR and state organizations of ex-soldiers. On February 12, 1909, Hodgenville, LaRue County, and the nation celebrated a gala national holiday, one unseen since the 1876 centennial of America's birth. The 1909 Lincoln centennial celebration was responsible for the publication of several sets of beautifully colored and embossed Lincoln postcards specifically published for the centennial. Displayed on these two pages, and on p. 111, are four examples of these postcards printed by different publishers. Patriotic postcards continued to be printed and sold for a while longer, but the general public would never see another year like 1909. The beauty, artistry, and craftsmanship found on Lincoln's birthday cards were never duplicated.

ACKNOWLEDGMENTS

In order to provide many of the illustrations used in this book, I have drawn extensively from postcards and photographs in my personal collection. I have similarly been able to locate much of the research material for the LaRue County and Lincoln text by reviewing books in my library and "re-discovering" old magazines, brochures, and *LaRue County Herald* newspapers that I had stored over the years in filing cabinets.

Pictures, information, and/or services have also been furnished by the following, to whom I extend my gratitude: Linda Back, Mary Berry, Kay Bondurant, Teresa Brackett, Russell Brooks, Kathy E. Brown, Paul Brownfield, Juanita Cottrill, Elsie Creal, Mike Dorsey, Alma Ford, Gary Gardner, Nancy H. Goodin, Allie Handley, Antinette Hawkins, Charles Hayes Jr., David W. Hayes, Nannie Johnson Head, Beverly Heath, Dixie Hibbs, Joyce Howell, Edgar E. Kinsey, Janet Marcum, Mike McCombs, W.L. McCoy, Jean McCubbin, John T. Meers Jr., Randy Newberry, Marilyn Ovesen, Mildred Payton, John Poteet, Willard Skaggs, James D. Smith, Mildred "Punkin" Sprowls, Homer Trumbo, Ruby Trumbo, James H. "Buz" Turner, Tommy Turner, Betty Vance, Sam Walters, Lois Whelan, and the hard workers at Packages and More in Elizabethtown.

My genuine appreciation is extended to official LaRue County historian James D. LaRue Jr., for his enthusiastic and insightful assistance. His knowledge of Hodgenville's people, businesses, and buildings during the period from 1880 to 1930, together with the use of photographs from his impressive collection, helped make each day I worked with him an enjoyable and memorable experience.

—Carl Howell

In 1983, when I first began collecting early images of Hardin County, it was a dream of mine to someday publish a book (or books) containing these "windows to our past," so that all present and former Hardin County residents could share in the unique heritage of this county we call home. Through the cooperation and encouragement of many present and former Hardin County residents, the "Images of the Past" collection has grown far beyond anything I could have ever imagined. To the many people who have opened their doors, sharing with me their personal recollections, stories, photos, and old newspaper articles, I extend to you my sincere thanks for helping me realize this dream.

Perhaps two of the more cooperative and interesting people I've had the pleasure of knowing were Margaret Richerson and Guy Winstead. Both of these extraordinary ladies opened their hearts and minds to me in a way that I shall never forget. With words of wisdom and encouragement, and always willing to help, they often amazed me with their detailed knowledge and love of Hardin County's past. I sincerely hope that in some small way, through the work I do here and in the future, I will pay a just tribute to these "dedicated preservers" of Hardin County history.

Though limited here as to size and space, I've attempted to represent as many Hardin County communities as possible. For many, these names and places will re-kindle old memories of childhood and a simpler place and time, while others will be viewing for the first time the people, places, and events that have been part of the heritage that we share as Hardin Countians.

—Don Waters